WEATHERVANES
of Great Britain

WEATHERVANES
of Great Britain

Patricia and Philip
Mockridge

ROBERT HALE · LONDON

© Patricia and Philip Mockridge 1990
First published in Great Britain 1990

Robert Hale Limited
Clerkenwell House
Clerkenwell Green
London EC1R 0HT

British Library Cataloguing in Publication Data

Mockridge, Patricia
Weathervanes
1. Weathervanes, to 1988
I. Title   II. Mockridge, Philip
739

ISBN 0-7090-3722-8

Set in Ehrhardt by
Derek Doyle & Associates, Mold, Clwyd.
Printed and bound in Great Britain by
Butler & Tanner Ltd., Frome, Somerset.

Contents

Illustrations

Acknowledgements

How does one begin to thank several thousand people, each of whom supplied separate items of information? We can only group them – all those librarians and archivists and museum staff, experts in their fields, local government officials, firms' public relations officers, clergy and church councils, who submitted to our questions and written queries with a good grace.

Of fundamental importance, naturally, has been the immensely informative contact with weathervane designers and makers of every kind. Making no distinction between amateur, semi-commercial, skilled craftsmen or large firms, we should like to list here those who in very different ways have been particularly helpful: John Allen, Brentor, Devon; Cyril Ashley, Staplow, Hereford & Worcester; Don Bales, Northwold, Norfolk; John Bennett-Williams, Piddlehinton, Dorset; Mr and Mrs Boulton and Jim Bailey, Erme Wood Forge, Ivybridge, Devon; Mr and Mrs Ronnie Carter, Simonstone, Lancs.; Bill Cordaroy, East Ruston, Norfolk; Frank Dean, Rodmell, Sussex; Frank Foley, Victoria Forge, Wakefield, Yorks.; Eden Fowler, Bisley, Glos.; Mr and Mrs David Harvey, Ivinghoe, Bucks.; David Hedges, Burwash, Sussex; Tony Hodgson & Partners, Terrington St Clement, Norfolk; Hubbard Bros Ltd, Norwich, Norfolk; Hyders Ltd, Plaxtol, Kent; Ray James, Baughton Forge, Upton upon Severn, Hereford & Worcester; L.C. Jay & Son, Norwich, Norfolk; Raymond Lister, Cambridge; Mr and Mrs Hector Moore, Brandeston Forge, Brandeston, Suffolk; A.V. Nicholls, Lower Swell, Glos.; Overton's, Rockland St Peter, Norfolk; Brian Owen, Templeton Forge, Dyfed; Sam Parsons, Wells, Norfolk; Andrew Ritchie, Musselburgh, Lothian; Anthony Robinson, Stanton upon Hine Heath, Shropshire; Eric Stevenson, Hoveton, Norfolk; Denis Trinder, Filkins, Oxon.; Graham Walker, Theddlethorpe, Lincs.

Countless other private individuals have spent time speaking, telephoning or writing to us, directing us to other weathervanes known to them, sending pictures or information and even the results of extensive research. Some gave us useful access to photographic vantage-points on private property. Our thanks to all these people. To those disappointed by finding in the book no obvious record of their efforts we offer the assurance that theirs is the nine-tenths of the iceberg that underlies the one-tenth that has surfaced here.

Finally we thank our daughter Rachel for her help in preparing the typescript.

Introduction

At a guess, most readers will have picked up this book out of curiosity rather than an established interest in weathervanes, for, despite their dominant position, weathervanes are only beginning to attract attention once more.

The first purpose of this book, therefore, is simply to increase awareness of these objects which have ornamented our rooflines for centuries. Their immediate impact is considerable: immense variety of form, executed with highly skilled craftsmanship or unsophisticated care, frequently with humour, sometimes with real beauty. The interesting stories or legends attaching to numbers of them are a bonus.

Old weathervanes survive largely through accidents of association with significant buildings or people. Local affection may have preserved a curious specimen; remoteness may have deterred vandals or poverty prevented renewal. But with age comes fragility. The second purpose of this book therefore is broadly conservational. It would be splendid if it were the norm rather than exceptional to record weathervanes, repair them sympathetically, maintain them *in situ* to contribute their lively motion to the landscape, and preserve the too-fragile or apparently redundant in collections. Not all weathervanes are of fine-quality materials or refined design, of course, but sturdy construction, historical associations and downright oddity all have their value. Even at their lowest estimate as bygones, they manifest the materials, taste and ideas of their period.

The third purpose is to direct the resurgent interest in weathervanes towards the creation of new ones of quality. The artistry and craftsmanship of past centuries have not evaporated; the tradition of erecting weathervanes with, say, civic emblems, or those that are decorative and well adapted to their buildings, is worth continuing. If vanes are made from modern materials or if in their use of traditional materials they reflect contemporary ideas in their lines and in what they show pictorially, then Britons of 2090 will be able to extrapolate from them our skills, tastes and values, just as we do from vanes of 1890. They may deplore what they see – but would surely deplore still more a period with no weathervanes identifiably its own.

To stimulate this enlightened interest we have aimed to touch as many chords as possible. Thus we have concentrated on indicating the immense variety of what is to be found, how skilfully made, significant, beautiful or amusing this display is, where it is to be found and how it came to be there.

To this end, owners, librarians, curators, PROs, even interested passers-by were accosted with a string of questions. What is this building? Who owns it? Who erected the weathervane? When? Why? Why to this particular design? What does it depict or signify? Who made it? Of what? How big is it? What is its history of repair, replacement, transfer etc? What is its present condition? And occasionally, When, and why, did it vanish? Blank astonishment; 'No idea'; '*What* weathervane?' was one answer. At the other extreme, several accounts, all apparently equally authoritative, would flatly contradict one another. Both were such frequent responses that we drew the sad conclusion that it is already too late to collect reliable information about a great many weathervanes. Thus the emphasis on what is here *now* rather than on scholarly history.

A word or two of caution. The book is concerned with weathervanes. We are *not* experts in heraldry, zoology, botany, agriculture, symbolism, field or any other sports, maritime or transport history, careers, national and local history and legend, metalcraft or aesthetics, though needing to touch on all of them. Scholars and experts in any of these fields may well be affronted or aggrieved by our sins of omission and commission, and we accept that greater specialized knowledge on our part might have modified our response to particular weathervanes.

We are also aware that gargantuan meals are indigestible. Nonetheless, quantity seemed paramount, so that readers might have as much as possible with which to compare weathervanes they find for themselves. We are no arbiters of taste, and beyond the judgement exercised in whittling down material within the compass of a book-cover, our evaluation is tentative, as befits what we believe to be the first attempt at a nationwide study of the subject. We hope that readers seeking within the book material comprehensive enough to suggest the potentialities of the subject will accept it as a primary source or springboard. It is offered on the assumption that subsequent students, delving more deeply into certain aspects or genres, or able to make more authoritative judgements from a bigger sample, will profit from our errors and omissions and improve on it.

Although we drove over 25,000 miles on main, secondary and unclassified roads all over mainland Britain, this represents a little less than a tenth of the national road network. Taking into account the number of weathervanes along those 25,000 miles that were hidden by undulating ground or estate boundaries, too distant or on rear outbuildings, swamped by new development or tucked into pedestrianized areas, quite apart from weathervanes missed through a chance turn of the head, our sample is obviously below ten per cent. Even so, our total 'haul', ignoring duplicates, approached 3,000. Any unfortunate gaps in kinds or numbers of weathervanes noted in a given area may simply reflect that chance led us on less productive routes. Again we rely on the sheer quantity of examples we have given to enable people to match what they find against what is to be seen elsewhere. Many of our general assertions will also probably be overturned by localized tendencies and exceptions.

Grouping the weathervanes regionally would have meant much repetition but arranging 3,000 weathervanes into subject groups proved unexpectedly difficult. Apart from puzzling decisions about the unique and quirky, a fish is a fish, cogs are machinery and a grasshopper is an insect – but all are symbols. Fire-engines, trains and bicycles are vehicles but may also represent an occupation, a hobby, or local history. Various animals may be themselves, or heraldic devices, or puns on somebody's name. Often genuinely multiple reasons for the erection of a particular weathervane make it equally at home in several groups. Generally we have tried to make common-sense decisions based on the overall effect of the vane. A naturalistic lion is 'wildlife'; if it is rampant, holding something or holding its elongated tail over its back and grinning, it is clearly heraldic. A lamb is an animal; a lamb with a flag is heraldic and symbolic. Complete consistency is impossible, especially if hard facts about a vane's origin are in short supply. If a weathervane is not included in what seems the obvious group, it may be either because we have discovered something about it that has made us put it elsewhere, or because we failed to discover something that seems obvious to those in the know.

Inevitably the book concentrates on weathervane motifs, because their movement is what takes the eye and gives the weathervane meaning. But it must be remembered that the motif is not the whole weathervane. Unless the motif is exceptional in some way, a blacksmith-observer will ignore it and focus on what accompanies it. Spindles, mounts, finials, arms, letters and scrolling often test craftsmanship more than a motif and express it with nearly as astonishing a variety. These aspects of weathervanes, therefore, have received independent consideration in Chapter 6. The logic of this position is that motifs must claim some prior consideration, so the two main ancestral groups of motifs, cocks and heraldry, with its immediate derivatives, are looked at first. Decorative enhancements then make some sense. Subsequent chapters on other groups of motifs can then assume an awareness of their possibilities and scope without the distraction of constantly referring to them.

To illustrate this essentially visual subject, most previous writers have opted for more illustration through drawings. They can also be 'doctored', with motif, arms and decoration all deliberately aligned to display each to its best advantage. Success depends on the skill and accuracy of the artist. Pot-bellied horses, or motif and decoration recorded separately and later re-assembled without reference to their respective sizes or the pivot point, give a false impression. Photographs, although costlier and therefore fewer, correspond more closely to how most people actually see weathervanes – that is, with all the attendant difficulties of distance, angles and obstructions, modified by the assistance of binoculars or telephoto lens. This closer, enlarged view reveals details sometimes surprisingly subtle but sometimes disconcertingly crude, like close-up views of stage costume and make-up. Except for *2.1* and *2.2*, all the photographs, blemished as some are by the hazards of wind, rain, snow, sunglare, gloom, roosting birds, obstructions, perspective and often sheer distance inherent in such a project, are our own. Many are multi-purpose, illustrating points made in other chapters as well as in their own. Unless the text indicates otherwise, it can be assumed that we have seen any weathervane mentioned.

Blacksmiths and makers are referred to briefly in the text, but many of them more fully in the acknowledgements.

1 Weathervanes in Our World

Beauty and craftsmanship are increasingly valuable commodities in the late-twentieth-century search for that elusive 'quality of life' that material prosperity alone has so signally failed to create. The beauty and craftsmanship of weathervanes, freely exhibited on the British skyline for centuries, are only just being rediscovered. A weathervane pleases by its fitness for its purpose, however oddly placed, by its often superb execution in enduring materials, by its astonishing individuality, above all by sudden, unexpected beauty that gives a lift to the heart. Such pleasure is valuable. The object that gives it should be cherished. A good weathervane is more than merely eyecatching. It is decorative, intriguing and stimulating at sight, quite apart from any additional interest that may emerge on closer acquaintance.

The craftsmen who created these pleasing objects have almost all been anonymous, though certainly far from unsophisticated. From ancient times the blacksmith's skill has been venerated. Did he not work with iron, sent from the gods in meteorites? Assisted by the elements of fire and water, he subdued it with fierce blows against a strangely but superbly contoured anvil, using few, unchanged tools. Subtly curved horsehoes seemed little short of magical. He created sturdy tools – scythes, axes, shovels – so that other men could exercise their skills, and boot-scrapers, firebacks and firedogs, hinges and latches and other utensils for domestic use. But beyond such utilitarian objects he could often produce stunningly intricate and delicate gates, locks and ornamental work, including, as a small part of his output, weathervanes (*1.1*).

1.1   Blacksmith forging scroll, surrounded by his
ornamental work: Victoria Forge, Wakefield, Yorks.

Until well into this century every community had its blacksmiths. Every community of any size had several, for, except in areas completely dominated by some local industry such as basketry, blacksmiths far outnumbered other craftsmen, even after more specialized metalworkers had set up independently. Their weathervanes, like everything else they made, showed their skill and pride in work well done. They were solidly, not flimsily, made, of strong materials and were balanced to work efficiently.

These were important attributes, for many a weathervane was so awkward of access that it received only infrequent attention. The luck of more regular maintenance fell to those more easily reached or regarded as a valued part of the building. Survival may also have been helped by a sheltered location or distance from the polluted atmosphere of an industrial centre.

Not until this century did this ancient craft come under threat. Those forges that switched to succouring traction and later internal combustion engines represent a small fraction of those that closed down. Very few traditional blacksmiths persisted. Today's climate is more promising, with increased demand for well-made iron objects; the new British Artist Blacksmiths' Association recognizes that such objects must also be well designed.

Good work is costly but, like all genuinely hand-crafted goods, it is now highly regarded. Two extraordinary commissions from David Hedges, a Burwash blacksmith, shed an interesting sidelight on the reputation abroad of British ornamental wrought ironwork. One was for a house name – to make an eighteen-foot-span arched entrance to a Wyoming ranch. The other was for a rooster and a galleon, 'in sections not above two feet so that they can go in my suitcase'; they were carried off to Australia, the astronomical transportation costs simply brushed aside.

One of the joys of weathervanes, however, is that they are well within the capacity of people to make for themselves. This has probably always been so, but because they are usually made of ephemeral materials, they are often short-lived. However, those amateurs with the courage not to use a standard pattern often achieve great individuality and charm (*1.2*).

The point to remember is that no weathervane is there by accident: it has been ordered or made or bought by someone's deliberate choice, and for some particular reason. It may be that fashion decreed such an architectural embellishment; it may be beautiful; it may have some individual relevance or reference. That being so, one might reasonably expect weathervanes to figure in records of buildings, repair bills, architects' plans, guide-books, business firms' histories etc. Not a bit of it. In towns where the standard practice is to insert new, smaller shopfronts into the ground floor of large old buildings, ownership becomes fragmented or tenancy often shortlived. If some faceless property company administers the whole block by remote control, an

1.2   Individual charm: bird-table scene, Aberaeron, Dyfed.

economically unproductive weathervane becomes a very unconsidered trifle. Private houses also change ownership, and any word-of-mouth information passed on about a weathervane becomes amazingly garbled. Even Sir Nikolaus Pevsner lamented that he had been unable to 'provide the elucidation readers may hope for' on quite outstanding buildings. So no wonder mere details such as weathervanes never seem to feature on, for instance, estate agents' particulars.

The National Trust, diocesan offices and Redundant Churches' Fund, although attentive to all the items within their care, do not have identifying lists of all their weathervanes. Occasionally, individual churches record a weathervane's erection, repair or replacement, but usually a vague 'thought to be eighteenth-century' or 'believed to be the original' is as positive as most accounts will venture. Proud detailed accounts of such civic achievements as Peterborough Town Hall describe minutely the portico but ignore the weathervane surmounting it. Even the Royal Commission for Historic Monuments will conclude paragraphs of precise architectural description with the vague comment 'surmounted by a wrought weathervane'. A brief indication of pennant, banner, arrow or some other device would be so much clearer.

Visual records are little better. The artist's imaginative or indeterminate blob is matched by the architect's impressionistic dash, while photographs or TV shots are usually cropped immediately above the roofline. With such poor documentation, no wonder the siting of some apparently incongruous weathervanes cannot be accounted for, and what others represent remains a complete mystery.

It comes as no surprise that, with little official notice or care being taken of them, weathervanes are liable to succumb to the whims of fashion or be discarded during urban renewal. Mere age takes its toll, especially when compounded by neglect. An apparently interesting abstract pattern turns out to be just the strengthening bars of a vane that has crumbled away. Vanes that cannot revolve freely may wrap themselves round the spindle or be bent sideways by wind pressure. Ship silhouettes on Southwold church, Suffolk, and the pub Junction 23 in Loughborough, Leics., suffered these afflictions. If parts snap off (in Norfolk the 1680 weathervane on the Pinnacle Tower of Great Yarmouth's town wall has lost its pointer), imbalance and strain result (*1.3*). On some buildings ivy or creeper ramp over the vane; it is happening to a lovely Arab mare and foal at Plumpton, Sussex (*1.4*), and on the cricket pavilion at Lurgashall, Sussex.

Weathervanes have other natural hazards to contend with too. Birds broke off the date 1930 from beneath the pennant on Rodmell church,

1.3 Pointer broken off and not
replaced: Town Wall,
Great Yarmouth, Norfolk.

1.4 Encroaching vegetation:
Plumpton, Sussex.

Sussex – watching them trampolining on the heraldic pennants of Thorney Abbey, Cambs., makes it easy to see how. Recent hurricanes felled a good many, including the cock of All-Hallows-by-the-Tower, City of London, which brought the top six feet of spire with it, providentially impaling itself upside-down in the roof instead of crashing into the crowded concourse below. Bent cardinal arms and letters are often the legacy of storms. Lightning has shattered several church vanes, and the fine cock in Smithfield Market, City of London, though preserved, is no longer *in situ* after a fire destroyed the market halls in 1958. Somewhat less dramatically, plastic weathervanes, placed too near a chimney, have been known to melt.

As if natural hazards were not enough, weathervanes face attack from other quarters. The Smithfield cock's scars are honourable ME109 bullet holes from World War II, but hundreds of weathervanes have been colandered in target practice. Their clear outlines, their challenging but not impossible distance, their responsive spin recording a hit before they return to their original position, have made them irresistible – especially, if hints are to be credited, to vicars' sons and soldiers on leave. The challenge to climb on or ride weathervanes is part of standard weathervane mythology. Saddest of all is sheer mindless vandalism, as endured by the Happy Eater restaurant vane at Thirsk, Yorks, and the camel above the shopping precinct at Wadebridge, Corn. Removal *can* be genuinely motivated: a fine hunting weathervane went from Norfolk to Leicestershire as a bequest. But simple theft is now a threat. The weathervane on Piltdown Golf Club, Sussex, just vanished. And in the USA there are even several examples of 'vane-napping' – by helicopter. The most audacious was the holding to ransom of America's most famous weathervane, the grasshopper on Faneuil Hall, Boston.

The assumption that the money would be forthcoming interestingly indicates the developing duality of our response to weathervanes.

Certainly they present a challenge to both thieves and vandals, but as a sign of individual status or community prosperity they are also a source of pride. Their associations, aura of tradition and age, and skilled workmanship arouse an affection and admiration which are beginning in places to counterbalance their neglect. Thus, when they are damaged or threatened, there is concern. However, repairs often have to rely on enthusiastic and capable individuals rather than Authority. Norwich Fire Brigade, for example, dipped into their own pockets, and one of their own members repaired their delightful weathervane (*14.10*). There is no doubt that weathervanes can create or cement a sense of community and arouse fiercely possessive pride.

1.5   Popular pre-war motif of the Rural Development Commission:
Theddlethorpe All Saints, Lincs.

Another recognition of the developing regard for weathervanes comes
in the hundred designs in the metalwork section of the catalogue from
the Rural Development Commission – until recently CoSira, the
Council for Small Industries in Rural Areas. About one fifth of these are
pre-war designs, when the organization was the Rural Industries
Bureau; their originator is unknown. The remaining eighty or so have
been created since 1952, mainly by Mr Zigmund Schramm. Although
he often had considerable freedom, each was a specific commission,
subsequently included in the catalogue, with working drawings available
to other blacksmiths. The more successful of them, chiefly
representational, humorous and genre scenes, have been widely
reproduced. Fig. *1.5* is a popular pre-war Rural Development
Commission design.

The USA leads the world in its attention to the preservation of
weathervanes. In Britain awareness is growing of the desirability of
preserving artefacts that show 'the way we lived then'. As part of a total
town- or villagescape, best preserved *in situ*, weathervanes must surely

merit the concern of local preservation societies, the Victorian Society, CPRE, Civic Trust, even the Department of the Environment's preservation orders, as much as letterboxes or street fountains. Now we are catching up with the value and interest of our own past, it should be possible to collect records of weathervanes, with those of other artefacts, into reference libraries, local museums, county record offices, county photographic surveys and the like.

Sometimes weathervanes too fragile to be re-erected have been preserved inside their own buildings, as in a number of churches, and they are finding their way into museums. The Victoria and Albert Museum has a few good ones in its metalwork collection, though not all are British. Local museums are acquiring single weathervanes of local interest, but there is considerable scope for imaginative public collection and exhibition. Indoor display is not easy. Private American collectors mount weathervanes on stands or fix them to walls, but without movement and the surrounding sky they become lifeless.

Americans collect weathervanes with a dedication that is not yet evident in Britain. They see them reflecting the art, taste and social history of an era, and recognize that, even if not very old, they will probably never be made again: many would be far too expensive and few would suit contemporary buildings. They find the folk-art products entertaining and characterful, but primarily they look for what they find beautiful. If the form, subject, style, patina, quality, condition *et al* are satisfying, the weathervane becomes a desirable object.

As always when something becomes collectable, it becomes worth someone's while to fake it. Carved wooden weathervanes are easy to replicate, although an unweathered end-grain is a giveaway. That particular problem seldom arises in Britain, which has relatively few wooden weathervanes, but metal ones can be artificially antiqued. Rivets rusted in, iron oxide bleeding from rivets, and a pitted edge are difficult to re-create from new, however, and luckily the whole process is too time-consuming and costly to be very worthwhile at current British prices.

But the cheapest way of amassing a huge 'collection' is to emulate big game hunters, put away the gun (or chequebook) and hunt with binoculars and camera. No jumping to the tune of market pressures or economic stringencies then.

Because so many weathervanes in every region are inevitably missed, only the very broadest generalizations can be ventured. First, the effect of the terrain is noticeable. Mountainous regions have few weathervanes. By responding to a wind funnelling either up or down the valley but never across, they give no true indication of how thick a coat is needed or which beach will be sheltered. Exposed coasts are thought to test a weathervane's construction too severely. The sparse populations of moorland areas erect few, and those few tend to be repetitive.

Second, regional variations in architecture are reflected in both the number and variety of weathervanes. Areas with church spires, for instance, specialize in cocks, but with no arms to indicate the four cardinal compass points. Church towers produce greater diversity of style and are more likely to have cardinal arms and decorative iron to balance their mass. However, such towers as Yorkshire's with crocketed pinnacles or Avon's with a tall cone on one pinnacle are likely to be regarded as already sufficiently ornamented. 'Scottish baronial' buildings favour spiky finials, fixed ornaments at their highest points, or Victorian quasi-heraldic products. Glasgow's skyline is pierced by numerous weathervanes, some of them very fine. Edinburgh, however, joins Perth and most other Scottish towns in opting for finials. Since some Welsh towns do the same, it may be another recognition of the distorting effect of hilly terrain on weathervanes. Urban Scottish skylines hammer home the influence of some of the greatest nineteenth-century architectural iron-founders, such as Macfarlane's at Glasgow and Carron's at Falkirk. Although their products were sold throughout the British Isles, there is a real concentration of them near home.

1.6   Local heraldry; Bear and Ragged Staff: Edgbaston Cricket Ground, Birmingham.

Certain preconceptions about weathervane distribution have to be modified. Some cathedral cities, e.g. Norwich and Chester, do have many weathervanes, but Gloucester does not. Again, several Birmingham and Warwick weathervanes display the bear-and-ragged-staff of the earls of Warwick (*1.6*), but the Bedford arms do not dominate Woburn, nor the Percy arms Alnwick. Tenby, a pretty, touristy town, lacks weathervanes; industrial Leek is full of them.

Weathervanes breed: not just in Greater London or York or Blackpool but in such villages as Haddenham, Bucks., and Aldbourne, Wilts. A kind of chain reaction produces all foxes in one part of Staffordshire, all cocks on Dyfed farms around Carmarthen and Llandeilo, a skyful of three-dimensional cocks above Stirling, Central. The mere presence of an interested blacksmith may not only boost the local weathervane population but create a recognizable 'family' of foxes or scroll shapes. His favourite iron or copper or gilded work will characterize the area.

Regions vary in where they deem weathervanes a fitting adornment. For example, in 200 miles of driving in Warwickshire and Northamptonshire we saw weathervanes only on public buildings, not a single one on a private house. In the south, farms are keen to display them, but not in the north, nor in Worcestershire and Shropshire, apart from round Hay on Wye. Some local authorities, at Wivenhoe, Essex, and Thrandeston, Suffolk, have recently insisted on weathervanes on new or restored buildings. So perhaps a new pattern of grouping will emerge through the planners. Our impression that there are more good weathervanes in East Anglia and Sussex probably reflects the fact that we know East Anglia best, while Sussex weathervanes are the best documented. The implication is that readers will find as good a 'collection' in their own favourite haunts.

Another preconception to be abandoned is what constitutes a suitable weathervane site. Our list of the kinds of constructions ingenuity has so adorned approaches 200 and is doubtless far from exhaustive.

Religious buildings are the obvious starting-point, including less obvious ones like corporate chapels, missions to seamen and cemetery gatehouses. And there are some surprising weathervane subjects here – beady-eyed foxes, astronomical symbols and Disney lambs among them.

Public buildings offer a profitable hunting area – all the town halls and administrative offices, the old buttermarkets, Victorian corn exchanges, modern shopping arcades; public service buildings from police stations to public lavatories, surgeries to sewage works; educational buildings, from nursery to adult level; theatres and libraries, collections and exhibitions in anything from a single upstairs room to the Victoria & Albert Museum. Historic city gatehouses, town walls (*1.3*) and tollbridges may all have weathervanes. So may places of public refreshment and entertainment, the plushest hotel or the bingo hall on the pier. Then there are surprises on kiosks, bus stations, underground station entrances, road depots and seafront shelters.

Many of these public buildings will have been dignified with turrets or lanterns or cupolas with a weathervane as the finishing touch. At their best, such weathervanes harmonize with their setting. Schools, for instance, may have suitably classical pennants or Victorian Gothic banners or display the school badge, which may itself derive from local arms, as does Kirkham Grammar School's dove with olive branch in Lancashire. The seemingly so apt quill pen vane, however, has never achieved in Britain anything comparable to its American popularity.

Cupolas or turrets also dignify certain kinds of commercial enterprises. Banks, for instance, may occupy some venerable edifice like Lloyds in Winchester's eighteenth-century guildhall with its elaborate contemporary banner (*5.4*). Victorian Gothic Barclays and NatWests may still fly weathervanes initialled for London & County or Parr's banks which they have absorbed. Other commercial premises make far too long a list, but shops, breweries, watermills, fish-curers, garden centres, boatyards, vineyards (*1.7*), service garages, factories and sculptors' studios give just a flavour of it. All these commercial weathervanes are endangered by urban renewal that sweeps them away unless the building itself is valued. They can, however, be among the quite small architectural details which help to integrate old and new and which give great slab-sided modern developments human scale and visual interest. But the peaceable dove with olive branch above the oasis of St John the Baptist's Church, Crawley, Sussex, makes both an ironic and a poignant comment on the frenzied civilization that now whirls about it.

Rather less subject to radical changes of function are sports venues: weathervanes on clubs and pavilions, hunt kennels, pigeon lofts, racecourse towers etc are reasonably secure from redevelopment threats.

The safest weathervanes are probably those on castles, stately homes and their ancillary game larders and shooting lodges. Here they are likely to be restored if they disintegrate: at Island Hall, Godmanchester, Cambs., the entire eighteenth-century cupola was rebuilt to the original design, complete with simple pennant, to their mutual enhancement. Vanes on ancient almshouses, like the superb wyvern on Sir William Turner's Hospital, Kirkleatham, Cleveland, are also highly regarded.

1.7 Vineyard weathervane: Stitchcombe, Wilts.

In contrast, the most vulnerable are the most numerous: weathervanes on ordinary modern estate houses, 'urban executive' residences and humble rural cottages. Here weathervanes come and go with the occupants, reflecting not diminishing but changing weathervane interests.

Erecting a private weathervane poses a dilemma. On the house roof it gives most enjoyment to the neighbours. For the owners' benefit, it has to be transferred to a barn or summerhouse, pigsty or dovecote, stable or garage. Most visible of all may be a mast, freestanding or rising from a gatepost, like public ones in parks or on harbour walls. There are even telegraph poles ... And the list of ingenious perches stretches to include clock tower, lock-up, memorial, drinking-fountain, sundial, icehouse, sluice-gate (*1.8*), ventilation shaft, bird table and sewage pumphouse.

In the modern environment weathervanes have to compete for attention on the skyline they once dominated. No doubt there have always been deceptively shaped treetops, but this century's telegraph poles, spotlights, lamp brackets and above all TV aerials, especially with roosting starlings, are major distractions. The enchanting village of Castle Combe, Wilts., with all its TV sets operated from a central aerial, thanks to the demands of a film production, reminds us what a perfect weathervane roofscape would look like – but it has none, perhaps because it is a valley village. Cocks peer over Slough's concrete monoliths with quite startling effect. From Blackfriars Bridge, the City of London flaunts cranes and highrise office blocks: old City church weathervanes are now silhouetted against buildings, not sky, except from close beneath. However, there are modern gains too: those same tall buildings offer vantage-points, which together with binoculars and telephoto lenses permit close-up views of meticulous craftsmanship formerly granted only

1.8   Humour of sluice-gate vane, in context (*left*) and in detail (*right*): Denver, Norfolk.

to the birds. And pedestrianization is a boon for leisurely examination, otherwise possible only during evenings and weekends.

If the numbers and positions of weathervanes surprise us, they also remind us how inconceivably important before our centrally heated, mechanically transported age the weather used to be. Domestic comfort, farmers' crops, the safety of fishing expeditions all relied on wind awareness. Small wonder then that primitive painters often saw weathervanes as disproportionately huge, unlike many modern architects who represent this ornamental top-knot by an ill-defined squiggle. International trade needed wind information too: the Glasgow merchants used the fine gilt sailing-ship on their Steeple, and the Bank of England its weathervane with interior dial to predict the arrival time of trading-vessels, with its knock-on effect of financial dealings. Electronic gadgetry has taken over serious weatherforecasting, but people still use weathervanes to interpret how good local conditions are for field-spraying, fishing, garden bonfires. Those sports club vanes acknowledge how wind can affect not just wind-dependent activities – gliding, sailing – but ball games and athletics too. Ventilating glasshouses, ringing birds, dressing for a country walk, even choosing a picnic site can be decided by a glance at the weathervane. One customer even told a blacksmith that she wanted a weathervane to tell her which way to put the baby's pram.

Ben Butterworth's *The Weathercock*, a Ladybird book, makes the interesting assumption that even very young children will recognize a weathercock. Villagers make wise decisions based on the wind-direction it indicates, but mistakes when it is broken, so it is rapidly restored. The book offers an accolade for weathervanes as functional accessories in twenty-five brief sentences.

Although the 1980s emphasis has moved to weathervanes as more attractive than useful objects, such decorativeness has its own function. An increasingly mass-produced and impersonal environment has spawned the craze for 'personalizing' everything. Ultimately, this is self-defeating – 'when everyone's somebody, then no one's anybody' – but it expresses an intensely felt need. A weathervane can certainly give individuality to an otherwise uniform house. Inevitably, much of what is available is itself mass-produced. Fine, provided that economy and manufacturing constraints are not allowed to dictate crude products. It is perfectly possible to mass-produce weathervanes with basically good designs, not necessarily complex but well-proportioned and elegant. Better still is expert craftsmanship to an original design. That is real personalization.

The multiple impetus of designer's ideas, maker's skills and client's requirements makes every weathervane a compromise. Obviously, its weight, strength, durability etc must comply with the demands of its function and suit constructional processes at a cost-effective level. Unostentatious skill in using contrasts and balancing lines and masses will underlie a satisfying appearance. For such reasons, absolute authenticity has often to be sacrificed. A fox must resemble a fox, and a ship a ship, but fanatically accurate reproduction, though satisfying the craftsman, may well not make an effective weathervane. Details are often better modified, simplified or even implied. (The deliberately stylized is usually distinguishable from the merely inept.) Simple profiles promote at-a-glance at-a-distance understanding better than complex replicas. A final influence on design is a sense of architectural fitness. For each City of London church Wren rebuilt, he designed an individual weathervane. Christopher Dykes Bower has done the same for his new parts of Bury St Edmunds Cathedral, Suffolk.

Partly because the height and aspect and environment of a known site exert their discipline and because the client states his precise requirements, competitions are a fruitful source of weathervane design. A national competition in 1880 produced London's Natural History Museum in South Kensington with its four fish weathervanes; a local one in 1920 the rebus village sign at Westcott, Surrey. Three delightful owl scholars on Kingston Junior School, Sussex, and the dramatic 'Black Shuck' at Bungay, Suffolk (*17.1*) were both competition-winners designed primarily by children. Weathervanes made during school examination coursework are often proudly erected after assessment.

Wren judged the size of the dragon for St Mary-le-Bow Church in the City of London (*2.6*) from a wooden template. It is still often best to decide pragmatically on length of cardinal arms, size of lettering, the distance between arms and motif to avoid visual confusion, and the desirability or otherwise of coloured details.

Any attractive result, unless it is incomprehensibly personal, is likely to be copied – and apparent errors are thus perpetuated. But ducks rising downwind and deplorably undisciplined gundogs may be design compromises; the globe on a horizontal axis seems more like a mistake. Slavish copying is less common, however, than all sorts of modifications which the maker thinks create a more efficient, more decorative, more fitting, more (or less) realistic, more personal, easier-to-make or cheaper weathervane. Even if he makes six exact copies of a motif, he can vary arm shape and size, lettering style and size, scroll work, finials, surface treatment and proportions, to create six vastly different vanes.

'Custom-made' weathervanes generally mean some permutation from within the blacksmith's established range, or an individual motif above his standard arms and ornamentation. The styles of different forges may thus be recognizable no matter how far from home modern transport and advertising have taken their work.

But it is the completely one-off weatherwave that gives blacksmiths the greatest opportunity for imaginative, dramatic or delicate work. They delight in the challenge to show how their skill can leap the chasm between vision and execution.

2 Historical and Technical Background

Considering that weathervane history spans some 2,000 years, there are few hard facts or dates. Nothing is known of the stages by which experimentation led to weathervanes as we know them. The very first recorded weathervanes are already fully fledged, as sophisticated in concept as any that follow. They work on the same principles and are made of the same materials and by the same processes as are used for the next nineteen centuries. Throughout all that time there is, therefore, no observable development from the primitive to the advanced. Their 'history' consists largely of charting trends or waves of fashion. Only new industrial processes and materials brought any radical change.

Apart from a few important developmental landmarks, therefore, culled chiefly from contemporary references earlier than any weathervanes that survive, this survey chiefly attempts broad guidelines to the distinctive features of each century's weathervanes. Individual examples of note are considered according to their genre. In Britain actual weathervanes can be studied going back through 600 years, though they do not survive in significant numbers much before the eighteenth century.

Awareness of wind-direction was part of primitive man's survival kit. It taught him to sense impending storms, hunt from downwind and make fire with comfort and safety. Several civilizations had come and gone, however, before any permanent form of wind-indicator is recorded.

In about 48 BC, a Greek astronomer, Andronicus of Cyrrhus, built what has become known as 'the Tower of the Winds'. Its base still stands near the Athens Acropolis, a 45-foot-high octagonal tower, each

2.1   Erecting a weathercock on Westminster Abbey, 1065: Bayeux
Tapestry.

of its eight sides carved with the god whose wind it faces, to indicate the
eight points of the compass. Some twenty-five years later, Vitruvius, in
De Architectura described the actual weathervane that topped this tower
as 'a bronze Triton with a rod in his hand'. This half-fish, half-man sea
deity, son of Poseidon, more usually controlled the winds by blowing on
a shell. Vitruvius continues: 'It was contrived so as to turn in the breeze,
always facing it, and holding its rod as a pointer directly above the
representation of the wind that was blowing.' It is claimed that such
precise description implies a new invention as yet unnamed. On the
other hand, it may well suggest a well-established custom of fusing
function and decoration, for this was a bronze sculpture, anything up to
eight feet long on what was actually a quite complex weatherstation,
incorporating sundials and a water-clock. Whichever is true, from this
weathervane or its fellows descend our familiar representational
weathervanes, including the cocks which we can regard as one 'parent'
form in Britain.

Within a decade of Andronicus's Triton, the Roman Varro wrote in

2.2   Oldest British weathercock, with whistle tubes,
c. 1340: Ottery St Mary, Devon.

De Re Rustica of his aviary weathervane, though he did not describe its motif. It controlled a pointer on the ceiling inside, where the eight cardinal winds were marked 'as on the horologium at Athens'. Other writers mention a Triton in Rome, a copper horseman in Syria, a human figure in Constantinople and others. Clearly, these ancient weathervanes were fine, sophisticated creations.

In Britain, weathervanes in the shape of full-bodied cocks were familiar enough by the eighth century to provoke this Anglo-Saxon 'riddle' – a poem describing an object without naming it:

I am puff-breasted, proud-crested
a head I have, and a high tail
eyes and ears and one foot,
both my sides, a back that's hollow,
a very stout beak, a steeple neck
and a home above men.
                    Harsh are my sufferings
when that which makes the forest tremble takes and shakes me.
Here I stand under streaming rain
and blinding sleet, stoned by hail;
freezes the frost and falls the snow
on me stuck bellied. And I stick it all out
for I cannot change the chance that made me.

Michael Alexander, *The Earliest English Poems* (Penguin Classics, 1966)

This familiar adornment of the church steeple is repeatedly said to have been imposed in the ninth century by a papal enactment. Evidence is elusive, but the cock certainly emerges very early as a symbol of both human frailty and Christian vigilance. Its asymmetrical form requires it to swivel if it is not to succumb to the first gale. The earliest cock weathervane ever discovered is of this vintage. It was found in Brescia in Italy in 1652 and was inscribed '*Dominus Rampertus Episc: gallum hunc fieri praecipit anno 820*' – 'Bishop Rampert ordered this cock to be made in the year 820.'

Weathercocks are mentioned or pictured in manuscripts with increasing frequency from the tenth century. Wulfstan, for instance, enthuses over Bishop Swithun's golden cock at Winchester: '*Ornatu grandis; regit; superbus; nobilis imperium*' – 'Grand comb nodding, proud, noble, he rules his empire....'

The Bayeux Tapestry illustrates a cock being mounted on Westminster Abbey at its completion in 1065 (*2.1*). By 1091 English vane-makers were evidently highly enough regarded to be sent to France to repair the damaged cock of Coutances Cathedral.

Non-representational weathervanes have a very different ancestry. At dates ranging between about 1400 BC and the fourth century AD, small flags decorated the staves and spears of Ancient Egyptian, Greek and Roman soldiers, and streamers flew from their buildings. The Bayeux Tapestry shows eleventh-century European soldiers with similar spearhead flags. By the ninth century, fabric flags had already become quadrant metal vanes on Viking ships, similar to those used on Scandinavian churches during the next two centuries. Medieval England developed these military flags, with certain permitted shapes for different ranks, into a full-scale heraldic system. The heralds also governed the erection of them in durable metal weathervane form, though weathervane licensing seems to have slipped through the net by 1485, when Richard III incorporated the College of Arms.

By 1300 the terms '*gallum*' and '*ventrilogium*', 'weathercock' and 'weathervane', have become interchangeable. Alongside heraldic banners, churches have continued to erect their cock weathervanes. A twelfth-century manuscript shows two on Canterbury Cathedral, while repair records indicate one on St Paul's by the mid thirteenth century. Soft, malleable copper was the preferred material, for, although it needed bracing with wrought iron for strength, so did iron itself if it had been rolled thin enough to cut intricately. Moreover, copper did not, like wood, require the specially smoothed plaster of Paris foundation, known as 'gesso', before gold leaf would adhere properly. However, spindles, bearings etc, and later cardinal arms, needed wrought iron's strength and hardness. Surprisingly, cast iron, already successfully produced in Kent and Sussex by the fifteenth century, was not employed architecturally for a further 300 years.

Cocks and heraldic weathervanes have continued with little obvious change right through from the late Middle Ages to the present. Britain can boast one of each, still existing from the fourteenth century: a church cock at Ottery St Mary, Devon, from about 1340 (*2.2*), and a heraldic banner on Etchingham Church, Sussex, from a few years later (*2.3*), both further considered later. Wishful thinking attributes a number of others to the fifteenth century, including those on churches at Emneth, Norfolk, and Fotheringhay, Northants, (*4.2*), but scientific examination of the metal seems the only way to ascertain whether or not they have ever been renewed. None of these early church weathervanes has cardinal arms: devout Christians knew that their church lay east-west.

The ostentation of the later Tudor period produced a rash of weathervanes, particularly heraldic emblems and banners. The simple square banners, without pointers, were made dramatic by the enormous carved heraldic beasts that frequently held them. Hampton Court's have been renewed, but the one on the medieval kitchen at Stanton Harcourt, Oxon., may be even earlier. The Victorians resurrected the fashion on neo-Gothic buildings, and 'Queen's Beasts' were created for the 1953 coronation, though these held shields not weathervanes.

In contrast to flat banners are some splendid early full-bodied weathervanes. A number of elaborate ships, the lion on Brighton Brewery (*2.4*), the City of London's Royal Exchange grasshopper, the fish at Bradford on Avon, Wilts. (*2.5*), Sheffield Cathedral's cock and the fierce dragon at Newark Park, Ozleworth, Glos. (*16.13*), all thought to be sixteenth-century work, give some idea of the range skilled Tudor craftsmen could emcompass.

Erecting a church weathervane was a ceremonial occasion. Contemporary notes on the building of Louth steeple, Lincs., between 1501 and 1518, describe the weathercock 'hallowed' by the parish priest and his brethren,

2.3   Oldest British weathervane,
c. 1370: Etchingham, Sussex.

2.4   Reputedly sixteenth-century: Black Lion
Brewery, Brighton, Sussex.

' … and then the said priests singing Te Deum Laudamus with organs, and then the Kirkwardens garred ring all the bells, and caused all the people there being to have bread and ale'. It further notes: ' … that Thos Taylor, draper, gave the weathercock, which was bought in York of a great baron, and made at Lincoln'. Pious donation was often the origin of church weathervanes.

Ignatio Danti revived the idea of vanes with interior dials in sixteenth-century Italy. They have never been really numerous in Britain, but a few were made in each period from then on.

In the seventeenth century, dominated by plague and fire, Commonwealth and Restoration, the popular notion of date-piercing weathervanes first becomes obvious. Perhaps earlier ones have simply not survived. Dates should be taken with a large pinch of salt, for replication is so easy, as on Stourbridge School, West Midlands, where the 1667 banner is not original. A 1620 brewery vane at Lewes, Sussex, and a banner of 1680 (*1.3*) on the town wall at Great Yarmouth, Norfolk, appear to be genuine, but Yarmouth's has lost its pointer, a typical addition, as are cardinal arms, from the mid-seventeenth century onwards.

After the Great Fire of 1666, Sir Christopher Wren rebuilt much of London. A scientist (who had designed a weather-clock), he was equally an artist concerned that the useful should also be beautiful. So each city church whose rebuilding he supervised had its individually designed weathervane. The variations he devised on the swallowtail pennon with pointer can still be admired, for some survived the London Blitz, others were later reproduced and several Oxford and Cambridge colleges also have them. The gridiron on the City of London church of St Lawrence Jewry is attributed to Wren, but especially famous is his splendid full-bodied dragon on St Mary-le-Bow Church, 1679 (*2.6*). A humbler silhouette dragon on St Mary at Latton, Harlow, Essex, cocks on the cathedrals at both Chichester, Sussex, and Norwich, Norfolk, and a three-dimensional ship at Kirkcudbright, Dumfries & Galloway, demonstrate the seventeenth-century range.

From the eighteenth century onwards, weathervanes survive in quantity and variety. It was above all the century of the pennant, elegant on gracious eighteenth-century homes, simple for their stable blocks with ventilation or clock turrets, and vying with banners for eminence on public buildings. Llanidloes, Powys, has a dragon banner dated 1738 (*5.12*). More individual weathervanes include the visual double pun or 'rebus' vane of East Dereham Church, Norfolk, dated 1773 (*2.7*), and the Wakeman's horn at Ripon, Yorks, 1780 (16.7). The popularity of the domestic silhouette, too, pointed towards the far greater variety of motifs the next century was to bring.

For half or fully rounded weathervanes, although some casting was done in bronze, copper was still the most favoured material. The smith would hammer each half from copper sheet, gently stretching it into curved shapes but without making it too thin at any point. Working from inside, he hammered it onto a bed of pitch-and-plaster mix, or lead, or even a leather bag filled with sand, any of which provided the 'give' needed to prevent the copper splitting. Making each half, working by eye alone from a drawing, was difficult enough. Making both halves so that they fitted perfectly together for soldering demanded a sculptural imagination, especially if the form was not symmetrical, perhaps with a mane or tail swept to one side. Still more details, fins etc, could be applied externally to the rounded form. There are still craftsmen who can do such work, but the long, highly skilled man-hours involved mean

2.5   Reputedly sixteenth-century: above chapel on
Bradford on Avon's medieval bridge, Wilts.

2.6 Seventeenth-century; Wren's most famous weathervane: St Mary-le-Bow, City of London.

2.7 Eighteenth-century, double-rebus weathervane: East Dereham Church, Norfolk.

2.8 Nineteenth-century; idealized human
form: Burslem Town Hall, Staffs.

it is a method used nowadays only for special vanes, such as the dolphin
in Ludham, Norfolk, described in Chapter 13 (*13.10*).

Three-dimensional ships would have been started in the same way, as
they are today, with the hull beaten out in two halves which are then
joined, often smoothly but sometimes riveted to imitate a keel. Masts are
fixed to the keel, and the deck, cut larger than its final area, is fed over
them. Pressed into the top of the hull shape, it can then be secured,
again by a variety of methods, to the top edges of the hull. The holes
required to prevent the hull imploding from gases cooling as heat is
removed can be incorporated into the design as scuppers. Sails, beaten
from flat sheet, and rigging of copper wire, are added afterwards, again
always delicate, time-consuming and costly work, though the results can
be beautiful (*15.1; 15.2; 15.3; 15.4*).

Increasingly during the eighteenth century, however, copper was
being challenged by good English wrought iron, especially for flat vanes,
for which its greater strength made it more suitable.

The process of smelting iron with coke, developed by the Darbys of

Coalbrookdale early in the eighteenth century, heralded the most dramatic change in weathervanes for centuries. It was a real breakthrough, for since it took so much woodland to fire one furnace with wood, heavy taxes had been imposed on ironwork since Elizabethan times. One cause of the American Revolution is said to have been the restriction placed on American ironworkers to produce only pig iron for Britain, using their abundant wood to save their former homeland's. Weather-resistant cast-iron ornament, including weathervanes, could now be produced in quantity, at speed, by semi-skilled labour, and therefore much more cheaply, thus tapping a new market. Famous cast-iron manufacturers such as Coalbrookdale and Carron were in full swing by 1760; Kenricks was established in 1791, soon to be followed by Falkirk, Macfarlane's and many more. The first surge of American weathervane-making came towards the end of the eighteenth century. Not unnaturally, Paul Revere's fish, President Washington's dove of peace, and Jefferson's dial vane are deeply venerated.

Although, of course, copper and wrought iron were still used, cast iron was the real feature of nineteenth-century weathervanes. Early pattern books culminated in such enormous catalogues as Macfarlane's of 1871, 596 close-packed pages measuring 15 inches by 11½ inches in two hardback volumes weighing nearly thirteen pounds. Seventy-seven pages are devoted to finials alone. Weathervanes increase from a modest two feet six inches to seventeen feet six inches high, the larger ones rising from elaborate railed surrounds or iron ornament extending right along the apex of the roof. Builders bought the smaller cast-iron finials and weathervanes in bulk from such catalogues for their rows of speculative villas. They created repetitive images, but sufficiently separated by different repetitive images to give the impression of novelty and individuality. In this new middle-class urban market, mere quantity of ornament, especially in iron, conferred status on the owner.

The Victorians, seeking to counteract industrial squalor without sacrificing industry's exciting products, evolved a conscious theory: plainness equals deprivation; decoration equals beauty; beauty brings happiness. So when they had built their schools and almshouses and shops and railway stations in imitation of medieval Gothic colleges and churches, they smothered every surface with decoration and added quasi-medieval-heraldic banners to the pinnacles. Classical town halls received classical vanes. Image-conscious commercial concerns then also took unto themselves the respectable auras of these two styles. In addition, the nineteenth century borrowed every known historical and geographical fashion of architecture. Fountains became Indian temples;

jubilee clock towers resembled Chinese carved ivory. How irresistible to create cast-iron ornament, including weathervanes, to suit. Tiny square banners came with angular or geometric cut-outs, larger ones with vaguely Egyptian or vaguely Oriental designs. For convenience of manufacture, the organic shapes – for example, of vegetation – recognized as inherently beautiful and therefore life-enhancing, were often formalized and simplified. Curving lines finally blossomed in some flowing Art Nouveau banners. Cardinal arms, too, became curved or otherwise shaped. Formal Roman lettering gave way to cursive scripts, some more decorative than legible.

Nineteenth-century silhouette vanes were unlimited in subject range. Living creatures, including a few exotics, sporting images, trade signs, symbols, ships and mythical creatures abounded. Rounded forms were also cast in iron, particularly the more detailed sections such as cocks' heads. Hundreds of these were added to separately cast or die-stamped hollow bodies, and differently cast or flat-sheet tails. Particularly delightful are Victorian dragons, both cast in modelled form and lively and writhing enough to look modelled even when flat. The human form, formerly rare in weathervanes, now begins to appear over grand civic buildings, sculpted into suitably idealized angels and divinities (*2.8*). It is all larger and more abundant than life, overwhelming, ostentatious, sometimes vulgar – but what determination, what zest they had. That so much of this output has lasted commends not just ingenious Victorian manufacturing but the perfectionist industrial craftsmen whose pride forbade them to let pass rough seams or anything shoddy.

American manufactured (as opposed to folk-art) weathervanes also reached their zenith at this period. Usually copper, they were mass-produced in moulds, but hand-finished, to create fine pieces of sculptural quality. They are far more fully documented than British vanes, and a very high proportion are now in museums and private art collections.

Twentieth-century architecture has, on the whole, been less sympathetic to weathervanes. Defiant replicas of City of London church weathervanes destroyed in the Blitz are dwarfed by huge post-war commercial blocks. Even earlier this century, as private homes shrank or combined into blocks of flats, and gabled roofscapes lost favour, full-bodied gilt dragons were obviously less at home. Running foxes and classical pennants found low, square garages less congenial than the turreted stable blocks to which they were accustomed.

The twentieth-century answer was to develop for these lower viewpoints 'genre' scenes, i.e. figures in a setting of trees, grass, fences,

waves etc. Travel and hunting scenes and contemporary sporting epi-
sodes were particularly popular. Many paid too little attention to the fact
that even quite shallow viewing-angles shortened and fattened human
figures while elongating and thinning horizontal animals, and many were
far too complicated. The real requirement was to create a bold outline,
with more details implied than executed. This approach led fairly directly
to the vigour of cartoon figures and graphic art tehniques popular today.
Exaggerated lines can solve problems of perspective and proportion and
restore the vitality that some too faithful reproductions lack. Conscious
humour in weathervanes, however, has to be considered carefully, unless
the vane is regarded as expendable, for humour can soon pall.

Mild steel has proved a very satisfactory medium for these silhouettes
and other flat weathervanes. The image is drawn, or finer details are
scribed onto steel sheet, and key points are drilled out as a guide. An
oxyacetylene cutter, with a stepped nozzle to create the cooler flame
necessary for thin sheet, makes cutting quite intricate motifs relatively
straightforward (*2.9*). Much of the final effect depends on the initial
drawing. Figs. *8.11*, *13.8* and *15.10* give an idea of the delicate and
dramatic effects clever cutting can create.

Recently, maintenance-free and lightweight plastics and fibreglass
have made some inroads, but easily worked aluminium is now chiefly
used. However, if wrongly balanced, perhaps through damage, these
lightweight materials can spin so wildly that they can actually launch
themselves right off their spindles, which some makers, therefore, insist
on having longer than for an iron vane.

Despite architectural indifference and sometimes mediocre mass-
production, the century has created its own striking weathervanes. Who
would believe that Old Father Time (*2.10*) at Lord's Cricket Ground,
Greater London, to many people the definitive secular weathervane,
began life only in 1925? Hermes at Twickenham, Greater London (*2.10*),
the Town House's dramatic saint at Kirkcaldy, Fife (*16.9*), some lively
modern cocks and pugnacious Welsh dragons, gilded three-dimensional
sailing-vessels at Bristol, Avon, and Farnham, Surrey, 'built' in the 1980s
– all are twentieth-century craftsmanship. The two new ships are gilded,
but modern taste inclines to the antique, so some new weathervanes are
artificially aged; when gilding has worn, traditional copper ones are left to
develop the beautiful greeny-blue oxidization that the Victorians would
have found shockingly naked.

Home-made weathervanes are also a sizeable contemporary group.
Discounting the crudely inept, some are delightfully naïve, some uninhibited and idiosyncratic. Or, like the engine at Wells-next-the-Sea,

2.9   Cutting the motif for *17.6*;
Bill Cordaroy at work: East
Ruston, Norfolk.

Norfolk, (*14.2*), they may result from long, patient hours with fretsaw
and file. Time-consuming detail often signals 'amateur' in its best sense,
not stinting on labour to make a profit. To work on comparable terms,
the skilled craftsman must find a patron who will commission without
knowing what the ultimate cost will be – because the craftsman himself
cannot estimate how long it will take, especially if he is evolving
techniques as he goes along.

A weathervane-maker must consider all its parts – its shaft or spindle,
cardinal arms and letters, decorative additions, as well as motif. His
thinking will be much influenced by his intention and his material. For a
public building, tradition suggests the expense but durability of metals.
Copper's malleability offers great freedom. Copper sheet can be
fashioned into intricate acanthus leaves or details of quality, such as
hands with distinct palms and backs and separate fingers. Cocks can be
bellied out for lead weighting; copper rod can be twisted to make, for
instance, a unicorn's horn or drawn into wire rigging. Copper holds gold
leaf the most effectively. Iron may be wrought or cast. Wrought iron
worked hot (scrolling, for instance) has a quality of spontaneity born of
the necessity literally to strike while the iron is hot: it can then be
chiselled or filed cold to finish it. Cast iron, different in chemical
make-up, can be cast in moulds or die-stamped and achieve
considerable surface interest. Brass, bronze and other metals have also
traditionally been used.

Aluminium's versatility now gives it great popularity. Favourite
designs can be stamped from aluminium sheets like biscuits; it is easily

2.10 Twentieth-century; *left:* Father Time, Lord's Cricket Ground,
St John's Wood, Greater London; *right:* Hermes, Rugby Football
Union Ground, Twickenham, Greater London.

worked by hand, and molten aluminium can be poured into moulds to make rounded weathervanes. The quality of the initial pattern is crucial here. Carved in wood or built up on a wire frame with plaster of Paris or Polyfilla, both accuracy of line and lively surface detail may be sought. Patterns by Mary Moore for Brandeston Forge, Suffolk, cast by Jays of Norwich, show what subtlety of detail can be achieved.

The casting process, although complex, is surprisingly quick in the hands of a skilled team. In a half box the pattern, laid on its side, is half submerged in sand rammed firmly enough to hold its impression. Surplus loose sand is carefully brushed from the pattern edges so that it will later lift out cleanly, and 'parting powder' is dusted over the entire surface. Then, with a tube inserted to create a pouring-hole, sand is piled over the second side and firmed, and the 'lid' secured. When turned on its edge and opened like a suitcase, the box should reveal a neat impression on one side, and the pattern lift out cleanly from the other. Air-escape lines are scored from the points of the design, the mould is gently closed, and aluminium at 70°–80°C is poured into the prepared hole (*2.11*) until it bubbles out. Aluminium takes only about twenty minutes to cool sufficiently to be removed (*2.12*) for decorating and finishing. Clearly, since the sand mould has to be remade each time, this ancient process is too skilled and too slow for anything except short runs. Quantity production required iron moulds capable of virtually unlimited use.

Stainless steel is not an easy material, but its anti-corrosive properties make it popular today, especially for spindles. Other modern materials include plastics thick and thin, of course, perspex, fibreglass, plastic laminate, even hardboard. Theoretically, anything with some flat sheet strength could be employed. All have fairly obvious pros and cons. Vanes may utilize the best qualities of more than one material – bulky wood for a cock's body, sheet metal for its tail's large surface area, for instance. Combining metals needs care and knowledge. Smiths have described aluminium reduced to a powder by contact with steel, and copper corrosion accelerated by iron.

Though obviously good for DIY weathervanes, wood alone, flat or carved, deteriorates fast, especially if rain and frost penetrate. Constant painting both strengthens and protects it. A cock on Borough Hill, Thaxted, Essex, overlooking the mill from its summerhouse, is an interesting combination. The owner, a keen furniture-maker, made the ball of yew, the cardinals of oak, and the pennant of acacia, weighted with lead. The spindle is of copper, and the cock, under his gay feathering, of zinc (*2.13*).

Some quite extraordinary 'scrap' materials emerge. Cistern ballcocks frequently serve as intersections; the Elephant and Castle pub at Bampton, Oxon., uses horseshoes as cardinals and makes a barrel from a stack of washers; hot-water cylinders and fridge doors have provided flat sheet; cycle wheels make pivotal bearings; hubcaps, springs, every kind of discarded farm equipment, even a plastic shampoo bottle, have all contributed.

Amateurs improvising in this way are unlikely to be employing the hot forge-welded joints traditional in wrought iron. Work that would originally have been riveted, pinned and dowelled, or riveted and banded in a two-hour job, can now be spot-welded in five minutes. Skilled workers will still choose metal of the conformation most suited to the task: flat bar for certain scrolls, circular rod to create, for example, the spade handle and reedmace or 'bulrushes' of *17.6* at Ranworth, Norfolk. The details of such work , however, are to be found in technical manuals.

Ordinary observers of weathervanes will be more aware of the various surface appearances associated with different materials. Modern maintenance-reducing techniques, the hot-dipped galvanizing, stove enamelling or Teflon coating remain the exceptions. Perversely, people

2.11   Casting in sand. Pouring molten aluminium.

2.12   New casting ready to lift out of hollow mould: Jay's
Foundry, Norwich, Norfolk.

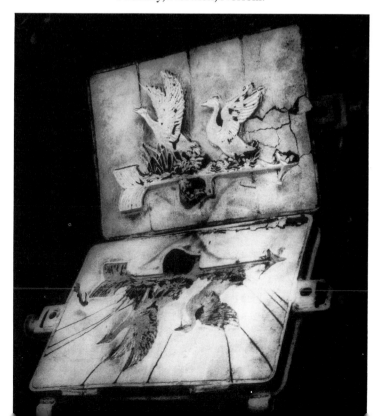

buying maintenance-free plastic weathervanes often paint them to give them some individuality. Plain silhouettes can be given detail, and sometimes the painted impression of modelling is very convincing, as in *11.4* and *13.4*, but the technique is misapplied to a loftily mounted weathervane. Reflective glass, copper nailheads, even leather and mica have all been applied for surface detail. Copper left unsurfaced develops a patina whose greener or bluer tinge stems from chemical reaction to atmospheric environment.

The surface most favoured through the centuries has been gilding, to impress and to beautify. It hid inferior metals; some cheats are now laid bare, for not all metals hold gold leaf equally well. Technical necessities, such as holes soldered after lead weighting has been introduced, are also hidden. Creating a seamless surface from 2¾ inch square sheets of gold leaf, each only 1/25,000 inch thick, laid onto an oil/size adhesive over the edges of piercings or the irregular details of a sculpted form, is costly in labour as well as materials, especially if more than one layer is applied, but should last about fifty years. Harpford Church, Devon, was recorded in the late 1950s as having a dove weathervane carved from pinewood overlaid with seventy separate pieces of copper, held by copper nails with soldered joints to prevent rain penetration. It sounds almost as though a carver was tempted to gild his wooden pattern instead of casting a mould from it.

Occasionally, surface interest can even be contrived from the strengthening bars that copper or thin sheet-iron vanes require (*3.4*). Usually, however, these straps are uncompromisingly straight: a black one horizontally across a simple, sweeping gilt cock-shape on All Saints, Compton, Leek, Staffs., gives the cock an oddly jowled appearance. Straps added after manufacture as repairs, even if deplorable artistically, add to the vane's historic interest. In general, however, restorers should work sympathetically with an old vane, not altering its proportions or removing, for example, traditional fleur-de-lys projections as a sop to some temporary fashion for a simpler outline.

Apart from surface corrosion, whether a vane needs repair or not is likely to depend on how successfully it pivots. Blacksmiths have their own pet methods and tend to deride all others. Subtle refinements are many, but the basic principle is that the spindle consists of a solid rod and a sleeve, one of which swivels. There are two main approaches. In the first, more usual method (*2.14a*), the sleeve drops over the spindle like a cap on a pen. In the second (*2.14b*), the sleeve is at the base, the spindle dropping into it; an extra 'umbrella' is needed to prevent rain filling the sleeve.

2.13   Summerhouse cock, zinc with a variety of
woods: Thaxted, Essex.

The simplest spindle has a sharpened point; but there are hardened
or phosphor-bronze bearings; there are steel pins with brass bushes;
there are glass marbles or ball-bearings in cups; there are ball-bearings
welded to the point and retempered in hot oil; there are ball races for
heavier vanes; there are bearings made of nylon rod for which the
lubricant is water. Some smiths swear by grease; one has a magic 'brew'
of graphite and plumbago which he claims will outlast the vane. The fit
must be tight enough to allow smooth rotation without rocking, loose
enough to allow for expansion and just enough friction for steadiness.

This is also achieved by the correct balance of the vane:
weight-to-area ratio is an element of both design and construction. With
its surface area and weight both wholly to one side, the banner still
works. But friction means wear, and perfectionists prefer a larger area of
motif, preferably more than two-thirds, behind the spindle to hold the
vane steadily into the wind, but roughly equal weight fore and aft. Solid
cast cocks' heads or lead-cheeked arrow points provide forward weight

(Hermes's pointer weight, at Twickenham, Greater London, is sixty pounds; *2.10*). Rounded copper forms may have experimental quantities of lead introduced, for example, through the nostril of the buck in *4.14*. The hole is sealed and quickly cooled; favourite equipment for this is apparently a cut potato. Vanes with horizontal width but with little obvious vertical tail surface, such as a three-dimensional flying gull or arms on an agricultural sprayer, need careful experimental balancing.

One maker's summary of his work seems worth quoting. Edward Reed, who made the vane at Ogle, Northd. (*16.5*) in 1948, gave these details:

> The figures are hand cut from ⅛″ sheet, balance being achieved by using steel for the stag and duralumin for the larger group. Whip, bit and reins, the last being double five stranded plaits, are of copper.
>
> The ironwork is hand wrot and clipped together. The spindle, which is solid, extends to the foot of the tubular column and rests on an adjustable, hardened steel cone. It is positioned by a ball-bearing at the top of the column which provides an oil bath for the whole mechanism.
>
> The top bearing is protected from the weather by a hand-turned duralumin cover, secured to the shaft by a vice nut bearing upon a split copper cone. The cover is stepped to prevent rain entering and provides for lubrication.
>
> The North and South points are represented by a Thistle and Rose, cut and worked in copper upon a steel frame. The flower of the rose was cut in one piece, and that of the thistle in four. The East and West points are plain scrolls, designed both to provide a basket for the floral pieces and to give the whole component the impression that it rests upon the roof ridge....

Successful weathervanes can achieve great size. Most are far larger than they appear. The angel at Burslem, Staffs, for instance (*2.8*), is five feet tall; in Dorset, Shapwick's vane (*17.3*) is nine feet long; the angel at Guildford, Surrey (16.9) is fifteen feet tall. (Many other dimensions are given throughout the text.) Occasionally a vane is unexpectedly small, like the cock at Ottery St Mary, Devon (*2.2*), at about two feet three inches. Perching starlings or pigeons often give valuable clues.

The corollary to size is weight, especially in older iron vanes, which weigh about three times as much as the equivalent size in modern aluminium. Even when the vane functions properly, the fixed parts take great strain. An experienced blacksmith will almost always add more iron than a theoretical designer specifies.

Comparing prices through the centuries is difficult without a complete matching scale of monetary values, though some prices are mentioned in various chapters as being of some intrinsic interest.

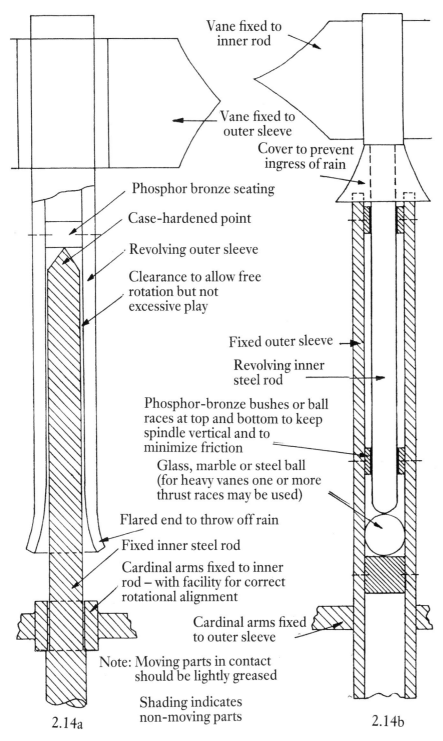

Vane fixed to
inner rod

Vane fixed to
outer sleeve

Cover to prevent
ingress of rain

Phosphor bronze seating

Case-hardened point

Revolving outer sleeve

Clearance to allow free
rotation but not
excessive play

Fixed outer sleeve

Revolving inner
steel rod

Phosphor-bronze bushes or ball
races at top and bottom to keep
spindle vertical and to
minimize friction

Glass, marble or steel ball
(for heavy vanes one or more
thrust races may be used)

Flared end to throw off rain

Fixed inner steel rod

Cardinal arms fixed to inner
rod – with facility for correct
rotational alignment

Cardinal arms fixed
to outer sleeve

Note: Moving parts in contact
should be lightly greased

Shading indicates
non-moving parts

2.14a   2.14b

2.14   Typical pivoting details, used in varying
combinations.

Obviously, in the late 1980s, £38 plus £14. 2. 0. for gilding sounds pretty cheap for Wren's eight-foot-ten-inch dragon (*2.6*) in 1679. In 1702 the Wakeman's Horn (*16.7*) cost £54. Harvey's Brewery in Lewes, Sussex, paid just 19s. 8½d. in 1756 for a second-hand vane. But realizing that South Shields' ship (*15.1*), at £108 in 1910, would cost £5,500 today gives those prices some perspective. Kirkcaldy, Fife, got a fine bargain in 1965 for £184. 10. 0: today £1700 would be nearer the mark. In 1967 St Michael's, Lewes, was able to repair the bronze spindle and pivot, and sandblast, zinc spray and regild its pennant, all for £124: in 1987, Norwich's three-foot fire-station vane (*14.10*) would have cost £160 for regilding alone.

Somebody, it seems, has always been willing to pay for the products of these largely anonymous craftsmen, working so confidently by eye and experience. The very popularity of their products spawned the quantity output of the late nineteenth and early twentieth centuries. Even contemporary blacksmiths are likely to be known only locally, or by the customer commissioning work from them. Their work, usually unsigned, is recognized by particular styles or shapes of arms and lettering, by particular production methods, and above all by quality, especially in the execution of scroll decoration, in which amateurs are usually less skilled. Although their names are so rarely publicized a few are indicated in the Acknowledgements.

The most superb design, materials and workmanship are all to no avail, however, if common sense deserts the new owner when he sets about erecting his weathervane. He may not be blessed with an ideal site, free of visual obstructions and wind eddies. But he *can* erect it with reference to the compass. A weathervane is a nonsense if its arms are merely neatly parallel to the house, or the north pointer indicates vaguely anywhere north of an east/west line. Magnetic north varies by several degrees between western Ireland and east Norfolk, so a vane should indicate not magnetic but true north. And perhaps it is unwise to rely too heavily on the alignment of other people's vanes in the vicinity!

3 Cocks

On the face of it the cock is too commonplace, too unadmirably 'cocky' to warrant the elevation it enjoys. But with this very early kind of weathervane we immediately meet the habit of erecting weathervanes that serve two or even three purposes – function, decoration and

3.1 Unusual early silhouette cock, *c.* 1500: Dunblane Cathedral, Central.

message. Which was regarded as having primacy depended on who you were.

The function of indicating wind-direction is admirably fulfilled by a cock. Not only does its large tail mean that for safety it *must* swivel – and movement is eyecatching – but at its natural point of balance it automatically swings head to wind. Even at a distance head and tail remain distinct; even in naïve, stylized, relatively uncock-like versions, its form remains decorative. Moreover, its message is multi-layered. Widely separated ancient cultures associated its dawn shout with the sun god; its alertness, pride and virility were manifest; ancient China and Rome revered the fighting cocks they bred. Gospel references to St Peter's betrayal of Christ eased the cock's passage from pagan lore to Christian symbol. The vigilance of both layman and priest against sin, the power of the Church in God's work, a reminder that the first morning duty is prayer were just a few of the Christian 'messages' attributed to the steeple cock.

Not surprisingly, therefore, references to church cocks start very early. The notably early bronze cock found at Brescia, references in Anglo-Saxon literature, the supposed ninth-century edict, manuscript illustrations and the Bayeux Tapestry have already been noted. From the thirteenth-century Durandus onwards, theologians elaborated with great subtlety on the cock's Christian significance. But already, before 1400, a 'Balade', attributed to no less a writer than Chaucer, uses it to jibe at woman's inconstancy:

> There is no feith that may your herte embrace
> But as a wedercock, that turneth his face
> With every wind, ye fare, and that is sene.

Symbolism may be carried as successfully by representative, impressionistic cocks, as by representational, lifelike ones. Early cocks usually lack legs and are often impaled, recalling the suggestion that Peter thus punished any cock with the temerity to crow near him. Simplified, often sinuous shapes persist right up to our own times, but not because smiths cannot re-create realistic cocks. An eighteenth-century French cock, now resident at the Victoria & Albert Museum, elevates the 'mere' weathervane into a superlative bronze sculpture.

To start with, cocks were probably the only form of church weathervane. They shared the respect accorded to the church building and were as carefully maintained. At least five regildings to Old St Paul's cock are recorded before it finally succumbed to gales in 1505. Even after other religious symbols or saints' emblems were used, all of which the Puritans found distastefully close to graven images, the cock weathervane never lost its hold.

The tenth-century Winchester cock already mentioned is the earliest recorded British example. The earliest known still to exist is a quite small one, only about two feet three inches long, still in use on the marvellous collegiate church at Ottery St Mary, Devon (*2.2*). It dates from *c.*1340. Although the tail, perforated by Cromwellian musket shot, was replaced in 1908, it was to the original design. The cast bronze bird, with v-shaped serrated brass comb, is substantially original. Two extraordinary trumpet-like tubes through the body amplified the notes of G and B, produced as the wind vibrated 'tongues' within them, and it became known as 'the whistling cock'. Attempts to silence it for the sake of nearby residents were only partially successful. It still moans a little in high winds. A rather primitive copper cock, full-bodied but with flat comb, wattle and tail, standing on Sheffield Cathedral, is probably the one for which John Darbie was paid 13 shillings in 1565. There is one reference, however, to its having an earlier date, 1428, on its tail. Both these three-dimensional cocks work well, so the trick of weighting the hollow breast with lead for proper balance was obviously familiar.

Another, quite different early example is on Dunblane Cathedral, Central (*3.1*). Bishop Chisholm, who inserted below the parapet bearing his arms two upper stages in the defensive tower to accommodate a ring of

3.2   Cock as pointer: St Ethelburga's Church, Bishopsgate, City of London.

bells, probably erected it, which dates it around 1500. The way it clings on for dear life prompted this local limerick:

> There was an old fowl of Dunblane,
> Who refused to sit down on the vane;
> This Chisholm decried
> But it hung on the side
> And surveyed all the precincts the same.

It is not a posture other church cocks have sought to emulate.

Perhaps the very universality of the cock lessened the potency of its religious symbolism. It sometimes became a mere adjunct to other elements – a finial, for instance. On the delicate 1671 banner at St Ethelburga's, Bishopsgate, City of London, almost overwhelmed by looming office blocks, it is reduced to a small, defiant bird on the curved pointer (*3.2*). Or attention may be transferred from the cock itself to something else: 'PAX 1713' cut into a Norwich cock commemorates the Peace of Utrecht.

Generally, however, dates and initials inscribed on a cock merely indicate restoration and those responsible. They come to light during subsequent repairs, and although they may cover a long timespan, they are fairly common. Not so the inscription on a cock at York. In 1645 it was ordered, presumably by Cromwellian icon-busters, that all the 'loose brass' in the Minster should be sold. Some must have been hoarded locally, for in the more relaxed atmosphere of the Restoration it reappeared, recycled into a weathervane. This stood on the Minster turret from 1666 until 1803 and although, sadly, not on show, it is still preserved. The sheet-brass bird has a double centre section, reinforced with iron to form a socket, and the plate tail has four separate feathers riveted on. Almost the whole consists of haphazardly arranged bits of inscription. Painstaking detective work last century reassembled the jigsaw into a virtually complete epitaph to John Moore, barrister of Lincoln's Inn, buried in the Lady Chapel in 1597.

A more conventional line in ecclesiastical economy is the transfer of a weathervane from one church to another. Winchcombe's fine, well-nourished cock is actually on permanent loan from St Mary Redcliffe, Bristol. The spire there fell in 1446, and this cock was for long attributed to the same date. In 1872 'the old weathervane' was deemed too heavy and large, at six feet, for the new slender spire and it moved to Winchcombe, Glos. Had it really been in store for over 400 years? The lifelike form struck the steeplejacks who last gilded it as more

3.3 Victorian mass-produced banner, metamorphosed (*right*) into a
cock: Ankerdine Hill, Knightwick, Hereford & Worcester.

like eighteenth-century work. By then, the intensely mystical interpretation of the stylized cock symbol was less powerful.

Realistic cocks, which we think of as typical secular weathervanes, also have their element of symbolism, representing the former ubiquity of poultry in every farm and cottager's yard. The easily visible barn was thought a suitable perch for farm weathervanes. Even when eighteenth- and nineteenth-century farmhouses were architecturally suitable, their owners increasingly aspired to something more elegant or individual than the farmyard Chanticleer. Ironically, they often chose banners from mass-produced catalogues. How very delightful it would be to learn when and why a favourite stylish Victorian banner on Tower House, Ankerdine Hill, Knightwick, Hereford & Worcester, was metamorphosed into an effective cock, simply by the addition of a head (*3.3*).

Although many farmers could have forged some sort of cardinal arms, easier still with modern techniques, few bothered. Assessing the general direction of the wind in relation to farm activities was the important thing, not being able to name it.

3.4   Design by John Sell Cotman for Knapton Church, Norfolk.

3.5   Modern mass-produced shrieking cock, distributed throughout
Europe.

To most of us a cock is a cock, but different breeds of poultry are sometimes distinguishable in weathervanes. Experts have identified a Silver Duckwing Yokohama at Lindfield, Sussex, on the summerhouse at Clock House, where a former owner reputedly bred them (*3.8*).

Cock weathervanes have appeared in some locations less predictable than traditional rural buildings. A Fort William distillery, Highland, the modern town hall at Watford, Herts., and Grandtully Castle, Tayside, are fairly diverse. In Berkshire, traditional three-dimensional cocks rear quite unexpected defiance above Slough's highrise blocks; Smithfield meat market in the City of London had a cock (why not a bull?) which crashed down in a destructive fire in 1958 and is now in an office. Oddest of all as a weathervane site must surely be a gibbet. A cock dated 1734 was placed on 'Jacob's Post' near Ditchling, Sussex, from which Jacob the Jew's body was hung in chains after his execution at Horsham Gaol for a triple murder at the Royal Oak Inn.

Undoubtedly, more cocks than any other creature acquire three dimensions and a gilded surface. Very broadly, these are ecclesiastical, while simple iron silhouettes are probably secular. But the overlap is considerable, with some quite grand cocks on schools or country house outbuildings, and quite primitive cut-outs on some churches. Cathedral cocks at Norwich and Exeter, for example, are not noticeably more handsome than parish church cocks at Ripe, Rhayader, Leuchars or Leamington Spa. Traditional three-dimensional cocks are still made – witness Guildford Cathedral's in the 1960s – but Bradford Cathedral's, of about the same date, his flat wings, held stiffly away from but parallel to its slightly rounded body.

Some cocks gain added lustre from a 'name', like Knapton's proud bird (*3.4*) designed by the local Norfolk artist John Sell Cotman in 1823 while he was employed giving drawing lessons to the daughters of the Big House. Recently it has been refurbished, courtesy of the offshore gas terminal at Bacton. Others acquire a unique shape, more curiously: the characterful bird protesting from the spire at Wimblington, Cambs., was discovered to be too large and was hastily snipped at all round before the scaffolding came down and rendered him inaccessible.

In late-twentieth-century Britain, cock weathervanes are again a most popular domestic choice. Several designs at a price anyone can afford are offered through mail-order catalogues (about one hundred years later than in the USA). This can result in their purchase for some incongruous positions on sophisticated or urban buildings where a pigeon or tomcat might seem more appropriate. Conversely, the shrieking cock (*3.5*), a most popular design widely available throughout Europe, looks incongruously modern on a rural thatched barn. Others come from abroad too: the 'O' for Ost cardinal letter beneath a cock at Helpston, Cambs., betrays its Austrian origin, while a little cast-aluminium cock-and-arrow is available in both Britain and the USA.

Mass production need not mean uniformity. Even though the nineteenth-century heyday produced thousands of cast weathercock bodies, the quantity of handwork involved in adding different heads and tails, and in finishing, expressed the period's prosperity and independence and prevented exact duplication. New owners of a mill at St Neots, Cambs., who found one of these cast cocks' bodies *in situ*, inserted into the hollow broken neck a flat zinc head of their own design. Sturdy plastic cocks come in several vibrant colours; one has a black body and hectic scarlet and yellow plumage, slashed so that the sky behind gives a fourth colour. Assorted feathering is also often painted onto other identically stamped-out cocks to render them more stylish or individual.

The continuing popularity of the cock weathervane is attested by the Rural Development Commission's catalogue. Its five designs, all secular, concentrate on the cock as a decorative image. Hence the inclusion of an unfamiliar 'gamecock' type. Every county provides examples of these, though here again individual blacksmiths, varying the proportions even fractionally, give them differing personalities.

Regional style is no easier to define than historical style, with much imitation of favourites across the counties, as across the centuries. One cannot help wondering whether one popular Victorian cock was a deliberate copy of an illustration in the tenth-century *Benedictional of Aethwold*, which it resembles, or some kind of folk-memory.

A real craftsman, however, given a free hand, can produce arresting weathercocks that are unequivocally of their period. Figs. *3.6* and *3.7* show two such examples. The cock made entirely of scrolls and curves was an imaginative pre-war creation, and after half a century on an outbuilding at Spronketts, Bolney, Sussex, it still works beautifully with only an occasional greasing. The strappy cock making uninhibited comments on passers-by at Dedham, Essex, was made for a Sussex garden folly in the 1960s.

Today's enormous population of weathercocks owes its astonishing variety to a number of factors. Wood, iron, copper and plastics differ in visual texture and working techniques. They will influence whether a cock is made in one piece or several, fully or partially rounded or flat. Different surface treatments have a different impact – oxidized copper,

3.6 1930s scrolled cock: Bolney, Sussex (*left*) and
3.7 Strappy fifties design: Dedham, Essex (*right*).

matt or glossy black, gold leaf, even an unexpected scarlet as on Balderstone church, Greater Manchester. The dual symbolic/farmyard background of weathercocks influences the shape. Designers vary significantly in the artistry with which they 'see' the details of the cock; a similar range is evident in the abilities of craftsmen executing the designs, not just in technical skill but in their capacity, for example, to interpret a drawing in sculptural terms. Finally, a further highly influential matter: the bird itself postures so extravagantly.

A few cursory glances aloft establish certain overall impressions. The simple, stylized serpentine cock can either sit up and beg or be elongated horizontally. The positioning of head and tail can make it look either chirpy or droopy; the same shape can be rendered lean or chubby. Cocks on churches at Winchcombe, Glos., and Stokesay, Shropshire, breast the air; that at All Saints, Hereford, almost overbalances. They can lean forward or recoil. Musselburgh, Lothian, has a town-hall cock that looks almost apologetic (*3.9*); Caley's Farm, Flinton, Humberside, one that is startled; South Ossett Church, Yorks, a neat and prissy bird. Whitekirk Church's cock in Lothian has an almost human face(*3.9*); Hartburn's in Northumberland looks like a sinister Knave of Hearts(*3.9*). At Beambridge, Ches., we have something more like a hen sitting on eggs(*3.9*), at Tenbury Wells, Hereford & Worcester, a child's 'potato figure' with looped tail(*3.9*). Some are taller than wide, some wider than tall. Naturalistic, sophisticatedly stylized and naïve cocks may be close neighbours. Some triumphantly

Hawkesbury,
Avon

Hove,
Sussex

Tabley,
Cheshire

Alconbury,
Cambs.

Rougham,
Norfolk

Barnstaple,
Devon

Cousley Wood,
Sussex

Meliden,
Clwyd

Newtown,
Powys

Eggington,
Beds.

Herne Bay,
Kent

Newton Abbot,
Devon

Lindfield,
Sussex

Wellingborough,
Northants

Llanrhidian,
Glam.

3.8   Cocks in endless variety …

Musselburgh,
Lothian

Beambridge,
Cheshire

Braemar,
Grampian

Tenbury Wells,
Hereford & Worcester

Wellington,
Somerset

Gloucester

Kneesworth,
Cambs.

Lakenheath,
Suffolk

Abingdon,
Oxon

Southrop,
Glos.

Gamlingay,
Cambs.

Hartburn,
Northd.

Haddenham,
Bucks.

Much Wenlock,
Salop

Hadlow Down,
Sussex

York

Martin,
Lincs.

Whitekirk,
Lothian

Kippax,
Yorks.

stamp the earth, others are helplessly impaled.

Four main aspects of the cock – body, head, legs and tail – contribute to these overall effects, and each can have great individuality. A small fraction of the variations, taken in conjunction with the drawings of 'typical' shapes (*3.8* and *3.9*), may indicate the fun available to readers who subject the examples they find to close scrutiny.

Bodies themselves are variable: spherical, oval, cylindrical, serpentine, almost triangular or reasonably naturalistic. The shape may be gently curved or almost a horseshoe, puffy or flat-chested, solid or an empty outline. Flat vanes usually ignore wings or suggest them by paint or perforations. On three-dimensional cocks the moulded wings may be held close, attached flat alongside with protruding wingtips, attached parallel to the body but at a distance, spread small like a sealion's flippers or wide like an aeroplane's wings.

Heads pointing skywards and through every gradation to a near nose-dive suggest different characters and moods. Beaks are primly closed, shouting protest, hooked like a parrot's, doubly curved like a crossbill's. With no crests, weathercocks resemble pigeons or turkeys. Crests may be sprays of feathers pointing forwards, upwards or backwards, plain triangles variously angled, something that looks like a serrated crew-cut, powder puff, horse's mane, Indian headdress … too large or too small, they alter appearance as drastically as a shaggy or shorn human hairdo. Eyes are often ignored. If they are pierced, the exact position and size need careful judgement. Moulded heads may have a suggestive hollow or knob, and there are several whose glinting glass eyes emphasize their vigilance. A famous American weathercock has eyes made from coins, updated at each renovation.

Realism is greatly enhanced by legs, especially with feet. Cocks can appear to have no legs (impaled cocks make no pretence), one leg (the spindle itself, perhaps with a little illusory feathering), two legs (shaft + 1) or three (shaft + 2), all usually chopped off at the ankles. Farmyard cocks, grasping a perch, strutting, running or raising one leg, are likely to have naturalistic claws, even spurs.

But the tails! These are the dominant visual feature, and their even greater variety can only be hinted at. Basically circular; semi-circular; triangular. Upswept; downswept; horizontal. Shallow or deep inverted U. Chopped off horizontally or vertically. Solid with grooves. Double, each half solid with grooves. Cut through. Separate feathers, parallel, at angles, curled. Feather duster. Tassels. Fingers. Cat-o'-six-tails. Grass snake. Toasting-fork. Trivet … Apparently limitless invention.

A mathematician might calculate the photo-fit combinations of the four elements – body, head, legs and tail – but there are dozens more. Decorative use may also be made of the need to rivet heads and tails to bodies, as in the scalloped feather effect of Gamlingay church's cock, Cambs. (*3.9*).

Church cocks may still stand with Cross and sphere, reminding us by

3.10 Ornamented Victorian church cock: Dryfesdale Church, Lockerbie, Dumfries & Galloway.

what power the Church claims dominion over the world. Farmyard cocks may crow at the sun or even the moon. They have perches and wheels; the less usual accompaniment of a trumpet at Thornton Hough, Merseyside, denotes Lord Leverhulme's crest. Flat weathercocks in particular often stand on arrows. Both forms may stand to one side of the spindle balanced by a half pointer. The original absence of cardinal arms gave way to cardinal arms heavily decorated, especially on church towers, whose massiveness could make an unadorned cock look puny. Dryfesdale church, Lockerbie, Dumfries & Galloway, dedicated in 1897, illustrates both the cock standing to one side and the elaboration (*3.10*). Sadly, the ornament on small domestic weathercocks is often trite and repetitive, taking no account of the site.

One other matter meriting consideration is their size. Weathercocks available in one size only from garden centres are really only suitable for single-storey buildings. Although Victorian catalogues offered an impressive range of sizes, many Victorian cocks still look too small. Nonetheless, on tall buildings even apparently small weathercocks are substantial – Hereford's All Saints and Norwich Cathedral cocks, both about four feet six inches tall, for instance. Inevitably they are also very heavy, for even if hollow the breasts are probably weighted with lead. Weights of fifty or sixty pounds are unremarkable: one foot alone of the Smithfield cock weighs 10½ pounds. Damage to themselves is not the only thing to be feared if they fall.

Their size, height and shape all lead to their being used for target practice. Breasts are dented, tails peppered, crests knocked off – perhaps this accounts for some of the odder shapes. They are also put to other, stranger uses. Dr Who *aficionados* may recall water spouting from church gargoyles and a gilt weathercock that whizzed round as a warning of evil. During filming, the villagers of Aldbourne, Wilts., had an energetic time running up the tower staircase with buckets of water and spinning the cock by hand.

It seems an undignified function. But the cock is self-satisfied rather than dignified: his 'dignity' and community value come from his symbolic associations, and his longevity – very few objects have been in familiar use for over a thousand years. He is also the first, and therefore most affectionately regarded, of a huge family of representational and pictorial weathervanes.

4 Heraldry

The second main line of weathervane development is implicit in the 'vane' element of the word, deriving from the Old English *fana*, a flag or banner.

Fighters no longer rally round the flag (except perhaps at football matches). A man's physical survival does not depend on his ability to recognize and interpret an armorial device. So, although heraldic weathervanes still have connotations of pageantry and tradition, they are primarily regarded as decorative objects whose historical associations are a bonus.

Even in its heyday, heraldry suffered from the fact that laymen used its strange esoteric terminology loosely. In later centuries slacker observation of heraldic rules led to even more slipshod description. By 'family crest', in particular, we usually vaguely comprehend any part of a coat of arms, supporters, helmet, coronet or household badge, not just the crest itself. Heraldic expertise, while not essential to the enjoyment of weathervanes, does enable some of those less obviously derived from heraldry to be recognized for what they are.

The purpose of heraldry becomes clear if we note two significant features of the Bayeux Tapestry: the small fluttering flags on approaching ships and on battlefield weapons, and the almost identical appearance of the two armies. The more all-encasing armour became, the more imperative also became some scheme of recognition. If a nobleman adopted some distinctive device on a tunic over his armour – his 'coat of arms' – then displayed this same device on his shield, banner and horse-trappings, and decorated his helmet with a personal crest, probably fashioned from boiled leather, he became distinguishable from

4.1 Painted and gilded Royal Arms on Tower
of London, possibly 1669.

everyone else. Rank was seemingly a military matter, determined by the
battalion a man could muster in the service of the king. By transferring
the chosen arms to flags of differing shapes, carried by the nobleman
himself or by his subordinates, sharp distinctions of rank could be
proclaimed.

Any knight on a medieval battlefield appears to have been entitled to a
'pennoncelle' on his lance. Contemporary illustrations suggest that these
were twelve- to eighteen-inch-long pieces of cloth, often arranged so
that the armorial devices were the right way up when the lance was
horizontal, during a charge. A 'pennon' was larger, 2½ to three feet, and
belonged to a middle-ranking knight. It was carried upright, sometimes
by an esquire, and of its three basically triangular shapes the swallowtail
became the most important. Banners were square, or tall oblongs, their
largest dimension about three feet and restricted to the highest military
commanders. All of them were strictly personal objects, denoting the
actual presence of the owner on the battlefield. They were the enemy's
obvious challenge, and the recognizable rallying-point for scattered

troops. Their loss was the greatest imaginable disgrace.

Heraldic weathervanes probably originated from the custom of soldiers' triumphantly mounting their colours on a stronghold they had successfully stormed. The middle-rank swallowtail pennon was particularly suited to having its tails cut off, whereupon it became a banner, to signify instant reward and ennoblement for battle prowess. Very early on, the French stiffened the top edges of their cloth banners to enable the devices with which they were charged to be seen more easily. (A relic of this transitional stage towards making a more durable rigid version persists in the projecting rod called a *schwenkel* still found on many Continental weathervanes and imitated by the Victorians.) It was only one small step to giving the banner permanence in metal, and a second to realizing how much less wind-damage a swivelling banner sustained. Revolving metal banners were established in Britain by the thirteenth century. It is likely that by strict heraldic rules the vane shape reflected the flag shape to which the owner's rank entitled him: a small triangle for lesser gentry, a swallowtail for middle-ranking knights, banners only for the upper crust. The shape of his weathervane showed a man's rank (unless ambition overruled his conscience); the arms on it showed his identity.

No matter what the colours of the arms, weathervane gilding was regarded as highly desirable. It literally dazzled with its implication of great wealth. Heraldic display is manifestly the primary purpose of such weathervanes. A subsidiary usefulness might decide their position: the weathervane at Stanton Harcourt, Oxon., for instance, was placed above the fourteenth-century kitchen and showed which louvres in the octagonal roof should be opened to release the smoke of the fires below.

Once the simple, recognizable devices on a shield were combined with several others through successive generations and marriages, a coat of arms with up to sixteen quarterings was too bewilderingly complex for use in its entirety as a weathervane. The market cross at Chichester, Sussex makes a good starting-point for comparing the varying effects of a single coat (Chichester), impaled arms – i.e. two coats side by side (Lady Faringdon, a benefactress), four quarterings (France and England, for Henry VII in whose time the cross was built), six quarterings (Bishop Story, instigator of the cross) and the Royal Arms with those of Hanover 'in pretence', which were added after 1801. Some are additionally decorated with projecting fleurs-de-lys. Like the Royal Arms on the Tower of London weathervanes, which may date from 1669 (*4.1*), they rely heavily on colour and gilding.

The coat of arms belonged exclusively to one nobleman. His retainers

4.2 Falcon and Fetterlock Yorkist badge: Fotheringhay Church, Northants.

4.3 Boar's Head badge of Richard III: Queens' College, Cambridge.

4.4 Swallowtail arms of Archbishop William Juxon, copy of 1660 original: Lambeth Palace, London.

might be distinguished by a badge, often derived from his crest. Because it was worn by so many and seen so often, it became better known than the owner's actual arms. Many are still extremely familiar – the White Harts, Feathers, Blue Boars and Boars' Heads of Britain's inn-signs.

Some heraldic weathervanes are doubtless very early, but since arms remain unchanged, only external evidence will confirm when during the last 600 or so years they were erected. The oldest is believed to date from about 1360, when Sir William Etchyngham erected a small replica of his banner, which has the relative simplicity of the oldest coats of arms, above his own Sussex church. 'Azure a fret argent', as pictured on the inn-sign almost opposite, is made in pierced form. Its present oxidized patina probably supersedes a gold-leafed surface. Repairs have been sympathetic (*2.3*).

Weathervanes of household badges are equally difficult to date. A sculpted falcon and fetterlock (*4.2*) stands on Fotheringhay church, Northants, recalling the House of York, some of whose members lie below. The hopeful association of this with the tower date of 1529 has not been possible to confirm. Similarly, Queens' College, Cambridge, has for centuries commemorated Richard III's benefaction by using his boar's head badge on table-settings etc. The weathervane, however, into which the boar's head silhouette is cut, probably dates from 1846. Eye, ears and tusk have been most imaginatively created by metal projecting into the 'space' of the silhouette (*4.3*).

4.5 Foley arms, now at Pudlestone Old Rectory, Hereford & Worcester.

An interesting survival as late as 1663 of a weathervane still indicating inherited military rank is that on Lambeth Palace, the official London residence of the Archbishop of Canterbury. Although William Juxon became Archbishop of Canterbury in 1661, and the weathervane shows his arms impaled with those of the See of Canterbury, it is not the aristocratic banner his ecclesiastical eminence might suggest but the middle-ranking pennon he was born to (*4.4*). In addition to its appropriate mitre finial, it has a pointer. These appear to have been added to many weathervanes from about this time. They make squarish banners more graceful and aerodynamic, and much easier to interpret from a distance. The Lambeth Palace weathervane, severely damaged in the Blitz, was later replaced as nearly as possible to the original design. Many heraldic City weathervanes were less fortunate and are now discoverable only in old illustrations.

One case-history can serve to illustrate a heraldic weathervane's tight-rope act between survival and destruction, interpretation and incomprehension. In the late seventeenth century, the Foley family possessed two Midlands estates. Paul, Speaker of the House of Commons, owned Stoke Edith; his younger brother Philip owned Prestwood. The latter's arms appear in a striking weathervane (*4.5*). 1703 was the year in which his father-in-law, Lord Pagett, appointed a Philip Foley to the Deputy Lieutenantship of Staffordshire. Some 120 years later, when Humphrey Repton's recommendation to add a cupola to the stables at Prestwood was being carried out, the accounts refer to an existing weathervane being regilded for it. Another century on, both estates passed to the same descendant, and Prestwood was sold in 1913. Both houses were destroyed by fire, but the Royal Commission of 1933 records the weathervane as being stored in the still-standing stables at Stoke Edith. It seems never to have emerged until the final dispersal sale in 1964, when it was bought, regilded and installed on an outbuilding at Pudlestone Old Rectory, Hereford & Worcester. The present owner, who researched it so diligently, disarmingly describes this history as 'conjectural'. But even the best-known and most highly valued weathervanes rarely have owners both concerned and knowledgeable enough to ferret out such a line of likelihood.

Students of heraldry regret that through the seventeenth, eighteenth and particularly nineteenth centuries the observation of strict rules of rank and privilege grew steadily more lax. Heraldry became debased into a scramble after decorative status-symbols, sometimes in embarrassingly poor taste. Nevertheless, the Foley vane shows that some good heraldic weathervanes did emerge. It is slightly unusual in its full shield with crest above: designs selecting just one element became commoner. Oxford's punning 'Ox-in-ford' shield provided the design for the late-Victorian town hall weathervane. The third Marquess of Bute cut his marquess's coronet into banners for Cardiff Castle and Castel Coch at nearby Taff's Well, Glam., both restored by him in the 1870s. A duke's coronet, from which rise symmetrically two arms brandishing ostrich feathers, is cut into a banner at Welbeck Abbey, Notts., now an army college. The fifth Duke of Portland probably put this vane above Stable Court when he built new ancillary buildings distant from the Abbey in his quest for privacy – a quest so phobic that the Abbey itself is riddled with 'secret' tunnels. The usual solid banner with cut device is sometimes reversed into a banner frame, empty but for the outline of a heraldic device suspended within it. Hidcote House, Glos., has a gilt eagle's head (*4.6*), and central Wrexham, Clwyd, what appears to be a talbot rampant made by this method.

Supporters and crests, chiefly animals and birds, are particularly suitable for use as 'free-standing' weathervanes, i.e. with no banner frame. Some heraldic creatures are reasonably realistic. Highmoor Mansion at Wigton, Cumbria, still has the Banks's six-foot 'eagle regardant with wings elevated … charged upon the breast and upon each wing with a fleur-de-lys'. Gilding must have made it very impressive. Sadly, the lofty bell-tower's quarter-chimes, different daily tunes, Sunday hymns and 'Big Joe' hour-bell audible twelve miles away have all gone.

Since medieval heralds had never seen an elephant, they gave it hocks like the domestic animals they knew. The elephant-and-castle weathervane that rises so improbably from a cowshed at Adderley, Shropshire, however, crest of the Corbett family who owned the land for four centuries, is obviously post-Jumbo, for the elephant is naturalistic under his howdah, or fighting 'castle'. In contrast, 'the pelican in her Piety', wounding herself to resurrect her young, is non-naturalistic. Borrowed from the King's Lynn Borough crest, it makes a superbly dramatic weathervane on the new courthouse dominating this Norfolk waterfront.

Lions are absolutely ubiquitous, rampant, sejant, passant and in every other posture devised by heralds. At Tatton Park, Cheshire, a cheerful gilded lion strides about with an arrow, the crest of the Egertons who, after 380 years, left Tatton to the National Trust. Oddly the three-foot copper lion weathervane which has surmounted Maxstoke Castle, West Midlands, since at least 1860 is prowling realistically, not the rampant lion appropriate to the Dilke family.

4.6   Emblem suspended within a frame:
Hidcote, Glos.

The disembodied animal heads that make somewhat unnerving
weathervanes arise from the popularity of such images as heraldic
charges. A boar's head crest, snout upwards, lurks behind the parapet of
Ripley Castle, Yorks. Unfortunately it no longer operates the dial on the
wall beneath. A wolf's head, impaled from behind by an arrow which
forms its tongue, faces downwind from the diagonal tower above the
stunning Priory of Cartmel, Cumbria. Given by the Knipe family, whose
arms show the wolf's head impaled but through the throat from in front,
it refers to Sir John Harrington, said (though there are other claimants)
to have killed the last English wolf near here. On Charterhouse Chapel,
London, the greyhound's head of Thomas Sutton, its founder in 1611,
has become the pointer to a pennon. The white hart's head crest of the
Domesday owners of Stanwell, Surrey, was placed above a gilt pennon
on the church in 1756, while a three-dimensional buck's head turns on
the arrow at Leathersellers' Hall, City of London (4.7).
    Dragons, wyverns, griffins, cockatrices and other assorted fabulous
beasts often had their origin in heraldry, though the connection may not

4.7 Buck's Head weathervane on the
Leathersellers' Hall, 1930, City of London.

now be recalled. However, although there had been a dragon on Bow
church previously, the obvious reference in the eight-foot-ten-inch
flying dragon there is to the dragon supporters adopted by the City of
London in 1633: both have wings marked with the cross of St George
(*2.6*). Wren paid 'To Edward Pearce mason for a carving of a wooden
dragon for a modell for ye steeple, and for cutting a relive in board to be
proffered up to discern the right bigness, the summe of £4. 0. 0.' And
later: 'To Robert Bird, coppersmith, £38 for making the Dragon.' It
surmounted a dominant spire: all other City spires were kept low. It had
drama too, for, as travellers topped the rise at Dulwich, there before
them was the London panorama, punctuated by Bow's white Portland
finger set against the dark dome of St Paul's. When William of Orange's
invasion was expected in 1688, London people are said to have looked
each morning to see whether the dragon announced a Protestant or
Catholic wind.

The red dragon, much favoured by Henry VII as emphasizing his
descent through Owen Tudor from Cadwalader, last native king of
Britain, still remains the emblem of Wales. Welsh dragon weathervanes
are numerous, their traditional attitude walking with one foreleg raised,

with wings and a blunt arrow tail. Though often quite small, they decorate buildings as diverse as Montgomery Town Hall, Powys, Owain Glyndwr Interprative (*sic*) Centre, Machynlleth, Powys, a Cardiff hospital, a pub at Criccieth, Gwynedd, (rampant, this one), a florist's at The Mumbles, Glam., and private homes all over the principality. Similarly the wyvern from Leicester's arms is found all over that city.

The eagle-headed variation known as a griffin makes an equally attractive weathervane subject. At Ombersley Dower House, Hereford & Worcester, formerly the twelfth-century courthouse, Lord Sandys' griffin stands on the tail of an arrow above a coronet (*4.8*), as it does in decorative relief on cottages in the village.

4.8 Griffin and coronet: Ombersley, Hereford & Worcester.

To a medieval herald, a seahorse was a horse with a fish's tail. As supporter to the arms of Ipswich, Suffolk, since 1561, a seahorse became the natural final flourish of Victorian civic pride on the 1867 town hall. Similarly, no live dolphin would claim kinship with a heraldic one. The dolphin's intelligence fascinated the ancient Greeks, who explained it by the story that dolphins were originally men, pirates whom the god Dionysus forced to leap overboard to escape the snakes with which he was punishing them for trying to sell him into slavery. Medieval heralds, unfamiliar with the genuine Mediterranean article, endowed dolphins with physical characteristics of inland and coastal fish they knew. Heraldic dolphins may therefore have gills, assorted numbers of dorsal fins, even scales on their bodies, which sometimes flick laterally with vertical tail instead of being 'embowed' or arched with horizontal flukes (even on the arms of the Fishmongers' Company ...). Brighton's or Blackpool's heraldic dolphins twirl gaily above schools and sea-front shelters. Families with the surname Dolphin rejoice in them.

Pretty well anything, animate or inanimate, that can be pressed into service as a charge, crest or supporter can become a weathervane. A copper silhouette of a bare arm brandishing a laurel branch, crest of the Burrells, decorates a building formerly attached to Ockenden Manor, now private apartments in Cuckfield, Sussex. After *c*.1700 the slackening of armorial accuracy led to greater variety of profile as the range of people erecting 'heraldic' weathervanes widened. Aristocrats and gentry were joined by a wider range of corporate bodies. Such old-established groups as the Cinque Ports, whose emblem adorns Fordwich church, Kent, and the City of London livery companies were joined by newer trading bodies. As late as the 1920s the Hudson's Bay Co decorated its building, (now sold) in Bishopsgate, City of London, with a beaver on an arrow, still turning so delicately as to belie its reputed eighty pounds weight. New civic arms are continually awarded that can be used in part as weathervanes. School badges prompt them – the dolphin above Clock Cottage, Barford, War., is so derived. Civic heraldry is sometimes borrowed by clubs. A member of Up River Yacht Club, Hullbridge, for instance, made them a weathervane shaped like a pointed silhouette windsock, and enclosing the Essex Shield with its three seaxes.

Many families have for generations used arms which they adopted without any formal grant by the College of Arms, such as the boar's head pointer with H in the banner on Burton Latimer Hall, Northants. A genuine error occurred at Lowestoft, Suffolk, which put a rose weathervane and crown finial on its Victorian town hall, probably in 1885. Only in 1913, when HMS *Lowestoft* was to be commissioned and

4.9 'Sour Plums' confused with the Fox and Grapes: Galashiels Council Chamber, Borders.

the firm chosen to make a commemorative plate queried the design, was it discovered that the rose and crown arms Lowestoft had used for 300 years had never been authorized. The prettily cut rose is double-sided but, alas, economical yellow – not even gold – paint has replaced the original gold leaf.

Splendid confusion surrounds the arms of Galashiels, Borders. In 1337 a party of English soldiers, gathering wild plums, was ambushed and annihilated by the Scots. The original arms probably showed just 'a plum tree fructed' with the sarcastic motto 'Sour Plums'. Unfortunately the official responsible for the town seal in 1868 (about the time the weathervane (*4.9*) was put on the new council chamber) apparently knew little of this history. Imagining the town's arms represented the familiar fable of the fox and grapes, he instructed the engraver to modify the tree into a vine – and first one, later two foxes crept into the arms.

Another mixture of history, heraldry and tradition underlies the eagle-and-child weathervane on Ormskirk church, Lancs. The eagle was adopted as Sir Henry de Lathom's crest to celebrate his tale of 'finding' his longed-for heir (actually his illegitimate son) 'abandoned' under a tree frequented by eagles. Later he added the child in a crib beneath it in an attempt to allay malicious gossip about the child's parentage. His descendants the Stanleys, created earls of Derby for services at the battle of Bosworth in 1485, were connected by marriage with the descendents of Orm, the early Saxon landowner. Over thirty Stanleys are buried in their chapel here, and they still hold the living of Ormskirk. The copper weathervane, on which a tightly swaddled child can just be made out in his crib beneath the eagle, probably dates from 1826, when the spire was rebuilt after a lightning-strike. 'The Eagle and Child' is another quite familiar pub sign.

How far all this is from the banner displaying a simple device for recognition. It even became popular to add personal details to civic arms, preferably on some edifice naming the philanthropic donor. Hospitals and clock towers are favourites. Cardigan Guildhall, Dyfed, is typical. When David Davies, a local shipowner, presented the tower, clock and vane, not only did the inscription commemorate his mayoralty but a large 'DD 1892' was cut into the oval banner, alongside the town seals, a ship and a castle.

A kind of symbolic understanding of some images replaces memory of their heraldic aspects. The lamb-and-flag, for instance, especially on churches, is more often interpreted as the Paschal Lamb than as the eleventh-century military emblem of the Knights Hospitallers. The town hall which Barry designed for Halifax, Yorks., is topped by an

4.10   Lamb and Flag, heraldry and symbolism: Halifax Town Hall, Yorks.

elaborately mounted lamb and flag (*4.10*). It still appears on the new Calderdale arms, but interpreted there as 'a general expression of the identity of the area as a Yorkshire wool-producing area'.

The invention, particularly by the Victorians, of a sort of quasi-heraldry, incorporated into decorative banners, interferes with the recognition of genuine heraldic devices. The banner on the Old School, Booton, Norfolk, looks merely fanciful but is derived from the Elwin arms: the Reverend Whitwell Elwin built Booton's astonishing church. The fleurs-de-lys in Lincoln Cathedral's vanes repeat those in the city's arms, but the fleur-de-lys is so frequently extraneous decoration that that significance may be overlooked. Similarly it may be the inn-sign that enlightens the uninitiated: that 'star' on the weathervane at Downham Hall, Lancs., is the 'mullett sable' of the Asshetons. It reappears on nearby Clitheroe's crest.

The banner on Clitheroe's civic hall illustrates another custom, that of enclosing the heraldic device – here a castle – within a shape far removed from the medieval pennon or banner. Clitheroe's is in an oval-tailed arrow, as is the Women's Institute badge-and-motto on the village hall at Yealmpton, Devon (*4.11*). The old arms of Perth, Tayside, appear in a circle on the Sandeman Library there. William Browne's merchant's mark and initials form a heart-shaped tail on the Hospital he founded in 1483 at Stamford, Lincs. Two striking circular weathervanes rise above the fifteenth-century gatehouse of Oxburgh Hall, Norfolk. The nineteenth-century one celebrates alliances between the Bedingfelds and the Pastons. Its matching partner is a happy marriage of old and new – the red eagle displayed, borne by the Bedingfelds since 1276, with the oak-leaves of the National Trust, who have administered Oxburgh since 1952 (*4.12*). Oxburgh's owner, who helped design this weathervane, is in fact a Herald at the College of Arms.

With one exception, these examples have presented their heraldic elements in the 'fane' or swivelling motif. The Ombersley vane (*4.8*), reminds us to look for heraldic elements in mounts or finials. The mount for the Victorian dragon on Brecon Town Hall, Powys, is a full coat of arms in vivid colour. At the Norfolk and Norwich Hospital, the Leicester Nurses' Home commemorates its benefactor in a simple banner weathervane rising from his earl's coronet in copper and gold; against all the odds, it survived wartime incendiary bombs. Finials for simple arrows have been created from the Royal and Ancient Golf Club badge at St Andrews, Fife, and at Fletcher Farm, Tottington, Greater Manchester, from a pierced and painted shield, surmounted by horns as a butchery trade sign.

4.11 Women's Institute badge and motto: village hall, Yealmpton, Devon.

4.12 Devices old and new combined: Oxburgh Hall, Norfolk.

4.13   Irish harp weathervane, developed from a signet ring: Brabling
Green, Suffolk.

Several stimuli are discernible in this century's revival of interest in
heraldry, and the many new weathervanes in this traditional mode. It is
genuine heraldry that pleases; because he is typical rather than
individual, the Rural Development Commission's 'heraldic lion' is not
popular. Since 1900 many civic arms have been granted, renewed or
modified. Especially if new civic buildings are involved – through the
1974 administrative reorganization, perhaps – a weathervane seems
fitting. Westmorland is no more, but the stylized oak tree from its old
arms is perpetuated in the finial of the arrow vane of the new county hall
at Kendal, now in Cumbria (6.9). On Hambleton's new district
headquarters at Northallerton, Yorks., the shield, supporters and crest
all turn on the arrow, although the shield is inexplicably blank.

Sometimes not a new building but a new setting can display a region's
historical associations to advantage. Because the 'Arth' syllable of his
name 'Arthgal' meant 'bear', the first Earl of Warwick adopted a bear as
his symbol. The second Earl added the 'ragged staff', the tree he tore up
to slay a 'fearsome giant'. This bear wields his weapon with less grace
than the county cricketers over whose ground at Edgbaston,
Birmingham, he has presided since 1938 (1.6).

A new weathervane depicting ancient arms can re-state corporate
pride. The nineteenth century knew this, and placed vanes at Trinity
College, Cambridge, displaying arms and mottoes used by Trinity for
300 years. A mid-twentieth-century rose-and-portcullis on King's

College, Cambridge, (*4.16*), serves the same purpose. A new college needs a new emblem to promote corporate pride: Oxford's Nuffield College weathervane helps to establish its collegiate identity.

Post-war Britons still display pride in their ancestry. At Burwood Hall, Mileham, Norfolk, the weathervane is the family crest of a lion holding winged spurs, supposedly the reward to an ancestor who helped the Bruce flee to Scotland. Moat Farm's vane at Brabling Green, Suffolk, was copied by Brandeston Forge in about 1960 from an ⅛ inch crest on the owner's signet ring (4.13). The apparent angel with backswept wings is the heraldic depiction of an Irish harp. At Bisley, Glos., the two-foot lion holding a deer's head, the Howard crest (*4.14*), came from a letter-heading. To Bisley craftsman Eden Fowler the embossed surface suggested a relief treatment, so he created the copper vane in two halves, seamlessly welded it and balanced it by introducing experimental quantities of lead through the deer's nostril. Julia Cooper, another of Bisley's craft workers, gilded it, and it was set to flash against its dark wooded background, having never moved more than 200-300 yards. And how agreeable that a neighbour chose a unicorn created by the same team (*4.15*).

Despite its iconoclasm, the twentieth century still erects Coronation and Royal Wedding vanes, though these are usually more symbolic than heraldic. There is also still considerable freedom of form: the de Montfort cinquefoil, for instance, makes the entire arrowtail of the weathervane at Leicester Golf Club.

Identical heraldic devices can inspire contrasting weathervanes (*4.16*). The rather solid rose pointer and portcullis tail in copper gilt, renewed in 1985, on St George's Chapel, Windsor, Berks., is much more staid in effect than the arrow with the airy double rose tail, and crossed portcullises in the mount. This was designed by William Haslop and made by Lister's for King's College, Cambridge, about 1954.

4.14   Lion crest: Bisley, Glos.

4.15   Heraldic supporter; unicorn: Bisley, Glos.

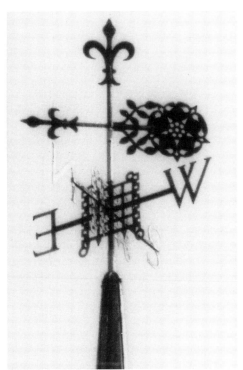

4.16 Two rose-and-portcullis designs: St George's Chapel, Windsor (*left*), and King's College, Cambridge (*right*).

A coat of arms is flat and so a good foundation for a flat vane. Only occasionally are some elements built up into rounded forms, as at Halifax and Bisley (*4.10, 4.14, 4.15*). By their very nature heraldic weathervanes are at their most effective if gilded or painted in the primary colours that dominate heraldry. A weathervane of the King's arms at Windsor is known to have been vividly painted as early as 1352. Weathervanes on the Tower of London (*4.1*), HM Prison at Lancaster Castle, the Jubilee Clock Tower at Chester, Chichester Market Cross, Sussex, and at Beaulieu, Hants, all glow with colour, and most glitter with gold leaf too.

Egalitarian America substitutes for this group of weathervanes huge numbers of loyalty-focusing eagles, Liberties and Columbias. In Britain, Union Jack and Britannia vanes are few: they are superfluous when local loyalties to feudal lords are so clearly recorded in heraldry. We lean very heavily on this aspect of tradition. Any State function would be unimaginable without state coaches, guards, trumpeters, uniforms. Though small, weathervanes, with their eye-catching movement, are a more permanent way of keeping heraldry before the public eye.

Certain criticisms can be levelled against heraldic weathervanes as a group, relating chiefly to recognition difficulties. Those who do not recognize the arms depicted may downgrade the vane as merely decorative. If elements only are represented, the owner himself is not always readily identifiable. An element may not even be recognizably heraldic – the swan on Longniddry Golf Club, Lothian, from the arms of the Earl of Wemyss, looks much like any other swan. And there will always be those who object to such signs of social status on principle.

On the other hand, heraldic weathervanes are among the showiest and most dramatic. It is often clear that a vane is heraldic even if it cannot immediately be interpreted. Animal banners on Louth Market Hall, Lincs., Brampton Market Hall, Cumbria, a parkside memorial at Tunstall, Staffs., and Carlisle station in Cumbria come to mind, as well as what looks like a complete coat on Old Cottage, Pearson Road, Sonning, Berks. All should be traceable. Heraldic weathervanes can still express, or even create, considerable civic or corporate pride. Above all, they add dignity, interest, attractiveness and colour to what can be, especially in towns, an increasingly dull and monochrome environment.

5 Banner, Arrow and Pennant Weathervanes (BAPs)

Using the inelegant acronym 'BAPs' is meant to do three things: to save cumbrous repetition of 'banner, arrow and pennant weathervanes' at every turn; to isolate this group of specifically decorative weathervanes from other groups whose motifs are likely to be of similar shape (notably heraldic, symbolic and historical vanes) and yet to underline how indivisible the three shapes really are. Considering them arbitrarily as three different shapes facilitates discussion but is ultimately unsatisfactory: so often subsequent examination makes today's arrow tomorrow's banner.

More than most other groups, the impact of BAPs depends on the integration of their motif with finials, mounts, arms, lettering and ornamentation. However, these five 'extra' components will be considered separately in the next chapter, since they belong not just with BAPs but with all other groups. The important point here is that any BAP may be found with any or all of these other elements in apparently limitless combination.

BAPs developed principally out of heraldic weathervanes and, with modifications, continue in an unbroken chain. What actually flies now may be a genuine seventeenth-, eighteenth-, nineteenth- or twentieth-century BAP. Or at any time during those centuries it may have been made to replicate or imitate an earlier one – not to deceive but to continue a tradition. Thus the points made about dating historical vanes in Chapter 16 apply equally to BAPs. A dated BAP may be a loyal gesture at a national celebration or a personal or parochial reference. It

5.1   A range of typical BAP shapes.

may be an entirely irrelevant copy 'because I liked it'. It may have inverted or reversed figures as a deliberate conundrum. The age of a BAP with no date may be arrived at through circumstantial evidence or inspired guesswork, aided perhaps by old pictures and fallible, sometimes conflicting, memories.

Initials pierced into BAPs may also help to confirm a date, not if, as at Selby Abbey, Yorks, they stand for patronal saints but if they can be identified as those of churchwardens, benefactors, builders, repairers, owners, firms etc. Some see in a man's enthusiasm for blazoning his identity or his works across the heavens a form of arrogance that deserves its come-uppance. Hence the unholy glee with which the initials AP in a vane at Peterhouse, Cambridge (now in the college office), were said to stand for Andrew Perne, a Papist, a Protestant or a Puritan. By modifying his views four times in twelve years, Perne managed to retain his office and even procure advancement successively under Henry VIII, Edward VI, Mary I and

Elizabeth. The jibe that a cloak was not turned but 'perned' was irresistible. Perne's protection of university members from persecution and his contributions to administration and scholarship were conveniently ignored. The AP may even stand instead for 'Aedes Petrus', a Latinized form of the college name.

The attractiveness of BAPs cut with dates and initials is greatly affected by the style of the figures and letters, their disposition within the vane's shape, and their proportions relative to each other and to the whole. Each one has to be judged individually.

The overwhelming feature of BAPs is their enormous variety. The reasons for this become clearer if we go through the mental processes of a man confronted with a square or oblong of metal to be turned into a decorative weathervane.

What shall he do with it? Gild it, or paint it? Elongate it, vertically in medieval or horizontally in later fashion? Even extend it into a streamer? Or cut off the four corners? Add projections, or depressions – or a mixture – shaped as knobs, squares, points, fleurs-de-lys, trefoils, straight

5.2   Chase Farm Hospital, The Ridge, Enfield,
Greater London.

or wavy spines, elaborate curls upon curls, a waving three-dimensional streamer, arrows, tridents, tiny scrolls? All of these can be added at the corners or along the sides. So can thick, huge framing scrolls to dwarf the banner itself or a thin wavy or scalloped frill to lighten it. Or shape the tail end: curve it in or out, split into wavy strips, give it a single central spine? Set top, bottom and/or one side at an angle for an asymmetrical effect? Curve the top and/or bottom in and/or out? Curve the whole thing into a bell, oval, circle or completely irregular shape?

So much for the outside. Internally, lighten the basic oblong with shaped slots inside the border? Cut into it dates and initials variously disposed, remembering that subsequent owners may not like initials or emblems of personal significance? Cut flowers with varying numbers and shapes of petals, with or without foliage; one or more circles, trefoils, quatrefoils, stars; hearts; fleurs-de-lys; pin-pricks? Or cut a central diamond, then ornament each of *its* edges? Go on chopping until more space than metal remains? Or cut out all except the 'frame' and 'suspend' the chosen shape within it, black on white instead of white on black? Curve its whole outline? Add curlicues until it looks almost like a curly dragon? Dispose gilt, black or colour variously about the pattern? Construct the entire banner from initials, with no frame or background?

If a pennant is required, only the early stages differ. Start this time with a triangle. Split tail into two, either slightly or right back to the spindle to create short tails or long streamers. Wave top, bottom and

5.3   Gas Board, Rochester, Kent.

inner edges of tails, or give them saw-teeth. Ripple the whole thing vertically instead of horizontally. Separate tails by a spiked, wavy or trefoiled 'tongue', or join them with loop or bar. Cut as for banners.

For appearance, clarity or physical balance (often nearly forgotten in creative excitement) a pointer may be needed. The easiest is a straight rod, which may be hollow or solid for weight. To make it decorative, develop the point into an arrow-head, a knob, a diamond, a trefoil, a star. Make the rod wavy. Give it a loop or hair-spring it. Give it kinks. Add a bird's or snake's head instead of a point. Give the straight rod hollow shoulders, squared or sloping. Or add C-scrolls where it meets the spindle. Or horizontal S-scrolls. Or both. Vary their numbers and sizes, double them, reverse them. Add curly 'wood-shavings' above and below. Move both tail and pointer away from the spindle and create a hollow central area, perhaps with its own scrolls. Make pointer hollow, shaped like a fountain-pen nib. Move pointer, whether straight or curved, from the centre to extend the top edge of the banner. Or the bottom. Or both, linked by a curve.

By now the miracles of variation that can be worked on the humble arrow will come as no great surprise. Bearing in mind that at least the simpler pointers described above can make the front halves of arrows, it is chiefly the tails that need further consideration. Even the plainest arrow can have a tail that is long or short, broad or narrow, with or without 'feathers' grooved or cut. It may be three-flanged like a dart or flared like a pressure-lamp flame. The shaft may be doubled to present the arrow in outline. Arrow and spindle can intersect through a sphere which may be hollow or solid. The tail may be almost circular or shaped as a star or heart. The whole arrow may be three-dimensional and developed into something approaching a stylized quill pen, fish, flying swan or dragon.

With all these BAPs, their proportions, their size in relation to the cardinal arms, the ornament, the building they are on and its height, and their visual separateness from the rest by a tall enough neck are all very critical, for the pleasure in them is an abstract one, derived from their rightness of design; there is none of the ancillary pleasure of the pictorial. Successes are numerous – because BAPs are numerous, far more so than any other group. They are certainly the easiest for amateurs to make, and because they are the group most adaptable to multi-function, multi-occupant buildings, they were the most suitable for mass-production. Cast-iron Victorian BAPs from Macfarlane, Carron and others are therefore legion, usually allied with equally mass-produced arms, lettering and ornament. All those in *5.1* are popular shapes. Today the Rural Development Commission offers six simple banner shapes with standard scrolls and letters to go with them.

Standard or otherwise, every region has literally hundreds of BAPs which have no particular meaning, no reason to be compared or contrasted with any others, but which make a significant decorative contribution. Unlike other chapters, therefore, this one ends with lists. From the hundreds of possibilities has been made an arbitrary choice of just seven or eight BAPs from each region (though not necessarily from every county), at least one of them illustrated. It is in no way a league table of excellence but broadly representative. The suggestion is that every region will have plenty of BAPs which, like these listed few, will for some reasons – shape, size, proportions, ornamentation, location, constructional distinction, ingenuity or sheer decorativeness – give pleasure and interest to anyone who examines them.

GREATER LONDON

Bermondsey, Southwark. South London College – elaborately decorated and mounted.

City. St Botolph's, near the Barbican – gilded, curved, cut and fringed.

City. St Agnes and St Anne, Gresham Street – Pennant with strange, beaky head pointer, 'A' finial.

Enfield. Chase Farm Hospital, The Ridge – tiered mount, shaped and cut banner (*5.2*).

Hampstead. 77 Fitzjohn's Avenue – modern arrow, vivid colours.

Totteridge. St Andrew's Church – initialled 1706 pennant apparently older than present building.

Twickenham. Kneller Hall Military School of Music – cut pennant, extensive scrolling.

Westminster. St Martin in the Fields, Trafalgar Square – cut and gilded, crown finial.

SOUTH-EAST (Kent, Surrey, Sussex)

Brighton, Sussex. St Mary's Roman Catholic Church, Surrenden Road – looped knobby 'arrow', cardinals above.

Eastbourne, Sussex. St Mary's Church – 1868 banner, churchwardens' initials, many fleurs-de-lys, serpent pointer.

Epsom, Surrey. Ashley Centre – 1980s arrow, 'C' tails in two planes.

Hawkhurst, Kent. St Lawrence's Church – gilded, much cut banner and pointer, very pretty foliage, scrolling and letters.

Lewes, Sussex. Harvey's Brewery – rediscovered 1620 pennant, formerly on church.

5.4   Lloyds Bank, High Street, Winchester, Hants.

New Romney, Kent. St Nicholas's Church – interestingly cut 1791 banner/pennant.
Rochester, Kent. Gas Board – arrow with reversed 'flame' tail (*5.3*).

SOUTH (Dorset, Hants., Wilts.)
Church Knowle, Dorset. St Peter's Church – simply cut, C in pointer.
Corfe Castle, Dorset. St Edward's Church – banner cut 1855, boar's head 'tail', open pointer and finial.
Salisbury, Wilts. St Thomas's Church – narrow triple-tailed pennant, gilt, strengthened in black.
Selbourne, Hants. The Wakes – Gilbert White's house; later silvery pennant, coronet and flower mounting.
Trowbridge, Wilts. Highfield, Hilperton Road – huge arched mounting, *c.*1900.
West Lavington, Wilts. School – knob-pointed arrow with open scrolled tail.
Winchester, Hants. Lloyds Bank, High Street – initialled and dated, gilded, edge ornamented, 'tongue' pointer (*5.4*).

SOUTH-WEST (Avon, Corn., Devon, Som.)
Bath, Avon. Pulteney Bridge – Gilt/black arrow, initials forming tail.
Beer, Devon. Beach House Hotel – double-ended arrow, letters cut into 'shields'.

Brixton, Devon. St Mary's Church – gilt, cut with chevrons, gilt perching bird.

Dunster, Som. Yarn Market – 1647 initialled banner.

Grampound, Corn. Clock Tower – copper pennant, sections riveted.

Hawkesbury, Avon. Old Rectory – initials and figures reversed and inverted in deliberate conundrum; carved knight mount (*5.5*).

Taunton, Som. Mary Street Memorial Schools – ornament above and beneath asymmetrical gilt banner; long, delicate pointer.

THAMES AND CHILTERN (Beds., Berks., Bucks., Herts., Oxon.)

Abingdon, Oxon. Stratton House, Bath Street – bird in fringed banner.

Cardington, Beds. St Mary's Church – large gilt flare-tail, hollow black pointer (*5.6*).

Fulbrook, Oxon. Meadow Lane – truncated black pennant with toothy jaws.

Hungerford, Berks. 'The Fire Place' – open arrow, probably 1880s, initialled for Hungerford Volunteer Fire Brigade.

Tring, Herts. St Peter's and St Paul's Church – traditional black pennant, hollow shoulders, 'wood shavings' on pointer.

Waddesdon, Bucks. St Michael's Church – arrow, star and half-moon on tail.

Ware, Herts. St Mary's Church – narrow gilt scallop, corrugated horizontally.

EAST ANGLIA (Cambs., Essex, Norfolk, Suffolk)

Bury St Edmunds, Suffolk. Cathedral – gilded banner, fleur-de-lys ornament, thickened pointer; pennant elaborately cut; both modern but in traditional style.

Churchgate Street, Essex. Old School – 1850s open black banner and pointer, much looped and tasselled.

Ditchingham, Norfolk. Chapel of All Hallows Convent – gilded asymmetrical banner, light-coloured ornament horizontally looped with knobs and corkscrews (*5.7*).

Great Barton, Suffolk. Church – eighteenth-century pennant, delicate open pointer and arm mounting.

Hartest, Suffolk. Stowe Hill – modern on old

5.5   Conundrum banner: Old Rectory, Hawkesbury, Avon.

5.6   St Mary's Church, Cardington, Beds.

5.7   Chapel of All Hallows Convent, Ditchingham,
Norfolk.

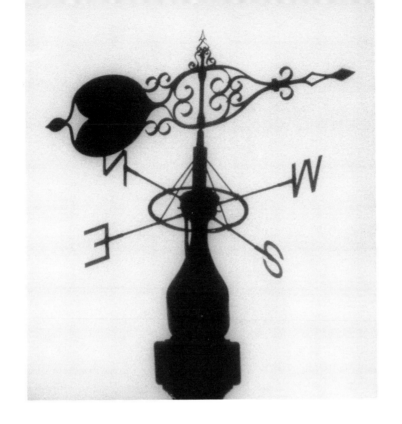

5.8   Guildhall, Derby.

5.9   St Philip's Cathedral, Birmingham, West Midlands.

mounting; arrow with half pointer, double irregular cross as tail.

Ipswich, Suffolk. Corner of Buttermarket with Upper Brook Street – copper arrow stylized into flying swan.

St Neot's, Cambs. Paine's, Bedford Street – imitation of waving fabric; a flour bag?

EAST MIDLANDS (Derbys., Leics., Lincs., Northants, Notts.)

Derby, Guildhall – large, elaborate open arrow, with horizontal solid heart tail (*5.8*).

Green's Norton, Northants. St Bartholomew's Church – gilded arrow with quill pen effect.

Kettering, Northants. Cemetery Chapel – gilded outline halberd-shaped arrow.

Leicester. Town Hall – gilded and cut with L and cinquefoil.

Mansfield, Notts. Metal Box Co. on inner ring road – gilt and black traditional pennant, with cut and open work.

Northampton. St Giles's Church – four gilded pennons containing suspended ciphers, three GRV, one EIIR; light scrolled pointers.

Wickenby, Lincs. St Peter's and St Lawrence's Church – open copper gridiron, cut oval tail with tabs.

HEART OF ENGLAND (Glos., Hereford & Worcester, Shropshire, Staffs., War., West Midlands)

Benthall, Shropshire. St Bartholomew's Church – fringed copper banner, bird on pointer; National Trust property.

Birdingbury, War. St Lawrence's Church – elegant open-fan-tailed arrow, gilded; knobbed cross similar to Birmingham Cathedral's.

Birmingham, West Midlands. Cathedral – open grid, heart pointer, boar's head tail from arms of local benefactor; probably eighteenth-century (*5.9*).

Cirencester, Glos. 7 Cecily Hill – arrow with plate tail; very elaborate twisting and scrolling (*6.6*).

Hidcote, Glos. Hidcote House – open gilded banner containing suspended eagle's head (*4.6*).

Newcastle under Lyme, Staffs. Keele University – simple outline pointed windsock shape with solid circle for tail.

Sutton Coldfield, West Midlands. 57 Somerville Road – Art Nouveau style.

Woofferton, Shropshire. Salwey Farm – black/gilt arrow, Gothic W in tail.

NORTH-EAST (Cleveland, Dur., Humberside, Northd., Tyne and Wear, Yorks.)

Alnwick, Northd. Town Hall – traditional black pennant, bird's head

5.10   Town Hall, Alnwick, Northumberland.

5.11   St John's Church, Workington, Cumbria.

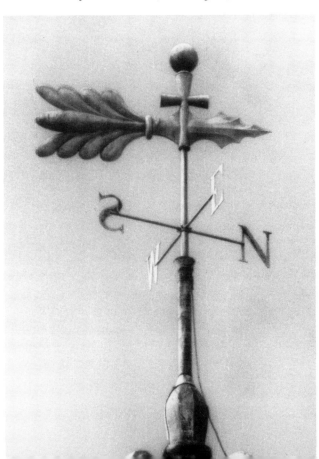

pointer; cardinal letters on roof (*5.10*).

Grimsby, Humberside. By No. 2 Fish Dock – arrow with cut trident tail.

Hexham, Northd. Abbey – plain solid gilt banner, curly scroll projections, open pointer.

Ledsham, Yorks. All Saints' Church – small open banner containing suspended foliage, matching that on arms.

Normanby, Humberside. Ex-coach house of Normanby Hall – plain modern arrow with suspended chevron tail; older base.

Pontefract, Yorks. Burtons – banner formed from letter B.

Tickhill, Yorks. Buttercross – cut-tailed arrow; fine elaborate mounting.

Yarm, Cleveland. Town Hall – simple 1710 arrow over elaborate scrolling.

NORTH-WEST (Ches., Cumbria, Greater Manchester, Merseyside)

Alderley Edge, Ches. Ryley's Farm – elegant arrow with heart tail; half-moon finial.

Kirkby Stephen, Cumbria. Church – 1753 fringed and edged banner.

Lancaster. Ashdown Memorial, Williamson Park – long narrow Edwardian cut pennon.

Lytham, Lancs. Queen Mary School for Girls – traditional pennant on open grid, with double wavy pointer.

Penrith, Cumbria, St Andrew's Church – 1759 pennant with serpent-tongued pointer, cock finial.

Salford, Greater Manchester. Education Office – curly foliate banner, foliage on pointer.

Warrington, Ches. Bridge Street, above Boots – four beasts in echelon with tiny initialled banners.

Workington, Cumbria. St John's Church – large solid gilt arrow, 'holly leaf' pointer (*5.11*).

WALES

Llandegfan, Anglesey. St Tegfan's Church – open-shouldered pennant, cock on pointer.

Llanidloes, Powys. Market House – 1738 animal banner (*5.12*)

Monmouth, Gwent. Monmouth School – small cut copper banner, probably 1865; 'turkey's head' pointer.

Nefyn, Gwynedd. Constitutional Club – arrow revolves inside oblong frame, which bears cardinal letters and initial finial.

Newtown, Powys. Agricultural House – hollow arrow, curved and flared cut tail; probably 1895.

Penarth, Glam. Portway Marina – new vane contrived entirely from PMP logo.

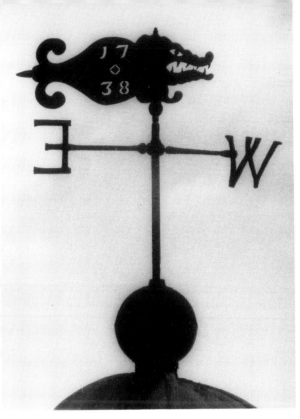

5.12 Market House, Llanidloes, Powys.

5.13 St James's Church, Penicuik, Lothian.

Taff's Well, Glam. Castel Coch – copper, cut with B for Marquess of Bute; probably *c.*1875.

SCOTLAND

Auldearn, Highland. School – half-moon tail decorated with stars.

Glasgow, Strathclyde. City Chambers – eighteen-foot-tall heavy cut gilt banner.

Glasgow, Strathclyde. St Enoch Square, ex-Underground entrance – four very curly banners, almost dragon-like.

Hawick, Borders. Henderson School – Entire motif from HHS.

Penicuik, Lothian. St James's Church – openwork rose and foliage tail (*5.13*).

Perth, Tayside. Canal Street Auction Rooms – open chequered banner with catherine-wheel tail.

St Andrew's, Fife. St Salvator's College – open gilt banner suspending St Andrew's cross; pennant tails; solid pointer.

6 Decorative Elements

This chapter deliberately does what should never be done – considers the decorative elements of a weathervane independently of its motif and even independently of each other. Remarks about cardinal arms and letters, scroll decoration, mounts and finials apply to weathervanes with every kind of motif. They may therefore be illuminated by the illustrations of any chapter. Considering them in isolation merely avoids the interruption of subsequent considerations of motifs by reference to these normally subsidiary decorative elements, except where they are particularly striking or important in the whole concept. Blacksmiths use these elements, rather than the motif, to judge a vane's workmanship.

If anything at all accompanies the rotating motif, it is likely to be arms indicating the four cardinal compass points. Churches, therefore, with their known east-west orientation (*pace* Liverpool Cathedral) often omit them. So do farms, where it is less important to name the wind than to recognize when it makes burning or spraying hazardous.

Theoretically only a north pointer is necessary, but such economy is less aesthetically pleasing than a balanced north-south arm. The north point may be defined by an arrow-head, fleur-de-lys, trefoil, diamond, star, cross, knob or stylized flower, with the south left plain or given an arrow-tail or crescent moon. When all four arms bear these devices, the north point may be longer or larger or contrasting in colour. At Etloe, Blakeney, Glos., a deliberate challenge of interpretation is satisfyingly resolved into a plain north-south rod, with the east-west axis turning up towards the sunrise and down towards the sunset (*13.14*).

Commonly, however, the four arms bear their appropriate letters. It is easy to under-estimate how tall letters should be, at even quite modest heights. Three inches is really the minimum even on a garage; on a three-storey building they can be eight to ten inches high. And lettering that is so intricately indistinguishable from the ornament as to be illegible is merely exasperating.

Lettering standards range from the ultra-particular to the indifferent. Nothing less than classic Roman lettering is acceptable on some roofs; near-enough-Roman, with different proportions or exaggerated serifs, satisfies many. But categorizing is bedevilled by the casual mixing of Roman or Celtic or Gothic styles with letters of no recognizable ancestry. The Victorians enjoyed developing fluid decorative lettering styles and cast thousands of curved or looped letters with trefoil ends. They also favoured wide fishtail ends to shaped pierced letters, a style still in use (*8.12*). Plain block lettering, its height, width, thickness and curvature infinitely variable, predominates this century. Various cursive scripts deliberately eliminate every possible straight line and sharp point. Some amateur efforts do so less intentionally, and the 'bent wire' impression spoils otherwise effective work. As always, materials exert their influence: wood demands thickness in all dimensions. Even car registration letters and self-adhesive metal letters from the DIY store are used, stuck onto supporting blocks.

Letters may be placed level with the arms, above or below them, extending them outwards or set across the arm ends like toast on a fork. A weathervane customarily seen from one viewpoint may have one letter reversed so that it reads correctly from that viewpoint. Further ingenuity stands the letters half way along the arms, actually impales them, slopes them outwards, hangs them on chain links (*6.1*) or encloses them within other decoration (*6.4*). At Alnwick, Northd., they stand independently on the town hall roof (*5.10*). At Brundall, Norfolk, they are not only tilted at 22½ degrees to match the spears but also slightly curved to match the circlet (*15.7*).

Weathervanes with letters differing from the familiar NSEW are always worth investigating. An 'O' reveals continental origin – but beware: in Germany 'O' stands for 'Ost', East, but in France for '*Ouest*', West. A thatched dovecote with arms labelled 'WES T' is a rebus village sign for Westcott, Surrey. 'DBC' and an arrow indicates Dunfermline Bowls Club, Fife, and 'WE B S', complete with artillery-man motif, advertises the Woolwich Equitable Building Society in Norwich, Norfolk. Most curious of all is a raven on Ravenshill, Dormansland, Surrey, erected during the Great War. 'G D T K', 'God Damn The Kaiser', it declared. Both raven and letters have been renewed, the latter now reading 'G B T Q', 'God Bless The Queen', a change probably made in Coronation year.

Unadorned straight arms are perfectly adequate and, for some motifs, desirable. Whether made of square bar, circular rod or flat strap, arms need to harmonize in thickness and in length with the shape of the motif above them and to be set well below the motif and well above the roof.

Immediately there is a tendency to 'improve on' these straight arms. Gently tapering them into the letters, or even through or beyond them, makes the vane look more 'finished'. So does giving them a central sphere to emerge from. Still horizontal and straight, they can be rippled, knopped, part corkscrewed, given a barley-sugar twist throughout. Partway along, or on the end, they may open into a circle or diamond to enclose the letters. A move towards shaping the whole arm comes with giving it an open shoulder. Perching the arms above the

6.1   Lettering hanging on chain links: Whitestone Pond reservoir, Hampstead, Greater London

motif is an eye-catching change, as is angling them steeply upwards and adding guards' flag letters to accompany the locomotive on a Home for the Elderly at Stalham, Norfolk (*14.4*).

This idea of pictorial arms can be extended. Thus each arm of a vets' vane at Bicester, Oxon., bears small animal silhouettes; nineteenth-century agricultural implements show a firm's products at Leiston, Suffolk (*7.10*); courses available at Worthing College of Technology, Sussex, are illustrated on the arms of its student-made weathervane; and a memorial vane at Horsted Parva school, Sussex, stands sporting figures on the arms in place of letters. Doubled arms beneath Derby Railway Engineering School's rocket vane are graduated to repeat the idea of the rocket's thrust. At an East Winch, Norfolk, equestrian centre additional riding motifs are placed between doubled arms. Similarly a weathervane at Hindon, Wilts., (*12.3*) completes its cricketing theme by enclosing the twelve-man team between the arms.

Arm decoration of these kinds is exceptional, however, compared with what can loosely be described as 'scrolling' – not necessarily orthodox scroll shapes but decorative lines and patterns placed around arms and/or spindle. Obviously there is no structural need for it: it is simply to give pleasure. How great that pleasure is will depend on how successfully the crucial balance is achieved between angle and curve, shape and line, weight and lightness, intricacy and simplicity. It may even be the decoration that gives substance to an otherwise unremarkable vane. Leaf-ended scrolls to echo leaves elsewhere on the vane, or such architectural details as matching roof railings, may also satisfy subconsciously. Although the originator's period or personal taste may not be shared by today's observer, an honestly consistent and integrated design demands some degree of acceptance.

Ornamentation may be restricted to only one axis, emphasizing a church's orientation or the fact that a building like the clock tower at Totnes, Devon, is seen from up and down Fore Street but not from alongside. Some people feel very strongly that decoration should be only below the arms, well clear of the motif. Others feel equally strongly that all the intersection angles should contain decoration, building up into some satisfying central three-dimensional multi-form. Individual cases may require the scrolling to emphasize horizontality or verticality, but always with an awareness that patterns that look attractive in the making can appear trivial or a scribbly muddle on high. Wren's principle of a template 'to discern the right bigness' might usefully be extended to test the effect of weathervane decoration. It is so irritating to find a weathervane half obscured by a high parapet or its own ornament. Really tall masts, given substance by scrolls, poise a Wisbech, Cambs., arrow above a barricade of buildings and render the church cock at Aberaeron, Dyfed, even more dominant. However, a tall, arched structure is

6.2   Ornament fused with arms: Stoke Bruerne Church, Northants.

unusually ornate for a private house in Hilperton Road, Trowbridge, Wilts. So is ornament crawling some distance down the roof, as on Anmer village hall, Norfolk, and on the buttercross at Tickhill, Yorks.

Really thickly encrusted horizontal ornament becomes indistinguishably fused with the arms. Church weathervanes at North Curry, Som., and Stoke Bruerne, Northants (*6.2*), and on South Molton Town Hall, Devon, share this rather heavy characteristic. A much lighter style places the scrolling under the motif, so they all turn together. The proximity of the motif then suggests replacing the scrolls with appropriate objects. So crooks under a shepherding vane at Salehurst, Sussex, and horseshoes under the shoeing scene at Rodmell Forge, Sussex (*8.1*), give them greater expressiveness. Dates and initials, too, replace scrolling, either swinging with the motif or fixed around the intersection. The VR on an obviously modern seated fox weathervane at Shipdham, Norfolk, identified not Victoria Regina but the former owners, Violet and Ron. They intended to remove it but hadn't the heart when they discovered that their successors were – incredibly – Victor and Regina.

Decoration can consist of the simplest straight bars. Connecting spindle and arm diagonally like umbrella spokes, they create angular geometric shapes. Even DIY shelf brackets were pressed into service at Eastbourne, Sussex (*11.8*). Twisted and duplicated and given curled ends and extra motifs, the effect is very complex at Ashperton, Hereford & Worcester (*6.3*). Introducing shorter horizontal spikes to indicate the intermediate quarter-cardinal points is popular; adding further spikes at different angles produces a bristling, conker-like central boss. Particularly in the sixty years before World War I, spikes softened to tendrils, as on Stratford-upon-Avon Hospital, War. (*6.4*), and fluid scrolls culminated in natural foliage or more stylized trefoils and quatrefoils.

For an idea of the indescribable variety, consider the basic C-scroll. The blacksmith can compress, stretch or twist it; make it thick, thin or graduated; give it infinitely variable curvature; poke it in the back; or turn it inside out. Fig. *6.5* suggests a few predictable results. Various combinations can build up height or width. Subtleties like snub, tapered, leaf-rolled or fishtail ends to the scrolls subconsciously increase our appreciation. The S-scroll is capable of almost more variations, and as for combinations of the two, with additional circles and linking curves – non-mathematicians fall out here.

Fig. *6.5* oversimplifies misleadingly, however, for it represents the decoration in only one angle. When every shape is repeated four, eight or twelve times, astonishing 'snowflakes' or geometrical and floral forms

6.3 Twisted arms and scrolls, multiple motifs:
Ashperton, Hereford & Worcester.

6.4 Curved arms, tendril scrolls, unexpected motif:
Stratford-upon-Avon Hospital, War.

appear. A few blacksmiths encircle the intersection with a broad horizontal hoop, with a smaller one above or below. Attaching scrolls to these instead of to the spindle creates Enfield Hospital vane's not unpleasant standard-lamp effect (*5.2*).

The last word in intricate decoration must be a group of enormous weathervanes made by Don Bales, a retired coppersmith. They require height and space. Above Woolmer's Agricultural Contractors, Outwell, Norfolk, the weathervane adds real excitement to the Fen landscape. A ten-foot span of leafy scrolls supports a variety of perching birds, and there are cups to catch the wind and spin, as in an anemometer, and little twirling balls for good measure. One hardly notices the motif (*18.6*).

The logical culmination of all this scrolling is to eliminate the straight arm altogether, and sometimes the intersection too, giving the weathervane a hollow centre. The simplest curved arms curve out and then up/down, or up/down and then out. The most elaborate combine rounded or kinked C-scrolls, S-scrolls in assorted sizes, circles, straight or concave diamonds, every degree of convex or concave linking curve, extra loops and curlicues – and then cardinal letters. Great swirling arms can give the same motif an impact decidedly different from straight plain ones.

Traditionally it is the ornament, including shaped arms, which characterizes the work of a particular blacksmith. Customers tend to specify exactly what they want on a motif but to leave the suppporting ironwork to the smith, who selects from designs he has evolved as pleasing and practical. So David Harvey's basically S-scroll arms (*12.11*) or the particular arm-tilt of Brandeston Forge (*13.2*), for instance, are instantly recognizable all over the country, and abroad too, now universal advertising and transport have obliterated the craftsman's strictly local boundaries. Arm shapes from forges long since closed may still declare the original kinship of weathervanes whose motifs have altered beyond recognition.

But again and again a blacksmith simply struck out weathervane arms as fancy moved him. Whether lapses of taste or unforced felicities of design result, shaped arms remain among the most eye-catching decorative elements (*6.6*).

The so-slight but so-endless gradations of arm curvature defeat description. With the reminder, therefore, that any blacksmith worth his iron can produce something characteristic but different and that *in situ* each shape is quadrupled, at the least, back to the drawing-board (*6.7*).

At times aesthetic, architectural or other considerations will suggest

6.5   Variations on the C-scroll.

concentrating the decoration into a mount – some form of self-contained embellishment fixed anywhere on the spindle below the motif. In practice the occasional impossibility of deciding whether a decoration is complete enough in itself to be described as a mount is unimportant, the distinction being made here merely for descriptive convenience.

Decorative mounts are particularly associated with Victorian cast-iron sprigs of leaves with assorted daisy, fuchsia or spindleberry shapes. Another more formal leaf or butterfly pattern has the rather sinister effect of eyebrows above hooded lids. These cast forms sprout from gable ends in a kind of posy, through which the spindle rises.

Above the amusement pavilion on Palace Pier, Brighton, Sussex, is an unashamedly frivolous mount – a mirrored dance-hall sphere. Whatever the directional vagaries of the white galleon silhouette above it, the sphere still goes on glinting and turning steadily – by electricity. Equally eye-catching for miles around is a huge golden sphere on the hilltop church of St Lawrence, West Wycombe, Bucks., right next to the Dashwood mausoleum. At the corner of Pall Mall, Westminster, Greater London, the mount is a similarly huge openwork sphere, the bands tilted like lines of latitude. These spheres completely dwarf their motifs.

But quite small figures and letters can also stand out sharply. The name 'Dr W A Byers' forms the mount beneath an arrow weathervane in Seahouses, Northd., and a memorial plaque describes the village's

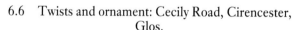

6.6 Twists and ornament: Cecily Road, Cirencester, Glos.

'all-weather friend and doctor for twenty-five years until his untimely death in 1981'. Mounts may also name a house or business.

However, actual words in a mount are less usual than images which, especially if the motif is insignificant, may convey the vane's main import. Heraldic mounts on Brecon Town Hall, Powys and the Norfolk & Norwich Hospital have already been mentioned. Similarly heraldic is the cock with a trumpet mount, the crest of the Leverhulme family, on Thornton Hough Church, Merseyside. Symbolic images are equally effective: crossed key mounts immediately identify St Peter's just as the fleece suspended beneath a pennant on Halifax's Piece Hall signifies the Yorkshire wool trade. Five arrows on the hotel of that name at Waddesdon, Bucks., make a dramatic black-and-gilt mount (*6.8*) whose family symbolism is described in Chapter 7.

In some highly integrated designs, mount and motif actually share the work of communication, each incomplete without the other. On the rebus vane at Watton, Norfolk, Wat, the flat gilded hare, is the motif, while the rounded 'tun' forms the mount (*7.3*). Henry VII's rose is in an arrow-tail, his portcullis in the mount of the weathervane on King's College, Cambridge (*4.16*). 'Indispensable' mounts of this kind are few, though a number expand on the idea of the motif. Thus the motif on the obelisk at Ripon, Yorks., is the Hornblower's horn, but the mount, the spiky rowel of a spur, refers to a local product (*16.7*); Hunt's chair factory at Stokenchurch, Bucks., uses a full-size red Windsor chair as mount, a small mass-produced 'hunt' rider as motif. The proximity of Brundall, Norfolk, to Roman settlements prompted a circlet of spears as mount for a Roman galley motif (*15.7*); reed mace ('bulrushes') and a turfing spade at Ranworth remind observers of the origin and landscape of the Norfolk Broads (*17.6*). At Pinchbeck, Lincs., a delightful misinterpretation of the architect's cross-hatching beneath an arrow with two doves created a basket mount, containing three squabs to represent the family's three children. Unfortunately the workman responsible for transferring the weathervane on Middle Holding, Ogle, Northd., from its previous location failed to recognize its beautiful thistle and rose mount as significant, so it no longer points correctly towards Scotland and England (*16.5*).

Heraldic supporters, or creatures in that style, provide logical but comparatively infrequent weathervane mounts. Since 1715 some interesting outline dragons have supported a rather small St George in action above them on St George's, Great Yarmouth, Norfolk. But Henry VIII ensured that heraldic stone beasts holding banners, such as he erected outside Hampton Court, should be fashionable. Although a

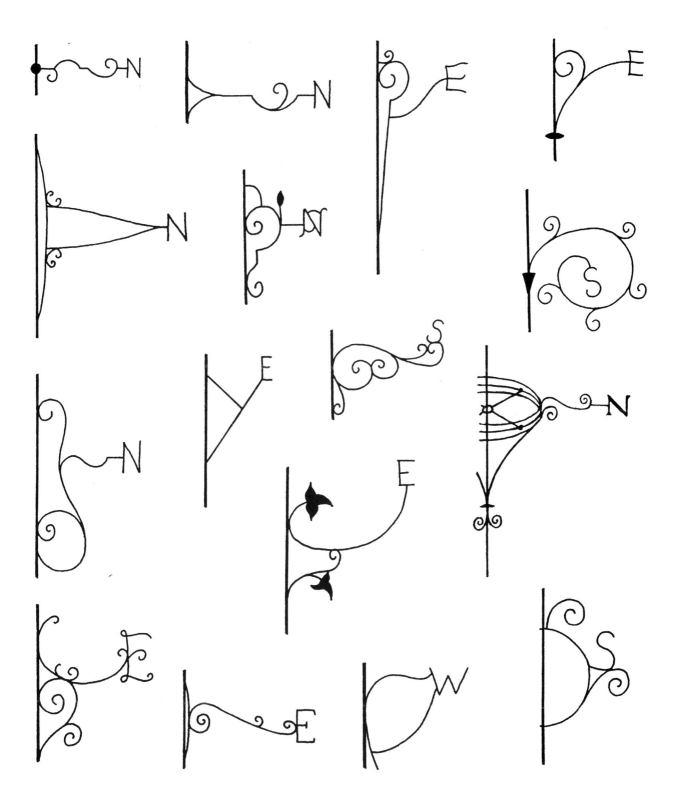

6.7　A few arm variations.

few may be genuine Tudor survivals, Victorian Gothic buildings, on which such beasts could appropriately be re-invented, supply most of them. The inherently decorative unicorn and eagle figure less than bulls, hound, griffins or lions; a phalanx of four looks particularly smart above Bridge Street, Warrington, Ches. A cottage at Thornton Hough, Merseyside, has what looks like the remains of a carved saint. Most curious of all is a carved stone knight on Hawkesbury Old Rectory, Avon. Its venerable appearance belies its 1970s origin. A conundrum weathervane and the commissioning of other quirky carvings encouraged the sculptor to create in this mount a sly resemblance to the owner. Entertainingly, he did not recognize himself (*5.5*).

Wooden pole masts are also sometimes elaborated into mounts, with top-masts, top-gallants, gaffs and shrouds. Alongside Falmouth harbour, in Cornwall, this raises no eyebrows, even with a fox motif. But an eighty-foot replica of Cowes' Royal Yacht Squadron mast is very startling looming over a bungalow at Wyton, Humberside. In the 1950s it apparently contributed to better TV reception; now the yacht motif it carries reminds the owner of his Solent sailing days.

Finally, finials. Many weathervanes do not have them; representation-al vanes, especially, themselves constitute the top part of the vane. But natural uprights in a design – a winning-post, a lamp-post, a ship's mast, a flag on a jump – can neatly incorporate the effect of a finial. Genuine finials may or may not turn with the motif; fixity or rotation depends on construction and is not in itself significant – indeed, it is scarcely discernible whether a knob or acorn finial turns or not.

The simplest finial is the unadorned spike, impaling an animal or projecting above a banner. On the Swan Theatre, Stratford-upon-Avon, War., it has been elongated and tapered to symbolize infinity (*7.7*). A spike is also easily hammered into a flat button top, rounded into a knob or twisted into a spiral. Generally, however, people prefer to add rather than alter, and fleurs-de-lys are clear favourites, minute or ponderous, in outline, silhouette or solid forms. Sidney Dye House, King's Lynn, Norfolk, shows how striking the three-dimensional treatment of a star can be (*13.1*). Finials consisting of spears, trefoils, wings, half-moons, tridents and acorns are all fairly easy to find. If finials echo floral mounts or leafy scrolls, the effect is very pleasing: Halifax Town Hall, Yorks, (*4.10*) and the triple ball design on the chapel of All Hallows Convent, Ditchingham, Norfolk (*5.7*), provide good examples. A trident finial above a converted church in Skene Street, Aberdeen, Grampians, suits its jolly dolphin pointer.

Using natural forms as finials seems unnecessarily confusing.

6.8   *Left:* Dominant mount at Five Arrows Hotel: Waddesdon, Bucks.
6.9   *Right:* Finial recalling Westmorland's oak tree: new county hall, Kendal, Cumbria.

Everyone expects a cock (especially), seagull, dove, eagle, a three-dimensional lioness, a cow or a shark to turn as motifs. Even a fancily cut lion and skeletal seahorse deceive. The horse finial at Isherwood Farm, Affetside, Greater Manchester, however, is no arbitrary decoration: he commemorates Manex, a beautiful Arab stallion, three times British National Champion and exhibited when the King of Saudi Arabia visited Buckingham Palace. In 1985, only ten years old, Manex was killed in a bizarre racing accident of which the owners can still scarcely speak.

When these finials, and more elaborate ones such as whole ploughing scenes and three-dimensional ships, rotate with an arrow motif, it is at least possible to tell which way the wind is blowing. But if they are fixed, the wind direction may be wrongly interpreted from the finial, and the small arrow swivelling manfully below may go unremarked. A larger arrow, intelligent contrast of black with gilt or colour, and good, clear vertical spacing may help to guide the eye aright.

Finials with associations are a pleasing group. For centuries people have topped weathervanes with crowns, often finely wrought, to proclaim loyalty to the Crown in general and satisfaction with coronations, jubilees or marriages in particular. Inevitably, superstition then linked damage to weathervane crowns with royal deaths and national disasters. But damage need imply nothing more sinister than rooks seeking surrogate elms. Coronets, mitres, spread eagles and other heraldic devices probably denote family allegiances. A stately home is not a *sine qua non*: Fletcher Farm, Tottington, Greater Manchester, places above its arrow the family arms with a pair of bull's horns to signify a butchery business. Community allegiance is declared by the defiant oak-tree of the now defunct Westmorland above Cumbria's new county hall in Kendal (*6.9*). The initial A survives as rotating finial above the reconstructed Wren church of St Agnes and St Anne, now serving London's Estonian and Latvian communities. Weathervane finials also express group allegiances. The Templars' lamb-and-flag surmounts the Temple church in the City of London; the scouting insignia represents the owner's involvement at Mill Peace, Weybourne, Norfolk (*7.4*); St Andrews Golf Club, Fife, displays its badge, quite apart from countless sports clubs using golf or cricket balls as finials. They declare the occupants' concerns as clearly as the crossed swords above a Scotsman's hotel on the sea-front at Morecambe, Lancs., or the logo finials of Lloyds Bank or the Co-op.

In the chapters that follow, the motifs described may have no arms, no letters, no scroll ornament, no mount, no finial. They may have some of these elements, or all. The modern trend to simplicity is fine if it is dictated by taste, regrettable if the motive is economy. Skimping careful touches like tapering arms into letters or finishing scroll ends properly detracts from the vane's quality. A well-made weathervane, which is an entity in which whichever decorative elements are used harmonize in style and proportion, gives lasting satisfaction.

7 Symbolism

Absolutely anything can symbolize something to someone. A high proportion of weathervanes considered in other chapters is, therefore, at least partially symbolic. Ploughing is an occupation, but a ploughing vane is often chosen as symbolic of a desirable way of life. Especially in the hinterlands of trade, many bird, animal, vehicle or implement weathervanes, though representational in appearance, are symbolic in intent. They say, in effect, Here be Friesians, or poultry, or a forge, or lorries for hire.

In Victorian times certain deductions could be made from the very style of a weathervane, irrespective of more overt symbolism. Any vane on a Gothic almshouse or library or Classical town hall strengthened the implication that these buildings harboured the morally or intellectually superior and the civilized. On a private dwelling it conferred status: the occupants had 'arrived'. The quantities that were made and erected soon invalidated the message but people continued to value the ornamentation as contributory to happiness, and often sought to make it reflect something of the building's function. Church weathercocks and heraldic vanes had created in the Middle Ages a symbolic habit of mind. Although modified with the onset of literacy, it has never fully died out. Weathervanes still express what buildings are for, who uses them, what work those people do and what ideas they hold.

Early weathervane symbolism was largely religious, and much survives, though now more vaguely grasped. Because the message is more important than physical accuracy, we still accept a stylized church cock and respond to the resonances of the world beneath and the all-powerful Cross above him.

119

A fish, the Greek word for which, IXΘYΣ, consists of the initials of the Greek words for 'Jesus Christ, God's son, Saviour', is a symbolic weathervane found on hundreds of churches. Most are just 'fish' but some makers depicted species they knew: hence the fat gilded sea-trout at Piddinghoe, Sussex, the salmon at Tweedmouth, Northd., and the supposed herring on St John's, Great Yarmouth, Norfolk. A half-silhouette, half-outline fish is appropriately fanciful on the astonishing St Conan's Kirk almost overhanging Loch Awe, Strathclyde. At Mildenhall, Wilts., a family erected its fish weathervane to be a sign to other Christians, as it was when persecuted Christians recognized each other through a temporary fish shape scraped in the sand by apparently random gestures.

7.1   Seventeenth-century key: St Peter's Cornhill, City of London.

The dove with olive branch appears on St John the Baptist's Church, Crawley, Sussex, and on Hethersett Church, Norfolk, with the serpent firmly trodden underfoot. Like many symbols, it was early incorporated into arms; in Lancashire, Kirkham Grammar School's weathervane is therefore from the town arms as well as symbolic. This symbol makes one of the most famous of American weathervanes, chosen by George Washington for his home, Mount Vernon, in 1787.

The Paschal Lamb is a popular symbol, lending itself to good full-bodied treatment, as on Halifax Town Hall, Yorks., (*4.10*), St John sub Castro, Lewes, Sussex, and St Mary's, Hendon, Greater London. It seems less likely on a bank in Guildford, Surrey. A pictorial ewe and lamb on Westwell church, Oxon., recalls biblical shepherd imagery, but a jolly Disney lamb frolicking atop a massive tower at Foulsham, Norfolk, has unduly secular overtones.

Ship weathervanes hammered home the ancient idea of life as a journey best undertaken in the ship of the Church. Flat representations, as at Wells-next-the-Sea, Norfolk, and Nefyn, Gwynedd, are most usual. Portsmouth Cathedral, in Hampshire, however, has a stunning three-dimensional Golden Barque, three feet five inches long and six feet tall. Its splendour is said to celebrate the triumph of the church

7.2   A family joke: Toad Hall, Bonnie Hill, Wivenhoe, Essex.

wardens of 1710 – the date its flag displays – when after prolonged legal wrangling with their vicar they succeeded in appropriating most of his income. (Doubtless they rejoiced less when he was later awarded £20 damages against them.) Because it spoke to homecoming sailors of safe return, symbolism slipped into superstition: whenever the Barque was lowered for repair, mothers flocked to lay their children in it, as a charm against drowning. Now it stands marvellously visible inside the cathedral on a plinth of *Victory* oak, with a replica aloft.

The sacred monogram 'IHS', prettily framed, makes a complete church weathervane at Wells, Som. The Hospital of the Holy and Blessed Trinity at Long Melford, Suffolk, however, shows the monogram surrounded by other symbols – stars, fleurs-de-lys (the Trinity), a heart (love), a dove (the Holy Ghost), the whole topped by the cockatrice crest of Sir William Cordell, the brilliant lawyer who founded these almshouses in 1573. It sounds ostentatious but is in fact restrained.

Satan is often symbolized in dragon form, and it might seem inappropriate to grant him eminence on a church steeple, but dragon weathervanes are warnings, for they represent dragons defeated – by St Margaret at Upton, Norfolk, by St Michael at Sittingbourne, Kent (both dragons are now inside their churches), or by St George at Orleton, Hereford & Worcester.

Of other individual saints' emblems, St Peter's keys are the most numerous. Crossed keys are usually pierced into a banner, but Bedford's single gilt key, horizontal and three-dimensional, is effective. The vertical one above St Peter's, Cornhill, City of London (*7.1*), is nine feet tall and believed to date from Wren's 1678–80 rebuilding. When last brought down, in 1900, it took two strong men to lift it. St Lawrence Jewry's gridiron, another notable Wren vane in the City of London, is back in place, restored after Blitz damage. Chobham church, Surrey, has another ornamental gridiron, but a version in Norwich with the saint actually spread-eagled on it for roasting was evidently too horrid for citizens to wish to replace it. Other saintly symbols are St Hugh's swan at Scunthorpe, Humberside, St John's eagle on Hurspierpoint College, Sussex, the anchor that was suppposed to hold St Clement submerged, on St Clement Danes, Westminster, London, the crossed arrows and crown on Moyses Hall at Bury St Edmunds, Suffolk. St Andrew scatters his cross not just over Scotland but throughout the land, but St David's dove is not evident in Wales. Many of these symbols would still find ready acceptance by at least a proportion of the public.

However, another group of weathervanes, because its symbolism

7.3   A punning vane; 'Wat' and the 'tun': old lock-up, Watton, Norfolk.

relates to particular families, is less readily accessible. But once elucidated, how entertaining.

The fan of five arrows (*6.8*) represents five Rothschild brothers, heirs to the banking empire, who scattered from Frankfurt to extend their financial domination of the eighteenth-century European capitals. A great-grandson, Ferdinand de Rothschild, built Waddesdon Manor, Bucks., and many other Waddesdon buildings, including the Five Arrows Hotel with this weathervane. A smaller family is represented at Intwood, Great Ellingham, Norfolk, by a row of four graduated cogs. It neatly expresses the necessity for each member to fit into the lives of the others without friction to create a smooth-running entity.

'You *are* a toad!' exclaimed an exasperated wife one day. Her husband promptly brought home a house name-plate, inscribed 'Toad Hall'. A one-time workhouse on Bonnie Hill, Wivenhoe, Essex, is the couple's third 'Toad Hall', at which their 'Tadpole' was born. For the new garage a planning-condition was imposed – some kind of finial. The indolent creature in *7.2* was the riposte.

At Chwilog, Gwynedd, a proud father celebrated the birth of his second daughter with their names and dates painted on either side of a weathervane arrow. Along it drives a Royal Mail van, its cartoon driver jubilant at his successful 'deliveries'. In a contrasting home-made vane at Rolvenden, Kent, an irate husband aimed his gun at the stork about to deposit a baby on the chimney. Ironically the stork remains unscathed: it is the man who has vanished.

The traditional gilded banner, cut with a heart to match those on the rain-heads at Levens Hall, Cumbria, symbolizes no such loving relationship. This 1984 weathervane recalls a gambling confrontation of three centuries ago, when the Hall supposedly changed hands on the turn of the Ace of Hearts. Intriguingly, local superstition foretells dramatic family changes whenever a white fawn ('hart') is born among the black park deer in the park. The owners disclaim any intentional reference to this, but rebus or punning vanes are traditionally popular.

Several towns have such weathervanes, at least two employing 'harts'. At Hartfield it decorates a Sussex coast, while East Dereham church, Norfolk, enjoys a double pun: on the arrow dated 1773 stands the 'deer' or 'hart', with a heart-shaped chain looped about it (*2.7*). Nearby Watton's seventeenth-century lock-up shows Wat, the hare, loping above a three-dimensional barrel, or tun (*7.3*). A weathervane at Cranleigh, Surrey, reproduces the crane symbol carved on the town fountain. An impressive embossed copper camel recently regilded, dominates Camelford, Corn. And the ox-in-ford from the shield of

7.4 A personal name-vane: Mill Peace, Weybourne, Norfolk.

7.5 Regional references; the Hampshire Hog: council offices, Winchester, Hants.

Oxford's 'canting arms' is on the town hall weathervane.

This approach makes an obvious springboard for house-name weathervanes, though generally these are straightforward illustrations – three trees for Pine Lodge, Everton, Notts., a silhouette map for North America Farm, Wivelsfield, Sussex, a demure crinolined pair for White Ladies, Piltdown, Sussex, a couple of purposeful monks at Great Totham, Essex, originally on Abbots. By extension, swans and dolphins, even some smiths and carters and mills, announce their owners' surnames. Mr Hands at Mill Peace, Weybourne, Norfolk, hammered sheet aluminium into a three-dimensional model of his pointing-hand logo (*7.4*). Does the bull crowning Blickling Hall, Norfolk, recall its former owners the Bullens (Boleyns, if you prefer)? A fascinating vane that Erme Wood Forge remember making showed a musical stave and treble clef with the notes A C B – the initials of the conductor Sir Adrian Boult.

The misrepresentation of objects, either accidentally or deliberately, underlies quite a few weathervanes. Pound and Stocks Cottage, Filkins, Oxon., defeated direct illustration, so Denis Trinder compromised, with realistic stocks, but overhung by a £ sign. To a fenman the term 'Fen Tiger' means the aggressively individual and stubborn native. To one uninitiated blacksmith it meant the effective but hardly indigenous beast that lords it over Willow Grange Farm, Chittering, Cambs.

In 1955 the new council offices in Winchester, Hants., were crowned with architect John Brandon-Jones's design for a gilded beaten copper weathervane (*7.5*). It shows a 'Hampshire Hog' on a wheatsheaf representing other aspects of local agriculture. Both literally, in compliment to Hampshire's quality bacon, and metaphorically, as a nickname for a Hampshire native, the term 'Hampshire Hog' has centuries of usage. How amusing then that it may originally not have meant a hog at all but a hogget – a sheep or even colt of a particular age.

From Rocket Lodge, Cley, Norfolk, the maroons used to be fired to launch the lifeboat. Its rocket weathervane, a small outline, is of a type more likely to launch Star Wars. Another rocket weathervane, this time with a long, flaming thrust, adorns the Railway Engineering School at Derby. Comments believed to emanate from the architect suggest that, despite its location, this was nothing to do with Stephenson's famous railway engine *The Rocket* but an attempt to express a vision of speed. Its date of 1938 makes the star finial a strikingly futuristic touch.

Cartoonists have frequently enjoyed impaling eminent figures in a strange mutation of the weathercock, which then becomes a telling political jibe with all sorts of shady Vicar-of-Bray implications.

On a quite different plane, a copper repoussé cock was created for French Heritage Year, 1980, symbolizing all the arts. The tail 'feathers' were a lyre, a T-square, a pen, a paintbrush and a strip of film. Its development from a poster into a weathervane culminated in its ceremonial erection on the church steeple at Falaise in Normandy, birthplace of William the Conqueror.

Certain widely accepted symbols surprise us by appearing other than where we expect them. In Canterbury, Kent, for instance, the theatrical comedy/tragedy masks surmount a shopping arcade, not the nearby Marlowe Theatre where they would not have raised an eyebrow (*7.6*). Moon and stars have slightly pagan good-luck associations for a church at Waddesdon, Bucks. Conversely the horseshoe, that universal good-luck symbol partaking of the magical powers of the blacksmith, is a singular rarity.

Symbolism can be in the eye of the beholder. Thus one member of staff at Livingstone School, Bedford, claimed that its snail weathervane suggested the children's slow but steady progress, 'making haste slowly'. To another, less starry-eyed, it indicated that unregenerate children are still, like Shakespeare's schoolboy, 'creeping like snail unwillingly to school'. Father Time, too, prompts various interpretations. At MCC's cricket ground at Lord's, St. John's Wood, Greater London, he removes the bails to signify the end of play (*2.10*); detractors say that this is to remind men that their lives can draw to a close during the length of a cricket match. A more bitter irony must have prompted a prisoner, doing

7.6   Theatrical masks: a shopping arcade, Canterbury, Kent.

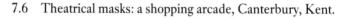

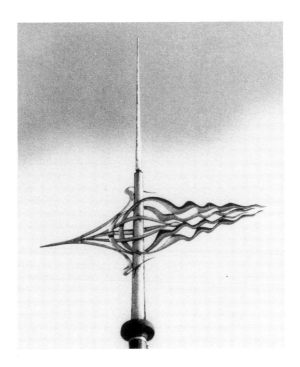

7.7   Abstract thought: Swan Theatre,
        Stratford-upon-Avon, War.

time with no bail, to make in the prison workshops, presumably from
memory, the Father Time weathervane that stood for many years on
Lewes prison, Sussex.

Small wonder then that sculptor Anthony Robinson found
Stratford-upon-Avon's new Swan Theatre a springboard for philos-
ophical thought. As he worked on its substantial pennants (each
three-quarters of a hundredweight and nine feet of stainless steel), all
sorts of insubstantial ideas arose and were caught (7.7). Globe-like lines
of latitude and longitude glance at the theatre *of* the world, and *as* a
world. Interwoven strands hint at rippling water, continuity and
harmony, the flames from which the new theatre arose, the flame of
genius. The vertical spindle diminishes towards infinity, timelessness ...
And well-met by moonlight these pennants release even more ethereal
notions.

The ideas embodied in a weathervane may have an unmistakeable
nationality. The impression of sun, moon, Indian with headdress and
pointing arm on Glebe House, Montgomery, Powys, is powerfully
American, and indeed the vane is a copy of a traditional American
design, acquired in California (7.8). Complete figures of Red Indians
and other patriotic symbols – fully modelled eagles with wing-spans

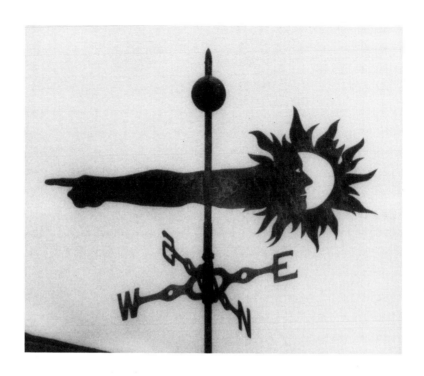

7.8   American symbols: Glebe House, Montgomery, Powys.

from seventeen inches to twelve feet, 'Liberty' with a painted or pierced flag – were made in quantity to express the enthusiastic new sense of American nationhood. Claiming that castles and palaces were two-a-penny in England but that the English were a bit short on wigwams, the American Isaac Singer, sewing-machine magnate and early instigator of hire-purchase, called his huge mansion in Paignton, Devon, 'The Wigwam' and inevitably gave it a Red Indian vane. Alas, it has vanished without trace.

Britain has few such symbols. A cheerful Union Jack banner with ornate pointer flies above St Mary's, Scarborough, Yorks.; its size suggests it was always intended to be so painted. The Britannia Pier at Great Yarmouth, Norfolk, and the Britannia public house at Northampton both have identifying weathervanes, painted and plain respectively. But these patriotic weathervanes are infrequent and certainly not mass-produced as America's were. In weathervane terms Britain's patriotism surfaces in legends like that of St George, and above all in heraldry.

A supra-national symbol, such as the medical rod of Aesculapius, is unexpectedly a rarity on weathervanes. A doctor placed one on his house tucked under the dunes at Waxham, Norfolk. A variation, a horizontally wriggling creature with forked tongue known as 'the Serpent of

7.9 Specialized educational symbol: Indian Institute, Oxford.

Healing', identifies the old York Dispensary, founded in 1788 to counteract squalid home conditions.

With this example we approach a huge group of weathervanes which 'advertise' symbolically what is going on in a community or building. (Those that actually *illustrate* it, with human figures, are chiefly occupational weathervanes, considered separately.)

Schools and colleges may identify themselves not just architecturally but with weathervanes. Badges or identifying initials are the simplest. More interestingly, the typist working on the initialled arrow, and the chef, house, lathe and ballcock on the four arms, indicate the range of courses available at Worthing Technical College, Sussex; the plumbing students made it. The copper plough, an apparently incongruous rural image on Austin-Rover's smart Marketing Centre at Studley Castle, War., recalls Frances, Lady Warwick's impulse purchase of the castle in 1903 to found a Women's Agricultural College, which functioned there until 1969.

Specialized educational establishments have produced some exotic weathervanes, very exciting on the British skyline. The former Indian Institute in Oxford, opened in 1883, still rejoices in its superb fully modelled gilded elephant, ridden by a mahout, with pale blue trappings beneath an elegant howdah (*7.9*).

Weathervanes can also identify another kind of community building – a Home for the Elderly. A resident at Bernhard Baron's Cottage

Homes, Polegate, Sussex, designed their touching symbol of a contented couple beside their home. Sometimes the whole community's activities are encapsulated in a weathervane. On Minehead harbour wall, Som., the coloured ship and woolpack suspended in a circular arrow-tail gain even more symbolic overtones through having been made by local youngsters on a Youth Training Scheme. Capturing 'the spirit of Lurgashall', Sussex, was the avowed aim in depicting Lurgashall green's chestnut tree, with a goose such as once grazed there and a crinolined goose-girl ('It's an old-fashioned place'). Similarly, oak and conifer woods, plough and pastureland, rabbit and bird symbolize the Welsh landscape pretty comprehensively, though unfortunately this competition design by Brian Owen of Templeton Forge, Dyfed, was never made.

The story of the grasshopper as a general trading symbol is told in Chapter 17. Most trade weathervanes refer specifically to the activity carried on either in the premises below or by someone living there. They inherit the traditions of trade signs from as far back as the heyday of Pompeii and Herculaneum. Although they no longer have to communicate to the illiterate they still make useful advertisements. The splendid agricultural weathervane (*7.10*) conveys in its seven-foot span of confident craftsmanship just how important the engineering firm of Garrett's was in Leiston, Suffolk. The implements on the cardinal arms indicate what was produced in their Long Shop, one of the first 'production lines' in the 1850s and now an industrial museum on which the vane has been reinstated. Firms on this human scale enjoyed weathervanes. Larger factories, automated and power-driven, seldom had them.

7.10   An agricultural engineer's products: Leiston, Suffolk.

Ploughs were important enough in Northrepps, Norfolk, for a 'gallus' plough, as made by the local foundry about 1860, to form the 1953 church Coronation vane. But ploughs are rare, considering how rural economy depended on them. Plenty of other rural tasks are symbolized, however. A tall pillar sundial in the old kitchen gardens of Sandringham House, Norfolk, supports what must be a besom, while at Ash Tree Farm, Old Newton, Suffolk, an agronomist's pair of disembodied wellies strides across the sky. For farm buildings at Washingford House, Bergh Apton, Norfolk, home of a former chairman of the local Farmers' Wildlife Advisory Group, Hodgson's made a pheasant, goose and tractor under trees, symbolizing both professional and conservational interests. The bee at Rothamsted Park Lodge, Hatching Green, Herts., marks the home of the research station's apiarist; a bee on a flower announces that at Scout Bottom Farm, Mytholmroyd, Yorks., bee-keeping is both business and hobby (*7.11*).

Not all country hobbies are so land-related, however. Church Farm, Weston, Beccles, Suffolk, has an owner keen on Country music, which explains the large guitar floating above his barn, and the smaller one he made for a friend of similar tastes at Ringland, Norfolk. If guitar-playing creates a thirst, plenty of refreshment is available. In Wiltshire, Stitchcombe Vineyard's owner-designed weathervane (*1.7*) promises well. 'Good ale available by the Toby-jugful' proclaims the weathervane on the Woolpack Hotel, Herstmonceux, Sussex. 'By the barrel-full,' amends Donnington Brewery's vane, Glos.: the arrow the owner himself made thirty years ago has a barrel, complete with tap, for its tail. Breweries, incidentally, are among the businesses whose weathervanes still actively contribute to the manufacturing process.

Mostly, however, trade weathervanes are unabashed advertisements. For instance, outside Herstmonceux, Sussex, Lime Cross Nurseries' elegant group of trees, and in Stanley Road, Teddington, Greater London, Sullivan Builders' initialled house announce 'This is what we sell.' The dripping tap on a Fordham, Cambs., garage and the three-dimensional coloured blow-lamp above Leicester Street, Melton Mowbray, Leics. (*7.12*), advertise plumbing businesses. At Chawton, Hants, at Kniveton, Derby., and at Oving, Bucks., removals and flat-bed lorries in distinctive firms' colours offer removals and haulage services. Although a modern luxury coach at Bourton on the Water, Glos., contrasts strongly with a horse-drawn timber waggon at Burn, Yorks., both deliver their message clearly. Some trade-symbol weathervanes are more imaginative than others. Instead of the standard anvil, for instance, Faygate Forge, Sussex, illustrates in vane form the old saying 'By

7.11 Beekeeper's vane: Mytholmroyd, Yorks.

hammer and hand all arts do stand.' Two hands, one holding a spray of vivid, outsize blooms, the other feeling how warm the minute greenhouse is, symbolize Southwater Nurseries, Sussex. The turkey on a farm at Holme Chapel, Lancs., is apparently oven-ready!

Trade-sign weathervanes are vulnerable when premises change their function: a coffee-pot cannot service cars, nor a penny-farthing sell computers. Other reasons have to be found to preserve them. One of these may be an appreciation of historical associations, especially those familiar from inn-signs – something like the old ram's fleece sign in which the animal is so uncomfortably suspended by its middle. On Halifax Piece Hall, Yorks., – a superb colonnaded quadrangle of 315 individual rooms from which cloth-makers sold their 'pieces' of cloth 200 years ago – the ram's fleece mount and pennant are presumably made secure by the historical importance of the location.

Several inn names have suggested weathervanes, sometimes replacing, sometimes reinforcing the conventional painted signboard. The fifteenth-century Dog and Partridge at Bury St Edmunds, Suffolk, depicts its name in a vane less old but still venerable; the Rainbow and Dove at Hastingwood, Essex, is suitably illustrated; and the Brentor Inn, Devon, presents the unmistakable landmark of Brentor Hill and its church. Less explicable is an eagle on the Swan at Pennsylvania, Avon. A crown weathervane at Long Crendon, Bucks., is one of many denoting a private home's former use as an inn. 'Good wine needs no bush' runs the proverb, and certainly these weathervanes have little in common with the general tavern sign of the ivy bush: they are specific and often unique.

Businesses of many kinds follow the same principle. They design weathervanes from some symbol people will immediately associate with the firm, in some cases the actual logo or trademark. The mirror-image Ns logo of the National Bus Co at Uckfield, Sussex, is too discreet, scarcely distinguishable from any other arrow point. Stylization can also be so extreme that a logo/vane, though visually pleasing, becomes comprehensible only after explanation, as with the germinating wheat seed on Harlow Agricultural Merchants at Latchmore Bank, Essex. Newly built branches of national chains sometimes erect weathervanes, at worst merely a token nod towards visual harmony with older neighbours. Better ones probably reflect local managerial drive. A pointer impaling an E and a star, a tail admonishing 'Safety' with a spread eagle above it, and star-shaped arm decoration form a splendid design on the old Eagle Star Insurance offices in Norwich. The Town Mill pub at Mansfield, Notts., has turned the field-gun symbol of Stone's Brewery houses into a weathervane. The Hertford branch of Bejam flies a cartoony figure created from a freezer cabinet, part of the firm's promotional material a few years back. W.H. Smith's DIY section uses a house-and-rainbow logo: the Colchester branch in Essex has turned this into a vane. The Co-op logo is a finial at Northampton.

There is no end to such weathervanes. Barrett's tree logo, used on all

7.12 Plumber's advertisement: Leicester Street, Melton Mowbray, Leics.

their housing developments in some form, becomes a vane at Long Stratton, Norfolk. The Lloyds Bank horse surmounts branches at Penzance, Corn., and Cardiff, while comic Happy Eaters urge motorists to pause at several branches of this restaurant chain.

Business symbols are designed for instant recognition. How ironic then to conclude with one that has become uniquely recognizable through initial failure. The medieval engravers of the Corporate Seal of Liverpool intended St John's eagle in compliment to their founder, King John. They produced the 'Liver Bird'. (An expatriate Liverpudlian keen

to make a Liver Bird turned out yet another unidentifiable creature ...) Liverpool does not apparently favour it as a weathervane but the Royal Assurance Co adopted it, and a good three-dimensional version still turns above their former offices in North Street, Brighton, Sussex (*7.13*).

Through generations of illiteracy, symbols communicated information satisfactorily on their own. People knew what the cock signified, what happened under a barber's pole, what the King's arms looked like on an inn-sign. Then, as heraldry, for example, slipped from daily use, forgetful or inventive sign-painting led to confusion. The sign at the Crown inn was still comprehensible; the King's Arms sign needed the words added for clarification. In weathervanes this still continues. The word 'Antiques' clarifies what the penny-farthing bicyclist, charming in striped trousers, tail-coat and topper, was selling from his premises in Weybourne, Norfolk. But the camp-site func-

7.13   The Liver Bird – an eagle *manqué*: North Street, Brighton, Sussex.

tion of a field at Theddlethorpe All Saints, Lincs., would have been perfectly clear from Graham Walker's pictorial weathervane without 'Caravans and Tents' in such painstaking iron lettering beneath. It is the final stage – 'The King's Arms' in words alone with no symbol – that conveys the information with little visual pleasure. A company's initials or name on a vane are functional and efficient, but not wildly exciting.

But in the 1980s visual messages bombard us from hoarding and screen. Instantly memorable images spring from the flourishing worlds of graphics and advertising. We respond to visual symbols. So shall we now see a new flowering of symbolic weathervanes?

8 Work and Leisure

Direct illustrations of people, doing jobs or enjoying themselves, convey information more immediately than symbols.

The human form's basic symmetry makes it ineffective as a weathervane unless placed behind the spindle. Even if the 'ground' element, without which human figures look distinctly odd, is given a pointer, the figure's direction needs clarifying by an outstretched arm or a trailing appendage like an open umbrella.

Occupational vanes illustrate chiefly outdoor, rural and individual jobs, and share an old-fashioned air. Accuracy often relaxes into hazy romanticism. The rural and nostalgic bias is explicable: indoor workers seated at desks, for example, though presenting distinctive enough outlines, can look out of place on weathervanes as the gale swivels them about and rain beats on their unprotected heads. Modern jobs often involve vast machines that dwarf the human operator. Individual craft skills, however, retain their mystique.

Another propensity of weathervanes using the human form is their humour – unintentional sometimes, with their cavalier disregard of human proportion and anatomy. But many deliberately use cartoon or caricature techniques.

The Rural Development Commission's patterns reflect these tendencies. There are rural occupations: a stable-lad, a man ploughing, a shepherd and a carter; a seated figure with carrots, basket and jug of flowers presumably represents horticulture. Three of the Commission's patterns are semi-comic: an elderly man and dog in a gale; a farmer chasing a fox which is carrying off his goose; and a doctor, scissors toppling from his Gladstone bag, stethoscope and fob-watch a-swing, running on tiptoe towards (or from!) some crisis – fun, but we have not found one. Two leisure designs show a couple dancing a minuet, and a cyclist, the only relatively modern touch.

Early weathervanes rarely used the human form. Nineteenth-century humans were usually transmuted into angels, abstract ideas or godly beings, in weathervanes as in statuary. So most weathervanes of ordinary people, even if engaged in obsolete tasks or wearing period costume, date from about 1900 onwards.

Three particular kinds of buildings share occupational weathervanes. Current business premises use illustrative vanes, like symbolic ones, as supplementary trade-signs. Former schools, chapels etc often have vanes indicating that former use. On private homes, occupational vanes probably demonstrate the resident's job rather than his place of work. Such a neat pattern is, of course, disturbed by frequent business or household moves, which leave weathervanes in or move them to incongruous locations.

Vastly increased mobility also carries weathervanes hundreds of miles as gifts or holiday souvenirs, especially designs like the Rural Development Commission's shepherd and ploughman, which are erected everywhere but represent simply *an* occupation, not *the* occupation of the resident. They tap our affection for the English countryside and a general sense of unease with twentieth-century life, and have considerable decorative appeal – that is, 'patriotism' or

8.1   Elongated farrier scene: Rodmell Forge, Sussex.

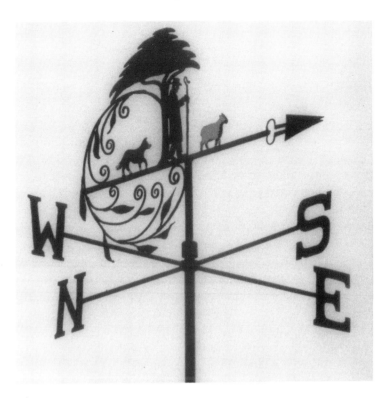

8.2 Adaptation of the Rural Development Commission's shepherd pattern: Plumpton College of Agriculture, Sussex.

nostalgia or aesthetics, not occupation, is the primary motivation.

Similarly, it is not really profitable to look for marked regional variations in a country as small as Britain. Any agricultural or industrial product needs the back-up of so many associated trades that any region can reasonably fly vanes illustrating any occupation with some hope of local relevance. There are not so much regional motif subjects – though a local smith may have his favourites – as recognizable regional styles, emanating from particular forges, as we have noted elsewhere.

The front-runner among occupations depicted on weathervanes is the blacksmith, fittingly enough in view of his king-pin position in community life for centuries. A smith at his anvil presents a strong, unromanticized silhouette, familiar within living memory in almost every community, still present in some, and full of the resonances of skill, strength and reliability. The Commission does not offer one – but what smith, past or present, needs others to show him what his own forge tasks look like? Blacksmith vanes are popular in both rural and urban settings, though forges, past, present or modified into vehicle service stations, are prime sites.

Lightweight and economical aluminium construction need not mean stiff-legged lifelessness. John Allen's smith, now at Ranworth, Norfolk, is suspiciously like himself hammering at a horseshoe held by tongs. A design refinement is the horseshoe with pierced nail-holes replacing the conventional arrowhead. Variations on this single figure at the anvil are the commonest form.

Two figures or additional tools begin to create more interesting cameos, though variable in the degree of realism they achieve. The example probably erected shortly after the forge at Shipton-under-Wychwood, Oxon., closed in 1942 adds a hearth and wheel but is rather static. At Hazlewood near Skipton, Yorks., a garage proclaiming itself 'Ye Anvil' still possesses blacksmiths' tools held in staples on a block, just as depicted in its weathervane, made on the premises in the 1960s. The Old Forge at Ide Hill, Kent, has a complete scene, made about 1970. Two smiths work at their anvil with assorted tools; the firebox adds extra windage. One of the most striking mobile scenes, though not a weathervane in the orthodox sense, is at Wakefield, Yorks (*1.1*). Set on a mast within an elaborately wrought frame are a flaming hearth with its hood, fixed, a blacksmith hammering a bar held by tongs, who rotates, and a hanging 'curtain' of linked scrolls that swings from the top. It is a real eye-catcher, advertising Frank Foley's Victoria Forge.

The blacksmith as farrier, in his leather apron and flat cap, figures on the Old Forge at Compton Pauncefoot, Som., and there are frequent representations of farriers shoeing anything from a pony to a carthorse. Baskets of tools or modern angle-lidded tool-boxes can give this essentially timeless scene a quite different sense of period.

To be visible on the weathervane, the farrier has to be shoeing the horse's back foot. Frank Dean at Rodmell Forge, Sussex, tells how he 'cheated' by photographing the groom holding 'Augustus' by his halter, the farrier at work, his tool-kit and anvil all extended into a line instead of in the tight-packed group of the real operation. Simple horseshoes decorating the pivot point focus the line. Its low position enables the appropriate hues of horse and clothing and the gently drooping cardinal arms to be closely inspected (*8.1*).

Because cartwheels were given metal 'shoes', blacksmiths and wheelwrights were close associates. Wheelwrights' shops survive only in such charmingly naïve vanes as that at Carleton Rode, Norfolk, with its short-legged figure tapping tentatively at one of three tiny wheels balanced on the anvil. In Heath and Reach's version, Beds., a sturdy wheelwright prepares, like the J. Arthur Rank gong-beater, to strike the completed wheel balanced on its rim beside him. However, on a small vane at Sandhurst, Kent, the Burwash blacksmith and wheelwright

David Hedges' interesting conception was to build the cartwheel up in stages just as he would a real one. So several wheel-spokes are in their hub, still without a rim, while the wheelwright hammers another one home, using a solid, three-dimensional hammer.

Between them, blacksmiths and wheelwrights permitted the efficient performance of many farm tasks, of which ploughing seems particularly to attract weathervane makers. Most use the Rural Development Commission's pattern (*1.5*). The scene it depicts was still familiar pre-war, when it was designed, yet it is criticized as looking too effortless and too decorative. Nonetheless, pivoted well forward and with deeper 'ground' for windage, it works satisfactorily and is popularly reproduced. It overlooks the Norfolk Showground outside Norwich, the delectably named Promised Land Farm at Wendlebury, Oxon., a stonily unploughable foreshore at Zennor near Land's End – every county in England has it but few in Scotland or Wales. It can become subsidiary to a house name, as at Theddlethorpe All Saints, Lincs., with Graham Walker's characteristic twiddly iron (*1.5*), or to complex ironwork such as Don Bales's at Eastmoor, Norfolk, or Westridge Farm, Cowfold, Sussex, though both these examples have two spirited horses. Another elaboration comes in the form of ridged 'earth' and a skittish dog (borrowed from the Commission's shepherd pattern) on the A158 near Horncastle, Lincs. Gilding suits the subject less than colour. This is subdued at Pasture House, Flinton, Humberside, but extremely vivid in the unlikely urban setting of Crome Road, Norwich, where the stables until recently still had eighteenth-century fittings.

Home-made attempts at ploughing weathervanes tend to come to

8.3   Poacher: North Wheatley,
Notts.

8.4   Cartoon builder's logo: Herstmonceux, Sussex.

grief with either spidery or rubbery horses' legs. Even so, the portly,
balletic ploughman opposite Emneth church, Norfolk, and the horse
apparently shod with concrete blocks opposite the Red Lion at
Woolverton, Som., share a naïve attractiveness. The Woolverton horse
ploughs towards the back of the vane. His bulk makes a practical
tail-piece, but it is another of these design compromises: ploughing
forwards, more conventionally, looks more comfortable. A cast
aluminum version at Church Farm, Thrandeston, Suffolk, not only
ploughs tail-wards but also shows one solution to the forest-of-legs
problem posed by a two-horse team – ignore the arithmetic and show
only four. Behind Eye Hall, Horningsea, Cambs., a nicely restored old
vane elongates the body to clarify the groups of legs. Although the full
quota of legs is well handled at Wishing Tree Cottage, Northiam,
Sussex, the 'tree' in question has been distractingly inserted between
ploughman and plough. Another ploughman enjoys his meal-break,
propped comfortably against a fence and watched by his unharnessed
horse. Brandeston Forge designed and made this cast aluminium vane,
striking in black and gold, for its own Suffolk premises. A more
unexpected find is a worker dressed for warmer climes ploughing with
oxen. It suggests southern Europe, rather than Green Farm, Compton
Dando, Avon.

   The most obvious reflection of our increasing unfamiliarity with
horse-ploughing is a weathervane in central Wallingford, Oxon. –
perfectly balanced but visual nonsense. The figure is attractively

coloured but appears to be pushing his plough unaided: a two-horse team shown in old pictures has broken off. This is just the surviving tail, moved forward so that it will still work, but meaningless. The British Trust for Conservation Volunteers who now occupy the building hope to restore the full design.

Like the ploughman, the shepherd has a somewhat romantic image. The Rural Development Commission's pattern is unashamedly pretty. The shepherd leaning on his crook, his capering dog, ewe and lamb are encircled by an enchanted grove of upward-swirling foliage. Little Bo-Peep cannot be far away. This decorative design is variously handled. There are faithful reproductions and may be more now that a small cast aluminium version is available. At the other extreme Water Lane House, Castor, Cambs., and Ogmore Farm, Glam., dispense with all that decoration, so it becomes at once much cheaper and a more strictly occupational vane. Most, like Orchard Farm, East Grinstead, Sussex, compromise with simpler foliage. More radical modifications appear in *8.2*. Leaves and tendrils sweep downwards round the tree; there is greater accuracy in a more staid sheepdog, correctly positioned behind the sheep, and an arrow pointer ingeniously contrived from old-fashioned hand shears. The evening-class student who made it at Plumpton College of Agriculture, Sussex, under Frank Dean's tuition, presented it to the college and was complimented on his work by its erection above the main entrance.

Sussex seems particularly keen on shepherding vanes. The pre-war example on Shepherd's, Bolney, a bustling scene on a pole at Plumpton

8.5   Appropriate design for the Gardeners' Royal Benevolent Society: Henfield, Sussex.

8.6 Popular school image: St Joseph's School,
Market Harborough, Leics.

Green, bought at a 1950s agricultural show, and another well-made
evening-class effort of the 1970s on a Salehurst barn all have shepherd
and dog; they differ mainly in the numbers of sheep.

Makers of cast weathervanes can easily imitate a fleecy texture, but
few have grasped the opportunity to show the shepherd's face, the head
and fore-part of a lamb under his arm on one side, on the other the
shepherd's back and the lamb's hind legs and wiggly tail. Only the
anxious ewe is identical on either side. Brandeston Forge produced this
design.

Other stockmen appear occasionally, leading bulls, herding geese,
feeding pigs. A drover drives a scrawny pig to market from a pig farm at
Bacton, Suffolk, both rendered desperate by pierced eyes and the wild
gyrations that betray too equal an area fore and aft. A lively American
version shows both figures marching along a meat cleaver!

Women's contribution to agriculture gets short shrift. There are
occasional milkmaids: the lass with yoke and buckets on Dairy Cottage
near Frant, Sussex, is central and symmetrical, the cow on the tail
providing the windage. Other bonneted figures with geese are
nursery-tale rather than occupational images.

The importance of working horses is much more seriously

acknowledged. Men trot alongside ponies and carthorses or train untamed creatures that rear threateningly. These designs are widespread, remarkable chiefly for their similarity without being exact duplicates. A pleasant Shire horse with trainer on an enthusiast's low barn at Grafham, Cambs., shows how this bold shape can benefit from colour on a low roof.

Although the object of all that ploughing was the harvest, harvest weathervanes are uncommon. An attractive reminder of old harvesting methods is on the building run by the Southern Counties Agricultural Trading Society (SCATS) in Robertsbridge, Sussex. The motif, renewed in the 1950s, is still connected through its 1877 'gears' to the painted wall dial (*18.4*). Other harvesters carry pitchforks or work companionably alongside the Rural Development Commission's prancing dog.

Profiting from the harvest depended largely on the miller. Yet the only true milling vane we have seen (distinct from representations of windmills) is at Ramsbury, Wilts. Here for twenty years a bowed miller has humped fat sacks towards a diminutive post-mill. Several forges list 'The Miller' as a subject, however.

Outsiders find some farming hazards amusing – witness the Rural Development Commission's farmer-chasing-fox-and-goose pattern – or alluring. The poacher as romantic outcast appears in David Harvey's 'Hunter's Moon' at Seer Green, Bucks., with his haul slung from a stick over his shoulder, his dog alert for another retrieval. The poacher beating an undignified retreat (*8.3*) on The Nook, North Wheatley, Notts., is unsentimental, full of delightful detail, unsophisticated in drawing but skilled in execution. Is he the Lincolnshire poacher, a refugee from across the nearby county boundary? 1868 seems an early date, and though motif and mount look Victorian, the house had no weathervane in a 1900 photograph.

These rural occupations constitute the bulk of occupational weathervanes. Many urban jobs, however, or those common to or connecting town and country, have their representatives, though again the emphasis is nostalgic.

Plenty of carters, as designed by the Commission and others, carry goods by road, while the inter-war builders of Kingston-upon-Thames Guildhall in Greater London put up a bargee, poling his heavily laden craft with his dog as figurehead. An antiques dealer brought to The Limes, Shipton-under-Wychwood, Oxon., his copper frock-coated chair-men, carrying their sedan chair with Georgian sophistication along a brass arrow.

Well recorded in weathervanes are the important tasks of many building workers. Bricklaying gives an opportunity for interesting stepped shapes alongside the human form, as at Pearson Road, Sonning, Berks. The painted hod-carrier at Lower Fittleworth, Sussex, made in the builder/owner's workshops about twenty-five years ago, was cribbed from the London Brick Co logo. The attitude and cap and overalls of the builder pushing his barrow to collect his pile of bricks in Heath Road, Warboys, Cambs., are deemed to portray the owner unmistakably.

Flint-knapping, an ancient building craft, stimulated a flint-knapper with nice cut-through definition working on his knees at Bishops Waltham, Hants. Obviously the house name, Gilbert's Knapp, traceable back to the early 1700s, dictated the choice of this copper design some thirty years ago, though it is now suggested that the name actually derived from 'knobb', meaning hill.

About 1890 Lister's made for a builder's carpentry shop a sturdy carpenter at his bench. Ninety years on he still planes away, unmoved, by one of Cambridge's ring-road roundabouts. John Allen remembers making a painter and decorator, while Ronnie Carter created a chairmaker for a furniture-maker's home at Bishop Thornton, Yorks. For Plover's Way, Oulton Broad, Suffolk, Hubbards made the interesting A-shape of the owner at his architect's board, inseparable from the cat he had rescued from a derelict building. And how intriguing the thought underlying a vane David Harvey had commissioned, combining an architect, a theodolite, kilns and the Parthenon.

All these straightforward presentations contrast with a cartoon builder at Herstmonceux, Sussex (*8.4*). His dungarees are made from flat, bronze-coloured sheet, but the rest of him is constructed in outline only. His central position with arm forward really requires a larger balancing arrow-tail. This cheeky figure, incongruous on a beauty salon, is actually the builder's logo of the property's owner.

Houses have gardens, all requiring maintenance. Adam the Gardener is one of Brandeston Forge's most popular cast-aluminium motifs. Another gardener with barrow and beautifully detailed tools, designed by architect John Brownrigg for the Gardeners' Royal Benevolent Society retirement home at Henfield, Sussex, proved so appealing that it is now familiar on the Society's promotional literature (*8.5*).

For populations both rural and urban, compulsory education was introduced in 1872. Schools at Brynsadler and Caerphilly, Glam., and Holme Hale, Norfolk, have weathervanes of a schoolmaster teaching

8.7   Artilleryman of *c.* 1800: Royal Services Club,
Whitehall, Westminster, Greater London.

8.8   'The unpopular priest': Deanery Garden,
Sonning, Berks.

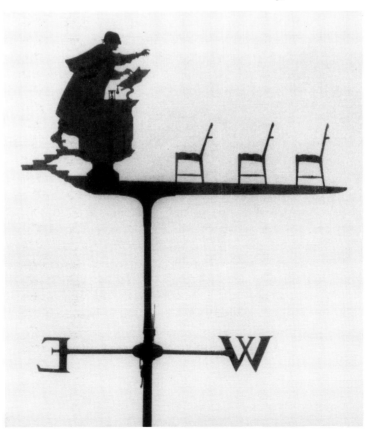

two tubby children (keeping a respectful distance), from a globe. Alas for their geography: the globe's axis is horizontal, not inclined. Holme Hale erected its painted vane in 1908, but an identical one at The Manse, Brayford, Devon, made fully forty years later, perpetuates the unfortunate educational gaffe. Interestingly, Brayford's coloured vane was actually made for their retiring headmaster by boys at Bargoed, near both Brynsadler and Caerphilly. Its colour gives it much more impact than their all-white versions.

The cane-wielding cap-and-gowned schoolmaster has proved a fruitful image for weathervane-makers. From simple admonishment on Bunwell School, Norfolk, he launches into full-scale pursuit above St Joseph's School, Market Harborough, Leics. (*8.6*). Here, today's parents are past pupils of the long-serving headmaster, and all shared the joke of the vane's design by a member of staff and its construction by Stuart Taylor, of nearby East Langton, in 1982. The old school road-sign provided the children's figures. A kindred scene decorates the Old School, Noke, Oxon., while dancing children tweak the master's mortar-board tassel at Edburton, Sussex.

Communities of any size require many goods and services. The physical need for food has provoked few weathervanes, though the Triangle, Haywards Heath, Sussex, does have a pieman to commemorate a bakery with old faggot-type ovens, here until the last war. As for clothing, John Allen's sewing-machine vane and an elegant lady bending her head charmingly over her lacemaker's pillow in Holt Road, Cromer, Norfolk, offer distinctly chilly comfort.

All sorts of other 'services' are illustrated in weathervanes. A lamplighter suits the Old Post Office, Minster Lovell, Oxon. Two firemen efficiently control a high-pressure hose above Thetford and King's Lynn fire stations – the gift of a Norfolk Divisional Commander determined, he declared, to make his men look up to him somehow. From W.H. Smith's Salisbury and Winchester branches, both opened in the 1920s, their Edwardian 'newsboy with a basket' distributes his newspapers at speed, one foot only on the quill pen that serves as a pointer. A cameraman filming a dancer constitutes a small copper vane above a cinema/bingo hall in Faversham, Kent. On Teddington Hospital, Greater London, a nurse in old-fashioned headdress, shaking a thermometer, approaches a shrinking, bed-ridden patient – binoculars needed here.

National defence is represented by the splendidly lively artillery man of about 1800, in action above the Royal Services' Club in Whitehall, Westminster, London (*8.7*), and a rifleman kneeling to take careful aim from Long Honey, Haddenham, Bucks. The startling Sudanese warrior riding his camel across the Sussex sky at Sparks Cottage, Northiam, denotes the distinguished foreign service of a former owner. David Harvey has made a deep-sea diver, but no modern servicemen appear: they would be invisibly encased in their machines.

Finally a clergyman offers his 'services' to rows of empty seats at Deanery Garden, Sonning, Berks., built for Edward Hudson, founder of *Country Life*, to designs by Sir Edwin Lutyens. Despite the vane's small size, the refined detail in the hymn-book ledges, curving pulpit steps, hour-glass etc is masterly (*8.8*). Although the assertion has not proved traceable, Lutyens is said to have written across the design, 'The unpopular priest: he ever speaks the truth yet turns with every wind.' Perhaps he had in mind that notorious turncoat the Vicar of nearby Bray.

Besides rural and urban occupations, a third group of weathervanes depicts people in leisure activities. Where this means sport, as it so frequently does, including portraits of known sportsmen, the vanes are considered in Chapter 12. Other portraits of historical figures of known appearance are studied in Chapter 16. Here, even if portraits – for example of owners – are intended, outsiders recognize the activity, not the person.

Most popular of these non-occupational weathervanes is a windblown figure. The classic form is a 'Quality Street' girl leaning backwards against the wind with her parasol blown inside out. Pennsylvania, Avon, Morton-on-Swale, Yorks., and Saunton Road, Braunton, Devon, have

8.9 Windswept girl: Saunton Road, Braunton, Devon.

8.10   Brownie/Scout activities: Horrabridge, Devon, and Plumpton
scout headquarters, Sussex.

it, the Braunton version with pretty white bonnet-edging, petticoat and frilly drawers, and a dog with streaming ears (*8.9*). Some versions make concessions to twentieth-century costume – a shorter red dress, yellow beret and scarf and black umbrella at Llwyngwril, Gwynedd; an even shorter skirt, no hat and high heels at Acle, Norfolk. But no real Marilyn Monroe.

The Rural Development Commission's masculine equivalent, an old man with flying scarf and a dog with tattered ears, is less popular. However, at Piltdown, Sussex, there is an entertaining, windswept man acquired from a 1938 agricultural show. Clutching in two directions at his reversed umbrella and flying top hat, he teeters on a pointer that has itself shrivelled in the wind. On Manor Farm, Barnham Broom, Norfolk, great vigour is achieved in a large design of emphatic diagonals, depicting two windswept figures. One braces himself forwards against the wind behind the shield of his umbrella; the other, flung round by the force of his umbrella snapping inside out, leans back against the gust, fighting to regain his balance. Surprisingly, their hats are still well anchored; the humorous accent this time is on the dog, trotting along the pointer with extreme nonchalance.

Other outdoor activities in weathervanes mostly continue this old-fashioned theme. A gentleman at Stubton, Lincs., rides in a cloak and topper, while the cycling clock seems virtually to have stopped in penny-farthing days. The figure cycling in topper and tail-coat above the sign 'Antiques' at Weybourne, Norfolk, pokes affectionate fun at the former owner, visible early each morning sweeping his shop-front in similar garb. Simple and detailed penny-farthing cyclists are fairly widespread. Even gardening is archaic: a Victorian lady cossets a lonely dwarf conifer with a watering-can at Ashington, Sussex. Walking the dog is less strictly 'period' exercise on a barn at Coddenham, Suffolk.

Children are not ignored. On Shoreham school, Kent, two children play tag – very like that road-sign again – while kite-flying apparently occupies them at Warningcamp, Arundel, Sussex. Ex-Brownies will recognize the cover picture of the Brownie handbook at Horrabridge, in an appropriate vane for a Guider formerly responsible for Devon's guide camps. Scouts will enjoy the figure in past uniform on Plumpton Scout Headquarters, Sussex: he is positively gleeful, with all his camping equipment topped by a kettle on his handcart. Both these vanes use the appropriate emblem as pointers (*8.10*).

Leisure may, of course, be devoted to more gracious pursuits. The Rural Development Commission's minuet we have yet to find, but there is a beautiful dancer (*8.11*) at South Wootton, Norfolk. Why this Home for the Elderly should have such a weathervane subject is not known, but the residents must derive great pleasure from the graceful figure, enhanced by pierced folds in the skirt and cascading cardinal arms.

A few weathervanes advocate less admirable pleasures. The old design of a man smoking at Wissett Hall, Suffolk, has been described

variously as eighteenth-century English, nineteenth-century Dutch and nineteenth-century American; take your choice. At Mill Road, Wells-next-the-Sea, Norfolk, a kilted Scot downs the last of his dram with a desperation that declares the barrel on the pointer to be utterly drained. Hubbard's gentleman in *8.12* has moved several times but is now contentedly settled at Howe, Norfolk, with his pipe and cat, perpetually watching the same programme. Long summer days in a deckchair under a spreading oak tree are idealized at Coddenham, Suffolk (*8.13*), given a 1920s air by the lounger's white flannels. But he should heed a vane placed, most extraordinarily, on a bird-table, at Harbour Lane, Aberaeron, Dyfed: choose your lounging spot carefully, it warns, or you may find yourself pursued by a

8.11   Lithe dancer for a home for the elderly, South Wootton, Norfolk.

8.12 Domestic entertainment: Howe, Norfolk.

8.13 Taking it easy, a retirement vane: Codden-ham, Suffolk.

bull, leaping over a field gate – to join the goose already there (*1.2*).

Two obvious points emerge from this survey. One is that, unless the significance of work-and-play vanes is recorded, it is forgotten. Even forty years ago people at Bampton, Oxon., were arguing whether the two weathervanes on their town hall represented a fireman and fleeing fire victim, or an Oxford proctor and fleeing student. No one actually *knew*. Still less will they, now that only one running cloaked figure remains. The other point is that, while some designs may be timeless, few weathervanes of quality really reflect contemporary life. Those that do, by gratifying our sense of recognition, give disproportionate pleasure. In the renewed popularity weathervanes are enjoying, what scope there is here. Why not a road-mender with pneumatic drill, a computer operator, backpackers, a disco dancer ...?

9 Domestic Animals

Whether herded, worked or kept as pets, animals were from early on natural candidates first for heraldic emblems and then for the pictorial weathervanes of ordinary men with no coats of arms. Moreover, although some animals are markedly ungraceful, they share certain useful weathervane qualities – obvious heads and tails to indicate direction, and legs which lift the body clear of any arrow and provide natural stiffening or weighting points.

Farm animals are among the easiest subjects, since little attempt need be made to suggest vitality. For the most part, bulls, cows, pigs and sheep stand stolidly on their barns like so many Smithfield bargains. Many are naïve, even crude, but they rarely inspire even professional blacksmiths to more than static silhouettes.

On working farms, animal weathervanes symbolize the income they generate. Other country homes display them either from sentiment or in defiance of overwhelming modern technology. Unlike cocks, however, farm animal weathervanes have not penetrated deeply into towns unless their farms have been engulfed by suburbia or they advertise the Dun Cow pub or something similar.

Virtually all farm animal weathervanes one sees will have gone up since 1800 but there is no obvious charting of historical breeding improvements or the changing popularity of different breeds. One or two distinctive anatomical characteristics can be added to a standard body shape, and economical farmers will indicate a change of allegiance to a different breed by repainting.

The Rural Development commission's farm stock patterns are fairly basic – three bulls and three cows just stand and a cow greets a barking dog in rather a cartoon grouping (*9.3*). There are two separate pigs and a third with two piglets. Extraordinarily, sheep are entirely omitted and poultry represented only by a turkey and one obviously farmyard bird among the cocks. These Commission weathervanes are ubiquitous, as are plenty of other designs too. Nonetheless, their variety and number are likely to be underestimated. The very nature of grouped farmyard buildings obscuring each other, tucked behind shelter belts or in hollows, set in the midst of their own land, renders their weathervanes invisible to any but the farm's own staff.

Cattle are the farm animals most frequently represented. Breeds with distinctive silhouettes are instantly recognizable: a white painted bull on Ashwicken Hall, Norfolk, is manifestly a Charollais. Entertainingly, even some farmers are at variance over the breed their weathervane represents. Identical nineteenth-century bulls are described as 'probably an Aberdeen Angus' at Merton Grange Farm, Gamlingay, Cambs., but at Home Farm, Ruddington, near Nottingham, as a Shorthorn, because Philo Mills, an American lace millionaire who built the farm, bred Shorthorns there. Another farmer who keeps Friesians at Great Holland, Essex, bought the weathervane from a retiring Shorthorn breeder. He finds the Shorthorn silhouette 'near enough', not even bothering with the illusion of black and white paint, which he feels would blur the silhouette against the sky. An additional quirk is that this

9.1   Belted Galloway, defined by paint: Gatehouse of Fleet, Dumfries & Galloway.

cow weathervane was advertised in the pets' column.

Especially to the non-expert, outline is less meaningful than colour. A plain black bull is less likely to indicate interest in Welsh cattle than the fact that weatherproof black paint makes for easy maintenance. But anything, of any shape, painted red or reddish brown with a white face qualifies as a Hereford: Court Farm, Boughrood, Powys, has just one of dozens. Anything painted patchily black and white is a Friesian. Their attractiveness varies widely. On the butcher's at Debenham, Suffolk, the animal is more white than black. Quoit Farm, Chew Magna, Avon, and Home Farm, Eynsford, Kent, both have good examples, the first denoting milk for sale, the second a pedigree herd. Only very rarely is a positive attribution made to a particular animal. On Witton Hall Farm, Norfolk, however, a Friesian bull is painted with the precise markings of a prize bull sold to the Milk Marketing Board 'for a fair bit o' money' about thirty years ago.

Occasionally, a local speciality is noted. Above a gift shop in the centre of Gatehouse of Fleet, Dumfries & Galloway, stands a vane of the striking Belted Galloway, black with a white band (*9.1*). Although Highland cattle would make splendid weathervanes with their great curved horns and shaggy coats, their popularity still seems restricted to china ornaments. However, rare breeds inevitably mean rare weathervanes, and these may well be the ones on farms veiled from public gaze.

Generally speaking, most observers are probably right in describing a weathervane as nothing more specific than 'bull' or 'cow'. They serve their purpose perfectly well. A sturdy example with a flimsy fence he could demolish with a flick of the tail stands on a farm above Snipe Dales Reserve, Lusby, Lincs. Beneath the yew tree at Irely Farm, Winchcombe, Glos., relics of Hailes Abbey, including the last wicked abbot in a gold coffin, reputedly lie buried. The tradition endows the guardian bull weathervane there with almost legendary stature. Croyde, Devon, produces a cow weathervane on a modern bungalow, while Buttsbury Lodge Farm, Stock, Essex, uses unpainted the same Rural Development Commission silhouette that made the Eynsford Friesian. A tiny bovine figure on the extreme tail of the arrow at Wickham Market, standing back to the Suffolk wind, makes a pleasing change. So do one or two charging bulls, a cheerful Hereford on Manor Fields, Shilton, Oxon., (*9.2*), and a copper trade sign, though not rampant, on the Rampant Bull Hotel, Cockermouth, Cumbria – indelicately situated opposite the cattle market and next to the abattoir.

For most breeds, there is little advantage in the textural subtleties achievable by casting. Cast vanes made at R.V. Nicholls' forge and Brandeston Forge's version with a calf concentrate on showing the lines of muscle and bone. Highland cattle would benefit.

Because no close relationship exists between men and cattle, they rarely share the weathervane stage. For Low Farm, Theddlethorpe All Saints, Lincs., however, Graham Walker created a bull led by a man, nicely detailed with his stick and pipe, and the rope leading to the ring in the bull's nose. Similarly, cattle are seldom combined with other

9.2   Hereford bull: Shilton, Oxon.

animals. The Rural Development Commission's cow with barking dog is popular (*9.3*) – in colour too at Northiam, Sussex – and a Friesian says boo to a goose at Beeches Farm, Isfield, Sussex. A weathervane made to enhance the veterinary surgery sign on Eastbourne Road, in Uckfield, Sussex, (*9.4*), places the cow in a row of other tiny creatures waiting for treatment, monitored by a small bird to forestall any queue-jumping.

Thirty years ago, a writer could state that pigs on weathervanes were unusual. Their ancient exaltation as symbols of fertility and good luck, and associated traditional customs like the Dunmow Flitch, make this surprising. Certainly, pig weathervanes are currently extremely popular, and less restricted to rural settings than cattle.

9.3   The Rural Development Commission's cow with barking dog: Semer, Suffolk.

9.4   Vets' surgery sign: Uckfield, Sussex.

Whether the slightly comic effect of so many pig weathervanes is intentional is difficult to say. Inquiring snouts and perky ears can give the cheekiest air to rotund porcine figures, on pig farms, as at Bacton, Suffolk, and Halton Holegate, Lincs., on mixed farms or on private dwellings. A cheerful pig tiptoes above Four Acres, Gipsey Bridge, Lincs., looking oddly cantilevered with front legs set far back and snout questing forward.

Longer or shorter bodies, ears pricked or drooping or forward, painted bands or markings will suggest to the knowing Landrace, Large White, Saddleback, Gloucester Old Spot. Far outnumbering all others, however, is the Rural Development Commission's pig-and-piglets and variations on it. The basic pattern, one piglet facing the sow, another running on ahead, looks very jaunty painted bright pink at Alderford, Norfolk, overlooking the old slaughter yard. Some variations show the piglets following the sow; many include extra piglets, five the highest score to date. One piglet sometimes indulges in unintentional greasy-pole antics. This design is also popular in cast form with slightly rounded surfaces.

A stylized but lively weathervane shows two pigs running under apple trees, as they did when Hugh de Poix designed it for his fruit farm at Broome, Norfolk, in 1924. Strong colouring – white pigs with black eyes and fat crimson apples embedded into the flat, dark green tree like so many cricket balls – further enlivens it (*9.5*). Lastly, a contented fat pig with an endearing twirl of a tail travelled about twenty years ago from a Connecticut antiques shop to the thatched barn at Ivy Cottage, Axford, Wilts. (*9.6*). Last century's specialist American weathervane manufacturers all advertised swell-bodied farm animals like this twenty-five-pounder. Because the moulds were made in several pieces, intricate detail could be carved. The texture of a ram's fleece, for instance, could stand the closest scrutiny.

By contrast, British sheep weathervanes are puny, despite the animals' historic and economic importance. Except for a few of the symbolic Paschal Lambs and one or two in cast aluminium with shepherds, they are flat silhouettes with no fleecy texturing. At least silhouettes on those farms where specific breeds are kept can be accurate, like the Texel the farmer himself made at Eastfield Farm, Hough-on-the-Hill, Lincs. But although Holmes Farm's weathervane at Lower Bentham, Yorks., started life as a Suffolk, it is no longer appropriately painted. Most are just rather approximate sheep. Unless accuracy is deliberately sought, firm shapes collapse into animals with the soggy physique of children's stuffed toys. An exception is the well-defined Disney type at Shepreth,

9.5 Hogs under apple trees: Broome Fruit Farm,
Norfolk.

Cambs., which gambolled across from the primary school to the village hall, exchanging *en route* associations of youthful innocence for those of the supposed 'shepherd's heath' of the village name.

Diversification from these three main stock-keeping activities is little represented, though a tiny tethered goat makes a cottage weathervane at Ingham Corner, Norfolk. Quite unaccountably, a goat-in-a-hoop, equally remarkable for its decorative iron (*6.4*), surmounts Stratford-upon-Avon hospital, War. But even the heraldic Bagot goat is not in evidence around Abbots Bromley, Staffs.

Of the ubiquitous poultry, only turkeys appeal to weathervane-makers. Reydon Grange, Suffolk, a turkey farm, uses the Rural Development Commission's pattern, and something very similar marks Turkey Cock Lane in Rye, Sussex. Simple painting dramatizes the turkey at Dynes Farm, Shalford Green, Essex. In Attleborough, Norfolk, a Home for the Elderly marks its former poultry market site with a striking weathervane made by Eric Stevenson in 1968. Two pecking chicks accompany the parent turkey, whose flared tail and half-spread wings are cut through with graceful feather lines.

9.6   American half-round pig: Ivy Cottage, Axford, Wilts.

Occasional vanes show chickens scrabbling in a farmyard, but modern poultry farmers, who still actually use weathervanes to warn them when ventilation in their hen-houses is becoming draughty, seem content with the most nondescript of cocks.

Duck weathervanes, if not obviously wildfowl, often resemble bathtub ducks. Duck and ducklings at Rose Villa, Flockton, Yorks., proclaim duck eggs for sale. At Aldbourne, Wilts., Duck Cottage has a delightful family of drake, duck and five tiny ducklings scrambling in all directions. Several other examples of this kind intimate an affectionate response to ducks that moves them towards the groups of creatures man keeps for his pleasure.

Chief among these, of course, are dogs, about which the British have become increasingly besotted throughout the last couple of centuries. Sporting dogs have always been the most favoured for weathervane representation, though greyhounds are no longer 'general', as they apparently were in the 1850s. The Rural Development Commission's sporting dogs are racing greyhounds, whippet, retrievers and pointer, but not lurchers or foxhounds. In combination with a man out shooting or a huntsman, all these obviously become sporting vanes.

On kennels, even hunt kennels, a dog vane might be thought a *sine qua non*. However, the Zetland Hunt Kennel vane at Aldbrough St John, Yorks., is a huntsman. Conversely, dog vanes are sometimes curiously placed. The pre-war greyhound seems not entirely at home on the dovecote of Grange Farm, Thelveton, Norfolk; a scottie is a mystifying emblem for a builder at Ashby de la Zouche, Leics. Country house stables and outbuildings prefer horses, foxes and decorative pennants, and it is private homes in urban or at least grouped settings that most favour dog vanes. In such positions the continuing predominance of sporting breeds reflects their changed status from actively sporting animals to household pets.

The nation's devotion to individual breeds, which first emerged in 1576, in *Of Englisshe Dogges, the diversities, the names, the natures and the properties*, results in careful delineation of those with distinctive outlines: many breeds are instantly identifiable. In addition to the sporting dogs, the weathervane line stretches from Great Danes and St Bernards, through boxers and collies, to miniature poodles, scotties and dachshunds. Familiar working dogs, such as Alsatians and Border collies vie with the less usual keeshond and bearded collie. The inference must be that every breed will be represented on a weathervane somewhere, though not from the Rural Development Commission's patterns, which are limited to an Alsatian and a dachshund.

It has to be admitted that in weathervane silhouette one labrador or sealyham or pug looks very like another. To the owner, however, it is Judy or Spot or Ben, whose photograph was tenderly handed to the blacksmith for immortalization. This makes the paucity of avowed mongrels doubly astonishing: the omission of their characterful numbers from the weathervane scene is inexplicable and disappointing. Only non-portrait dog-and-horse combinations, where the scene is the prime attraction, regularly depict non-pedigree dogs. Striking black and gold ornamented arms at Low Farm, Badingham, Suffolk, underline this decorative intention.

Poses characteristic of dogs in general – sitting, raising a paw, cocking the head sideways, begging (doubtless, somewhere, rolling over to be tickled) – vary the basic standing dog. Attitudes characteristic of a breed are a boon – bassets holding their tails so airily, pointers with tensely lifted front paw, poodles' sharply angular stance. They all look more natural standing on something. At Warwick Cottage, Corfton, Shropshire, however, the boxer's owner/breeder/maker has balanced his forelegs on the spindle, leaving his hind legs treading air. And some kind of anthropomorphism gives us a muscular spasm on seeing the greyhound at Thelveton, Norfolk, impaled vertically through its middle.

Fig. *9.7*, portraying two particular champion Great Danes the owner bred, and now at The Abbey, Skillington, Lincs., is exceptional in showing only the dogs' heads. The impression of highly strung movement is achieved by pierced eyes. One careless slip here and an animal can look demented or comic. Carefully done, however, cutting can, by demarcation, give almost a three-dimensional effect. The hair-thin line cut around the pendulous ear of a heavy old spaniel at The Limes, Bacton, Suffolk, is what defines the breed and makes him so lifelike. He sits as though the building were still a butcher's shop.

Painting is almost a must to indicate dalmatians and hounds: it adds great character to a splendid loping hound at Lacock, Wilts., (*9.8*) – belonging to a Mr Fox. On breeds like these, whose markings are variable, colouring serves to individualize. The greyhound Red Sand is named too at Barmby Moor, Humberside.

A hammered copper surface to simulate the dog's coat is an interesting departure on a vane John Craston exhibited at the Royal Show before delivering it to its rightly named home at Bassets, Old Newton, Suffolk. It has pleasing twisted, tapered arms and supports, and quarter cardinal spikes too, unusual in a dog vane (*9.9*). Apart from some most unexpected leafy ornament accompanying a bearded collie at Plumpton Green, Sussex (*9.10*), most dog vanes are either unadorned or given conventional unobtrusive scrolls.

Dogs are rarely shown with any possessions, though one, a labrador at Isleham, Cambs., has the spindle extended into a lamp-post finial, and a tiny red, black and white Snoopy has his kennel in Fairlands, Angmering-on-Sea, Sussex. They are also usually solitary, though a pet labrador and dachshund share a vane at Great Totham, Essex, and the Old Vicarage, Stonegate, Sussex, has the Rural Development Commission's group claimed variously as retrievers and setters (*9.11*) with four dogs of immense grace and vitality.

Although the urban veterinary practice at Uckfield, Sussex (*9.4*), must treat many of them, neither dog nor cat is among the farm animals on its weathervane. In fact, nowhere is the popularity of cats as pets reflected in cat weathervanes. Few seem to be portrait attempts; most are typical cats in typical poses or activities.

The back-view seated silhouette with dangling tail in Whittingham Lane, Broughton, Lancs., is a conventional single cat vane. Two cats on a chimney, with interesting crouched and stretched shapes, make the

9.7   Portrait of two Great Danes: The Abbey, Skillington, Lincs.

9.8   Painted loping foxhound: Lacock, Wilts.

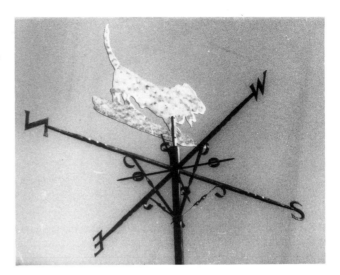

9.9　Beaten copper for a textured basset's coat: Old Newton, Suffolk.

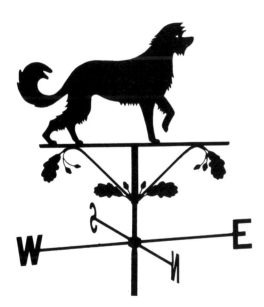

9.10　Bearded collie with unusual ornament beneath: Plumpton Green, Sussex.

9.11　A graceful Rural Development Commission group: Stonegate Old Vicarage, Sussex.

Rural Development Commission's pattern. Thorverton, Devon, and Crabbe Castle Farm, Wighton, Norfolk, enjoy this vane. A trio, two canoodling black cats and an arched, spitting white one, are entertaining at Nut Knowle Farm, Woodmancote, Sussex. The arched back is used again in a simple silhouette cat on Cleveleys, Mattishall, Norfolk, this time with a stylized head, turned sideways, with exaggerated cut-out eyes that one expects to blink in Disney fashion at any moment. Its Blackpool origin is entirely unsurprising.

Most common of all is a cat with mouse. The standard Commission pattern of cat chasing mouse, seen at Little Staughton, Beds., and East Linton, Lothian, is often treated with great freedom. The effect of the mouse standing or sitting facing the cat cheekily is vastly altered by the distance between the two creatures, their relative sizes and the cat's pose. At Stutton, Suffolk, the cat sits and pats the air unseeingly above the mouse's head. Generally, it crouches with rounded haunches and twitching tail, but looking comfortable rather than threatening. Rather solid, but interesting because cut from half-inch-thick plank and brightly painted, is the example on a farm near Alton, Staffs. (*9.12*). Perhaps because the cats are less successfully created than the mice, most of these vanes have an irresistibly Tom and Jerry effect. The ultimate in insouciant defiance is on Robin Hill, Rodmell, Sussex, where a bird turns its back on the cat.

Altogether, cat vanes are disappointing. Although much feline charm comes from sinuous movement and silky coat, these are not impossible to re-create in metal. Neither can the cat's slightly sinister associations be the reason: people do not shun witch weathervanes. It is an odd gap.

Groups of pets may occasionally be immortalized together. The Rural

9.12   Wooden cat and and practically tailless mouse:
near Alton, Staffs.

Development Commission's pattern of donkeys at Thursford, Norfolk, represents the two in the meadow; a beloved donkey and dog, Barley Mow and Jackie, greet each other opposite White Pond House, Baydon, Wilts. At Somerton Old Hall, Som., three sisters' pets, a Siamese cat, a dachshund and a Border terrier, remain permanently companionable on their weathervane, made at Erme wood Forge.

Theoretically, any domestic animal or pet could make a weathervane motif, but representations of smaller creatures, like rabbits or mice, nearly all seem intended as the wild creatures. Cage-birds get scarcely a look-in: virtually the only one we have seen is comedian Kenneth Horne's budgie at Alciston, Sussex. Perhaps these small children's pets are ignored because they are not such image-creatures as dogs – or horses.

10 Horses and Horse Sports

Since at least 2000 BC, when the Egyptians were already both riding and driving, the horse has occupied a unique place in man's history and in his heart. No other animal has been so revered for its beauty and grace, respected for its intelligence, exploited for its strength and loved for its responsiveness and character.

Weathervane horses are unlikely to be more than 200 years old, however. Heraldic horses could be older but, as they are depicted naturalistically, they are difficult to distinguish. Many date from the nineteenth century, especially cast ones, and there has been a great resurgence in popularity since World War II. Dating cannot be inferred from fashions such as tail-docking, which lasted up to 200 years. Even Woburn Abbey, Bedfordshire's most stately home, has no record of whether its stable weathervane (*10.2*), is contemporary with the eighteenth-century stable or later.

Naturally, horse weathervanes publicize the function of private, riding, breeding and racing stables, stud farms, mews and coach-houses. They define the past of houses converted from stableyards or service stations evolved from forges. A lofty water-tower with a full-bodied copper horse leaping across it, near Llanfechain, Powys, proves to supply an impressive stable-yard below. But why should the ventilation turret to public lavatories built in Burton Latimer, Northants, in 1898 be dignified by a copper running horse? A horse-and-dog vane seems too secular for the wooden louvred turret to St Michael's Church, Wortham, Suffolk, and very undramatic when viewed through the ruined embrasures of the adjacent circular tower, the greatest in the country. Cantering towards a man along an arrow dated 1931, a horse seems unorthodox decoration for a school's sports complex at Rhuddlan, Clwyd. At Tavistock, Devon, a man, resentful of what he regarded as a particular lady's interference in local affairs, sourly christened a horse weathervane topping a new supermarket 'the old nag'. The lady, more expert than he, took sly delight in pointing out that it was a stallion ... However, a horse from a mass-produced range suits some small workshops in Newton, Powys, for they occupy the Old Laundry of Pryce Jones, one of Britain's earliest mail-order firms.

As reliance on horses for work and travel has given way to their almost exclusively recreational use, they have come to signal the affluence and leisure of their owners. Hence the ubiquity of horse weathervanes now on private homes. Many are in towns, for riding still carries social cachet among urban dwellers. It implies a certain lifestyle: not '*Can* you ride?' but '*Do* you ride?'

Behind today's horse mania lies the folk-memory of those 4,000 years of association with horses. It helps to explain why the great majority of weathervanes show horses in some form of co-operation with man (though occupations and vehicles dependent on horses, and hunting, are separate concerns). On their own, however, horses are excellent weathervane subjects, whether in silhouette or full-bodied, adding to strong, recognizable shapes the possibility of conveying purposeful and inherently graceful movement. Is your preference for heavy horses, hunters, thoroughbreds or ponies, shaggy or smooth, long-tailed or docked? Somewhere there will be a weathervane of your favourite, standing, peacefully grazing, trotting or cantering, jumping or prancing or rearing or galloping.

Most are represented with some attempt at fidelity. But the conformation of the animals themselves is so variable. Thus a head can be reduced or a rump enlarged for better balance, and who shall say the result is actually wrong? Legs that are wobbly, rubbery, too short or too spindly or making arbitrary contact with the body, and heads disproportionately large or small betray real amateurishness. Even such oddities may have their own naïve charm. At the other extreme a true artist's eye may very subtly slim or elongate a silhouette to give the illusion of speed, and add vitality in a flying mane and tail. A tiny pin-prick perforation will suggest light catching the eye; anything larger makes the animal look as if it is about to bolt.

One of the most effective and popular designs is the ponderous, unambiguous silhouette of the work-horse. It is said that medieval war-horses, bred during the peak period of chivalry, were the ancestors of the largest of Britain's heavy horses, the Shires. Standing at seventeen

10.1 Portrait of Gardden Connell, pre-war Shire champion: Cardigan, Dyfed.

10.2 Working horse on stables at Woburn Abbey, Beds.

10.3 Heraldic horse, probably
1715: Denver, Norfolk.

10.4 Standard Victorian cast
horse on a 'wreath': Oak Street,
Windermere, Cumbria.

10.5   Good perspective in a silhouette
vane: Eastleach Martin, Glos.

hands, they plant their enormous feathered legs to haul loads of up to
five tons. The stocky, short-legged chestnut Suffolks and grey-black
Percherons and the Clydesdales bred in Scotland since the eighteenth
century are slightly less massive. Sheer strength made them
indispensable for centuries. 'Carthorses' pulled laden waggons and
coaches – a few still haul brewers' drays – eventually superseding oxen
as ploughing teams.

There is plenty of muscle in the Rural Development Commission's
pre-1952 design. Its wide-ranging sites include a vets' surgery on the
A41/421 crossroads in Bicester, Oxon., with other tiny animals on the
arms. Operative and past forges at Pode Hole, Lincs., and Roughton,
Norfolk, a saddlery at Surfleet, Lincs., a dairy that formerly used them
at Ashbourne, Derby: all have slightly different versions. In every case
the stance implies that it takes a good deal to get them moving.

Close family ties with heavy horses may well produce a portrait vane.
On Cwm Connell, Cardigan, Dyfed, the animal is a pre-war champion,
Gardden Connell (10.1), first prize winner at Royal and Royal Welsh
shows. The present owner's uncle was the shire expert; a nephew
reproduced the vane for O-level – already this family design has
spanned three generations. The white leg-feathering is an enhancement
here. Different in all respects is the dynamic working horse on the
stables at Woburn Abbey, Beds. (10.2). In his heavy but powerful
motion he gives credence to the theory of medieval war-horse ancestry,

which in turn makes the black and gold painting seem quite fitting.

Numerically, however, weathervane-makers have paid greater homage to lighter carriage horses, better suited to spanking along with light equipages, and to the hunters, riding-horses and thoroughbreds that have added so much pleasure to leisure. These lighter horses still stand in quantity on the coach-houses they embellish so fittingly. In Suffolk, Needham Market's charming docked horse with slender head is on what was the coach-house to Uvesdale Hall; the doctors' surgery at Snettisham, Norfolk, with a graceful gilt running horse above extensive iron ornament, was built as a coach-house about 1896. Confirming the subject's popularity, huge members of cast swell-bodied horses survive from Victorian and Edwardian days; northern counties and Scotland particularly favour them. Some may be later, but the copper one looking rather surprised to find himself on a confectionery and soft drinks wholesaler's in Diss, Norfolk, seems earlier than the building's date of 1924.

A high-stepping horse on a crown is almost certainly genuinely heraldic: on the former stable block to Crow Hall, Denver, Norfolk, this vane is thought to be the original from 1715 (*10.3*). The favourite twisted rod beneath cast horses is sometimes viewed suspiciously as a bit of social climbing, attempting to assume spurious rank by imitating the wreath under a crest. A kind of rocking-horse on the former stables to Hillside Old People's Home outside Lockerbie, Dumfries & Galloway, and the

10.6   Exmoor pony turns his back to the wind: The Forge, West
Porlock, Som.

white-painted one on the corner of Oak Street, Windermere, Cumbria (*10.4*), show the style.

They also illustrate how a horse at full stretch, hardly touching the ground, has to be impaled or, like the leaping horse on Llanfechain water-tower, Powys, uncomfortably balanced on its spindle. The Rural Development Commission's pattern-book continues this tradition by showing two unsupported leaping silhouette horses; all blacksmiths seem to impale them. Most of these galloping horses are extended comfortably, but the spiky mane and tail of the copper horse on Burton Latimer public lavatories in Northamptonshire give it a fearful air, and a farm at Llyswen, Powys, has had for nearly forty years a horse galloping quite frenetically.

The Commission's pattern of a horse rearing is successful; hardly any of the weathervanes made from it are. Fractional differences in angles, curves and proportions of limbs make it look awkward. A wild-maned horse on an outbuilding at Spronketts, Bolney, Sussex, however, is alive with graceful tension as he rears and pirouettes on one hind leg.

Apart from one rather clumsy modern mass-produced design in which the horse's hind legs are invisible behind a solid barrier, horses jumping without riders are not common. A splendid exception, with five-barred gate and hedge all in deep perspective, was made in the 1960s for Bouthrop House, Eastleach Martin, Glos. (10.5).

Most horses on weathervanes, however, appear in the standard actions of trotting, cantering or running with varying degrees of energy – and accuracy. Not until the 1870s did Edward Muybridge, a British photographer working in America, succeed in projecting a series of photographs rapidly enough through a 'zoopraxiscope' to establish the exact sequence of a horse's leg movements. A weathervane horse with 'wrong' legs perhaps predates that knowledge; other criteria of effectiveness will have to be applied by offended purists.

Though pleasant enough, even horse weathervanes that have caught the public fancy enough to be widely distributed are unexceptional. The same horse running over the same shaped arms is at Fleckney, Leics., Chipping Campden, Glos., and Starston, Norfolk; the last example looks different because the pivot point has been moved forward and the body braced. In another design, the next step will launch the horse into space, for the half-arrow pointer is at a lower level. Keen horsemen at Home Farm, Aspenden, Herts., have this vane, and on Shorne, Yelverton, Devon, it looks down at Dartmoor ponies grazing all around. Every county is likely to provide several examples of the most pleasing and elegant design, one of the Rural Development Commission's oldest

– a pair of horses, one with head raised, the other grazing.

Because so many horse weathervanes are undistinguished, the exceptions are doubly pleasurable. At Courtlands Stud Farm, Plumpton, Sussex, the former owner who bred Arabs until well into his nineties erected a white Arab mare running with a black foal, small but full of graceful action (*1.4*). A constant watch needs to be kept on this delightful weathervane lest the animals be strangled by the virginia creeper. The spirited Exmoor pony placed on The Forge, West Porlock, Som., about 1950, firmly presents his long, windswept tail to the wind (*10.6*). Facing downwind may be orthodox for the pony but is unorthodox for a weathervane.

Other weathervanes besides the horses grazing together emphasize their sociable nature. Her Majesty's Stud Office at Sandringham, Norfolk, is among the many buildings favouring the popular device of a mare and foal. The other frequent combination is a horse greeting or running with a dog.

Several unusual weathervanes, widely dispersed but manifestly all from one workshop, share a common history of having been bought at horse fairs, mostly in the early 1960s. All have various combinations of motifs, curly arrow pointers, curly-ended letters and large quantities of twisted scrolls and supports. The simplest, at Bridge Farm, Hanbury, Hereford & Worcester, and Valiant Equestrian Centre, Out Rawcliffe, Lancs., have a single jumping horse motif. Kimbold, Weeley Heath near Clacton, Essex, adds horses in different attitudes, with and without riders, on each arm. So do those at Holt Road, Horsford, Norfolk, and on Coltsgate Hill, Ripon, Yorks.; both these change the top motif to a mare and foal. Most elaborate of all is the hunting version at Ashperton, Hereford & Worcester (*6.3*), from which the overall impression of these highly idiosyncratic vanes can be judged.

Ordinary riding is the horseback activity most frequently depicted. Sometimes, in areas thick with road-signs warning motorists to beware of riders, not a single riding vane will be found. But some turn up quite unexpectedly in empty countryside, like a figure riding steadily beside the B1264 north of Northallerton, Yorks.

There are some obviously older examples. A tiny, fat horse carrying a rider apparently with no body below the shoulders is painted the bright blue and white of Cook's garage at Carleton Rode, Norfolk, where it has been since the premises were a forge early this century. A wasp-waisted rider in a topper on Tiptree windmill, Essex (*18.2*), leans insecurely backwards on his wild-eyed steed. Both these vanes have the appeal of quaint nursery toys. Many others must depict animals known to the

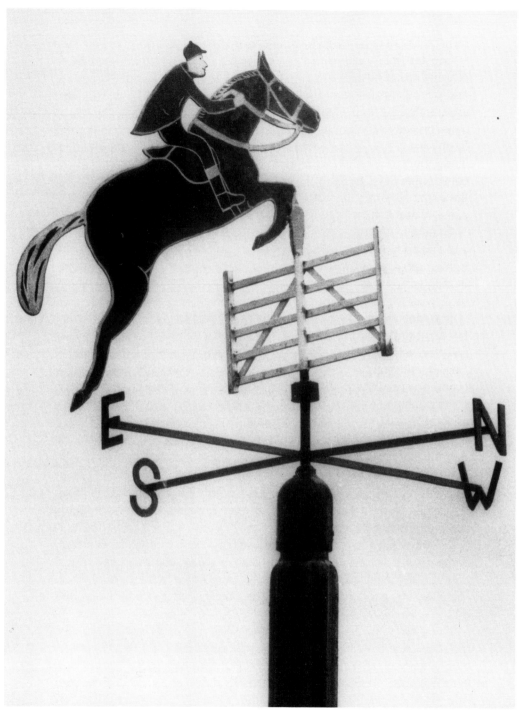

10.7 T-shaped vane, horse and rider clearing a physical barrier:
Frithville, Lincs.

owners, like the mare Go-go on Manor Farm, Northrepps, Norfolk.

Greater vitality is conveyed in weathervanes showing a horse and rider clearing an obstacle, for practical reasons rising or landing rather than in mid-air. These jumping vanes, apparently rather unusual in the USA, are among Britain's commonest. Several versions, of variable quality, are mass-produced. At the other extreme Forge Cottage, Aythorpe Roding, Essex, has a portrait of the owner on his horse jumping a gate. Uncle made the vane in the forge next door, and Sandy's aged eyes can still contemplate it in the intervals of contented grazing. In another personal design, at Rothbury, Northd., the horse jumps a stream, with the house name, Waterleap, in large iron letters beneath.

Generally any obstacle is shown in flat perspective. Between Sibsey and Frithville, Lincs., however, the gate makes a physical barrier, set at right angles across the horse and rider (*10.7*). This painted design was developed from an animal-feed merchant's advertisement and is one of three weathervanes on scrap lamp-posts at the end of the garden.

It is not always easy for laymen to decide whether a vane depicts hunter or show-jumper, a two-year-old hurdling or older animal steeplechasing or eventing. On Crowntailrigg, Bonchester Bridge, Borders, the solid fence with brush top marked with a flag would suggest eventing, even without the information that the family is involved in the sport at a high level. On another example, very attractive but very tucked away behind Hungerford High Street, Berks., an arched group of four horses competes at a flagged fence (*10.8*).

Some horses are born to run on the flat rather than jump. Competition between these flat-racing thoroughbreds, all said to

10.8   Group movement: Hungerford, Berks.

descend from three named Arab stallions, centres on the Derby, first run in 1870, and certain other fashionable meetings. Not all top racecourses have weathervanes, and the rather unhurried painted figure soaring above Ascot's grandstand is certainly eclipsed in realism by the recent vane on a modern office overlooking the Berkshire course but unconnected with it. Newmarket grandstand in Suffolk has had a full-bodied gilt horse and jockey at least since the 1870s.

None of the Newmarket's numerous racing weathervanes, some beautifully detailed, seems intended to represent a particular animal; rather they advertise the function of the training yard. This is in the strongest imaginable contrast to the USA, where every successful racehorse seems to have been individually immortalized in weathervanes. Possibly the horse and jockey vane at Brookfields, Sharnbrook, Beds., evidently newer than its mount, could have been identified by the jockey who formerly lived there. Although no particular animal is portrayed on a yard at Upper Lambourne, Berks., the jockey wears the late Lord Caernarvon's colours. Just occasionally both racehorse and jockey can be identified. 'Travel On', which won the Cherry Hinton Stakes at Newmarket, was portrayed by Denis Trinder for the owner at Kencot House, Oxon. The jockey, resplendent in the correct colours, is Joe Mercer (*10.9*). 'Appleby', winner of the Bedford Stakes at Newmarket in 1923, is unrecognizable in the horse on the Sussex stud at Cowfold, for the years have deprived him of both winning-post and his jockey, Steve Donaghue: this too was once a portrait vane. Doubtless famous Grand National and Derby winners are somewhere for the seeking.

'Individual portraits' can be created by the imagination. Thus to a Henley-on-Thames man the standard Rural Development Commission horse and jockey at the winning-post represents his late friend, a Japanese owner and jockey, and is to be painted in his colours.

The vertical line of the winning-post is a clever means of conveying a horse's speed, as on a little modern clock turret at Knaphill, Surrey. This is even truer at Barn House, Rodmell, Sussex, where two horses race along the rails towards it. The vane has so much life and action that it is astonishing to see that the larger horse is no bigger than a starling. Unfortunately, the cardinal letters are disintegrating, which suggests that the whole vane is becoming fragile. A rider flourishing his hat above his head as though acknowledging the plaudits of the crowd makes another small but beautifully painted weathervane on Tudor Limes, Redgrave, Suffolk. Neither the gesture nor the rider's clothing is normally associated with jockeys, yet the vane did stand for years on

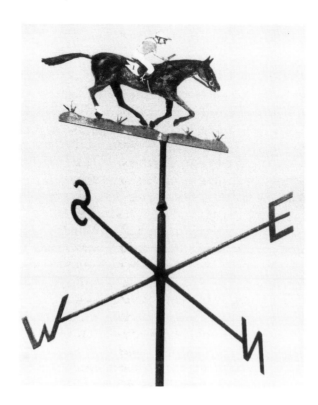

10.9   Joe Mercer rides 'Travel On':
Kencot, Oxon.

stables behind the Rutland Hotel in Newmarket.

If a horse is both fast and manoeuvrable it is suited to polo. Training and keep are both very costly, so this is a rich man's sport. Despite the status a polo weathervane can confer and the lively action it can capture, there are few of them, though David Harvey has sent his spirited version to Hull, Macclesfield and elsewhere.

The most extraordinary control of tiny movements from a large animal is needed in dressage. On Overmarsh House, Ness, Ches., the dressage weathervane depicts a horse bred by one generation, ridden in competition by the next and translated from photograph to weathervane by the third. Vanes on West Beech House, Pattingham, Staffs., and Tamarisk, Tredizzick, Corn., if not actually dressage, show a high-stepping performance that closely resembles it.

More stylish stepping occurs in a sport whose popularity has increased in recent years, carriage-driving. Because British weathervanes of carriage-driving, almost all copies of Rural Development Commission patterns, tend to look more workaday than sporty – unlike American examples – they are considered under

Transport, in Chapter 14. At East Winch, Norfolk, however, a simple rally carriage on the arrow combines with ridden horses on the arms to form a six-foot-six-inch advertisement for an equestrian centre. A livelier representation at Wotton Farm, Surrey, denotes the owner's hobby.

For many people the ultimate horse combines all the preceding qualities. He has speed, stamina and manoeuvrability, is bold enough to jump but can be controlled despite difficult circumstances and distractions. He is the hunter.

11 Hunting, Shooting and Fishing

Although somewhat dented, the image of the quintessential English country squire as a hunting, shooting, fishing type dies hard. Britain's ambivalent society resents class distinction but flaunts status symbols. These country squire activities, especially hunting, have for long attracted the wealthy, fashionable and competitive. Hence weathervanes suggesting that the owner participates in them are among the most popular, especially in rural and semi-rural settings.

Hunting for food and protection was very early formalized into enjoyment; much British hunting ceremonial and language can be traced to Norman aristocrats. In those days, however, and through the Middle Ages, 'hunting' meant stag-hunting. Richard Cœur de Lion kept staghounds; outlaws like Robin Hood poached deer in huge areas set aside for the royal chase. Men had given up judging a horse's capabilities by the colour of its eyes, but it still had to be a roan, with some white, to be deemed a worthwhile hunter. Elizabethan and Stuart sportsmen valued hounds more for their 'music' than their fleetness; indeed, hounds took so long puzzling out a scent that the hunt progressed at around two miles per hour.

Today, staghounds are almost unknown. Deer are stalked and shot, not chased. So specifically stag-hunting vanes are few. Two matched dogs energetically pursuing a stag identify an example at Hoveton, Norfolk, as a hunting vane despite the absence of human figures. Made by Eric Stevenson for the Director of the Rural Industries Bureau, later remodelled into CoSira and in 1988 into the Rural Development Commission, its absence from their catalogue is surprising: many of their designs originated in private commissions.

The single stag at Saxlingham Nethergate, Norfolk, swell-bodied and looking as though he has leapt off a Christmas card, also recalls stag-hunting. In this non-stag country, the specially bred quarry was released on hunt days only about ten minutes before the pursuit began. The object was a good run, culminating in catching the stag alive and transporting it back to Norwich ready for the following week. No wonder one stag allegedly turned on several hounds and drowned them.

Foxes superseded stags as quarry during the eighteenth century. Counties squabble over which had the earliest packs of foxhounds, but they were chiefly founded when fox-hunting blossomed under George I and his successors. The participation of prosperous lawyers, doctors, clergy, merchants – later immortalized by Surtees in the sporting grocer, Jorrocks – changed the character of the sport. Since the increasingly thoroughbred horses needed a good gallop, swift hounds were bred. 'Music' was sacrificed for 'staunchness', and packs became much larger so that at least one hound might be expected to pick up the scent without checking pace. Londoners, apparently, have cause to thank fox-hunting: the Duke of Grafton had such difficulty with Thames watermen as he tried to reach his pack of hounds at Croydon that he introduced a special bill into Parliament – and Westminster Bridge was opened in 1748.

Fox-hunting reached its peak in mid-Victorian times, dwindling towards the end of the century. But most hunting weathervanes date

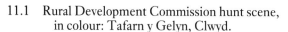

11.1   Rural Development Commission hunt scene,
in colour: Tafarn y Gelyn, Clwyd.

from the past hundred years, well after the heyday of hunting itself, perpetuating English tradition in an era of destabilizing social change. Certain hunts became particularly famous, but if hunting vanes are more numerous in the so-called hunting shires, it is only by a short head. Claims that some earlier hunting vanes owe their presence to the proximity of a particular pack of hounds cannot be extended to modern examples in Britain's extremely mobile society. The era depicted on hunting weathervanes may be discernible in styles of tack and dress, but it bears repeating that this is no guide to the age of the actual vane. Hunting costume is colourful and characteristic – but so minutely particularized. Those who paint their hunting weathervanes, and obviously the subject lends itself to colour, have every chance of offending hunting etiquette by sartorial gaffes.

This winter sport, almost invariably conducted on horseback, is controlled by the huntsman with his horn. His representation in the Rural Development Commission's pattern-book is widely reproduced. Another solo figure, a top-hatted horseman now at Sea Place, Goring by Sea, Sussex, formerly rode outside the Galleypot Inn near Hartfield, Sussex, inside which was displayed the full outfit of a famous Surrey Hunt First Whip. The rider on Sunny Mount between Tavistock and the Dartmoor National Park, Devon, is also probably hunting, having been erected by a former Master of the West Devon and Spooners. He might regret the way the present owner has fined down the horse's head, but the vane now works better.

Such solo performers are the exception. The typical hunting weathervane is a scene, one of the Commission's most popular half-dozen. It shows a fox, two dogs in pursuit and a horseman leaping a fence alongside a bush, surprisingly well furnished for winter – a holly perhaps. From the bypass to Tafarn y Gelyn, Clwyd (*11.1*), and by Lockerbie House Hotel, Dumfries & Galloway, it presents a lively silhouette. Its details can also be clearly picked out in colour, especially on a low site: Brooke Riding School at Stock, Essex, has an excellently detailed example with good decorative ironwork and lettering.

Minor variations on this design are also legion. A hedge replaces the fence or is placed behind the rider to increase windage; more or fewer hounds are differently disposed about the rider; the fox has escaped; the huntsman sounds his horn. Some of these variations are themselves duplicated, suggesting that any attractive hunting representation will be welcomed. A most beguiling hunt scene is on Sheppenhill Stables, Sellack, Hereford & Worcester. As the fox leaps off the pointer, pursued by a hound and a horseman jumping a fence, a yokel leans on his stick to

11.2   'Jorrocks': Stapleton, Yorks.

11.3   Pacing huntsman: H.M. Queen's estate, Sandringham, Norfolk.

watch and to provide extra windage. Although the painting is obviously fairly old, much detail is still clear. To heighten the charm, when a swallow perches on the yokel, the swallow is the larger.

In addition to full scenes, two other main groups of hunting weathervanes occur. One is characterized by a guilty-looking fox with trailing brush. In the standard version the horse stands alertly, the upright huntsman sounds his horn and the fox slinks off. Not a hound is in sight – and this on Zetland Hunt Kennels, Aldbrough St John, Yorks. Skilful painting gives the figures beautiful modelling. Nearby, on a Stapleton farm, and right across the country at Clock House, Corton Denham, Som., is a variant known as 'Jorrocks'. The horse's head is curved like a sock puppet's, his front legs mulishly vertical as his rider crouches forward urging him to great things – that is, movement. Both horse and rider are bulkily overweight. The fox still slinks (*11.2*).

In the other group, the horseman paces steadily after two hounds. One example of the design has travelled to Holwell House, Oxon., via Great Missenden, Bucks., from Flore near Daventry, Northants, where it is thought to have been made before the 1920s. An identical vane on buildings opposite Her Majesty's Stud Office at Sandringham, Norfolk (*11.3*), has not been dated. Copies with only one hound, or smaller, are at Toynton All Saints, Lincs., and on a barn at Risbury, Hereford & Worcester. All are painted with white horses and dappled foxhounds, apparently after a Leech illustration of James Pigg, Jorrocks' huntsman. On Picts Hill, Langport, Som., however, the dogs have near-dalmatian markings, and the rider's flat-brimmed hat and something more like an overcoat almost move it out of the hunting vane category altogether.

Of the multiple weathervanes described in the last chapter, the most complex, that at Ashperton, Hereford & Worcester (*6.3*), is the most obviously a hunting vane. Three riders are joined by a fox loping on the fourth arm. Hounds slaver at it from the scrolls below. The vane reflects deep family involvement in the sport as masters, whippers-in and eventers.

Complex though this is, it is all one weathervane. It has been known, however, for the huntsman to be on one end of the roof, a hound on the other, and the fox on the garage. One of the finest fragmented hunt scenes must be that at Capel, Kent. Here a fox, hounds and huntsman are divided among the tails of five oast-houses. Though diminutive, all are beautifully painted. Given the right wind-direction, the entire hunt streams across the evening sky in an unforgettably dramatic sequence.

The dramatic and decorative possibilities of good fox-hunting weathervanes make the hostility of the anti-bloodsports demonstrators

11.4 Late Master of the Dunston Harriers, Norfolk: John of Gaunt House, Somerby, near Melton Mowbray, Leics.

very saddening. Several owners have experienced damaged vanes or unpleasantnesses that have made them remove them.

But men's hunting instinct is very deeply engrained. If they do not hunt foxes, they will find something else to chase. Packs of otter-hounds, largely out of work once otter-hunting became illegal, are now enjoying renewed activity hunting mink. No weathervanes depicting these shaggy-coated hounds have come to our notice, but if attempts to reduce this latest scourge of British wildlife continue, mink-hunting vanes will doubtless appear. And a delightful footnote to hunting's aristocratic origins – one pack of otter-hounds is owned by Welsh miners.

Importing a quarry was such a tiresome business that the Norfolk stag-hunters mentioned earlier took to hunting hares instead. A portrait vane of the late Master of the resultant Dunston Harriers, in the correct dark green coat and again splendidly painted to convey the modelling of the grey hunter, stood until recently on the White House, Shotesham, Norfolk. Now it has been moved many miles, by bequest, to John of Gaunt House, Somerby, near Melton Mowbray, in Leicestershire. It exemplifies the dilemma posed by family association in conflict with local relevance (11.4).

Many 'huntsmen' may be harriers: only if the hare is shown, as on Walford Court, Hereford & Worcester, are they distinguishable. Hares can also be hunted on foot, using beagles, known in Britain since Roman times. A Rural Development Commission hare with a huntsman on foot presumably betokens beagles somewhere in the offing.

To most people, however, hares are pursued by greyhounds. These differ from other hounds in that they 'course' their quarry by eye, not scent. The Commission's pattern of hare and two greyhounds exudes muscular exertion. At Heath House, Newmarket, Suffolk, this is emphasized by sloping cardinal letters, sometimes an arbitrary device but here looking as if swept aslant by the animals' speed. In a rather fragile pre-war vane on Mill Farm, Great Ryburgh, Norfolk, two greyhounds course alongside each other, a confusing silhouette from afar but clarified by colour close to. A number of others claim to portray the owners' own lurchers or advertise the Hare and Hound pub, as at Ledburn, Bucks. Surprisingly the greyhounds on a barn at Twenty, Lincs., a ten-foot coursing scene which formerly bore the initials of the East of England Coursing Club, look very leisurely and unextended.

The greyhound track racing that has developed from coursing has such a following that more weathervanes illustrating it might be expected. The single standing greyhound at Barmby Moor, Humberside, bearing the name 'Red Sand' is probably a racer. For Vale View, Tring, Herts., David Harvey has made a portrait – a black greyhound called Alfie, correct in his red·No.1 jacket.

Numerically, hunting weathervanes cast a long shadow over those illustrating shooting, plentiful though these are. Again they are predictably less common in large conurbations. Perhaps more owners of shooting than hunting vanes participate actively in the sport, though whether they enjoy rough shooting, wildfowling, clay pigeon shooting or the classier pursuit of pheasants and partridges may not be clear.

Once again, creatures only occasionally appear without human figures. A German pointer and (presumably) pheasant at Waverton, Ches., declare the owner's interest, and a dog flushing a partridge from rough grass has advertised the Dog and Partridge in Bury St Edmunds, Suffolk, some say for 150 years.

Almost always a shooting vane shows a sportsman walking, waiting or firing, with his gun in the positions appropriate to those moments. One or more dogs may be seated, standing or returning with game. The Rural Development Commission sportsman, dating from before 1952, predominates. Firmly planted in his fitted jacket and gaiters, he aims horizontally from under his down-brimmed hat, accompanied by an alert pointer. Both man and dog are strikingly similar to a popular American design.

Make this figure thinner or fatter; give him a deerstalker or a flat cap (can the headgear at Carsluith, Dumfries & Galloway, be a Scottish bonnet?); give him a straight shooting jacket and boots; replace the

11.5   Sportsman with his dog: Burwash, Sussex.

pointer with a Labrador or springer spaniel; each impression is totally different. The social cameos range between shooting in formal dress over pointers to shooting in cap and tweeds over retrievers. Almost certainly, because the attitudes are relatively easy to photograph, many will be genuine double portraits. The round-hatted farmer with his dog at heel and gun broken on a farm at Cople, Beds., certainly is.

Inaccuracies in the dogs' attitudes and positions relative to the stage of the shot the sportsman has reached may simply betray ignorance. Equally, they may be deliberate modifications in the interests of a more shapely design. Shapeliness of any kind quite defeats some makers, but the vanes can still charm – like the sort of triangular man with his sort of square dog hastening in flapping raincoat after some long-tailed bird at St John's Chapel, Dur., or the sportsman and dog near Willingham, Lincs., militarily at attention before a whirling propeller. Somewhere,

11.6 Wildfowler: Bosham, Sussex.

according to Baughton Forge, there is a man aiming at a sort of Bugs Bunny grinning derisively on the pointer.

One of the most attractive shooting weathervanes is the vigorous portrayal in *11.5*. Recently David Hedges, the smith at Burwash, Sussex, who originally made it about twenty years ago, completely renewed the corroded boots and grass. At the same time an English springer replaced the earlier pointer, to reflect the different breed now favoured by the owner. The figure, stiffened with iron, is built up in layers of copper, so that the man has separate arms, and his coat flaps on either side of his legs. His period garb of brown leggings, green frock coat with gilt buttons, and black down-brimmed hat with light band is in clear but gentle colours. The largely white dog sets him off, and tiny pierced eyes gleam with concentration.

Fewer shooting than hunting vanes are built up into scenes with landscape as well as action elements. Wildfowling scenes at Seamore, Bosham, Sussex, and Fountain House, Eynsford Hill, Kent, are clearly from the same, possibly pre-war source. Their identical front halves consist of an open fence and a duck rising from a grassy bank. The Bosham sportsman and his dog have been caught napping, however: his gun is still slung over his shoulder (*11.6*). The better-prepared fellow at Eynsford is firing, and his dog eager to retrieve.

So much detail is included in a coloured shooting scene at the Pheasant Inn, Worth, Som., that it starts all sorts of story-weaving.

Pheasants rise from pine trees and bushes, a peppery-looking figure with plus-fours stuffed into his socks and a tufted hat takes aim, while a diminutive follower still holds the lead from which he has just released the retriever. Surely some local character must be delineated here (*11.7*). Once again, because it is on a low mast, painted features make a valuable contribution. Its slightly comic tone suggests that, despite its period feel, it is probably quite modern: the present landlords found it there.

The fishing activities of the British hunting-shooting-fishing squirearchy are far more sparsely represented in weathervanes. In this connection, 'fishing' should mean fly-fishing, for salmon, trout or grayling. Although the sport has kudos and is visually attractive, surprisingly few participants have translated their enthusiasm into weathervanes. Alan Knight, a Worcestershire craftsman, made for the fisherman owner of Combe Cottage, Finstall, Hereford & Worcester, a salmon swirling out of the water to take a fly. No fisherman is visible, but the fine wire holding the fly in position looks so like a fishing-line that the salmon appears to be hooked (*13.11*).

When fishermen are depicted, their rods bow to the weight of dream-sized fish. The moment at which the net is thrust forward beneath the tired fish is the favourite. The self-confessed fanatic in Park Close,

11.7 *Left:* Characterful, coloured shooting scene: Pheasant Inn, Worth, Som.   11.8 *Right:* Fly-fishing: Park Close, Eastbourne, Sussex.

11.9   Longshore fishing off Happisburgh: Brundall, Norfolk.

Eastbourne, Sussex, took his design from a photograph in a specialist magazine, so the balanced tensions of the man as he crouches to land his salmon are entirely convincing. His rod and fishing-bag and the pipe clenched between his teeth are finely detailed, and the muted colouring, especially of the water, makes this a most atmospheric motif (*11.8*). The mounting is also ingeniously contrived from parts of an old fishing-rod, appropriately enough, and DIY shelf components and brackets. On the outskirts of Bideford, Devon, another fisherman stands braced against the weight of his catch. No wonder: he has caught the point of the arrow, whose tail is the rock on which he stands. In his red waterproof, on a black rock and with a blue arrow representing the water, he adds gay colour to a low garage roof.

Fishing from a rock could be either inland or coastal sport. Most sea-fishing, however, is waterborne. Deep-sea fishing is represented by weathervanes of commercial fishing-vessels, longshore fishing from small boats by such entertaining examples as *11.9* on Willows End, Brundall, Norfolk. The owner's friend who made it has depicted Happisburgh's red-and-white shore lighthouse with truth, but the catch – perhaps – with tongue in cheek.

It is coarse fishing, however, that occupies most of the millions of British anglers. What a strange paucity of angling weathervanes, then. The characteristic umbrellas set up on river banks, with fishing-baskets and figures hunched on stools, offer interesting shapes for weathervane designs. But such angling vanes as there are focus mainly on fishing from dinghies. At Litcham, Norfolk, the rowlock, rudder and fishing-rod with its separate line and float are pleasing details (*11.10*).

11.10   Coarse fishing: Litcham, Norfolk.

Most vanes of this type, however, exaggerate the smallness of the boat and the alarming angles to which it tilts as some giant fish is played. In the prime example, the boat is considerably shorter than its occupant and clearly listing almost to the point of no return. But the real chuckle comes from its position – high, high up on the very top of the massive Denver sluice, Norfolk, that mighty piece of engineering that controls all the waters of the Fens. A past foreman placed it there forty years ago (*1.8*). In 1987 it vanished, presumably a victim of the same kind of bravado that crowns university pinnacles with inappropriate decorations. Replacement is only a matter of time. That subject, in that place, appeals too strongly to the English sense of the ludicrous to be resisted.

12 Sport

Ours is a sports-mad world. It is nothing new. A competitive urge seems as deep-seated as the hunting instinct. Even at periods of history when daily survival took considerable effort, men voluntarily added to natural physical challenges a deliberate pitting of their speed, strength, stamina and skill against those of others. They learned very early that training enabled them to dominate, not just for gain but for enjoyment. Thus Ancient Greece excelled in athletics and even enjoyed team games resembling football and hockey. Bull-fighting came from ancient Thessaly. Falconry was established in Britain by the eighth century, and competitive archery developed alongside medieval warfare. Real tennis began in the twelfth century, bowls in the thirteenth, and golf in the fifteenth.

After centuries of improvisatory development, it is only in the last couple of hundred years that regulating bodies have established these sports and games as we know them today. The Royal and Ancient Golf Club at St Andrews, for instance, was not founded until 1754 – after 300 years of play. Cricket rules were not formulated until 1774, and Test Matches began only in 1877. Much of the codification came through the influence of nineteenth-century public schools and universities, with their '*mens sana in corpore sano*' ethos. They regularized rugger in 1832, but until 1863 each school played its own version of soccer – no wonder there are some quaint traditional survivals – and hockey rules had to wait until the 1880s. Henley Regatta put rowing on the map in 1839, and in 1874 the British invented lawn tennis. In the nineteenth century Scotland also re-invented bowls, and Belgium sent us pigeon-racing. There was therefore a pre-disposition to formulate rules from the start for any new sports arising from new inventions, such as ballooning, motocross and car-racing.

It follows that few sporting weathervanes are particularly old. Because modernity and up-to-the-minuteness far outweigh nostalgia in sport, a sportsman's costume and equipment on a weathervane probably correspond to the date of its construction more than in most other groups. Accuracy is striven for. Failure to achieve it is more likely to reflect artistic weakness than sporting ignorance.

In this era of spectator sports, which bring together many who are interested but lack the space or ability to play themselves, the biggest grandstands and stadiums are notably deficient in sporting weathervanes. Perhaps club administrators feel that only one or two figures cannot convey a true impression of a team game. In designing the Rugby Football Union's weathervane at Twickenham, Greater London, in 1950 Kenneth Dalgleish neatly sidestepped this problem. His contemporary player is receiving a pass from Hermes, winged messenger of the gods. Beneath are the club's initials and serpents twined round a winged wand, symbolizing the power, wisdom and speed of the game. Roughly life-sized gilded figures and a contrasting dark green eight-foot-three-inch arrow, said to have a sixty-pound weight on the pointer, make it an outstanding feature on the east stand (*2.10*). It seems quite extraordinary, even in these vandal-infested times, that top soccer clubs have not emulated it.

12.1   'Norwich Canary', appropriately painted: Skedge Way, Blofield, Norfolk.

12.2   *Left:* Realistic players on the Town House, formerly the
Cricketers: Tower Ramparts, Ipswich, Suffolk.   12.3   *Right:* Cricket
equipment – and the team: Hindon, Wilts.

Supporters are less inhibited about erecting a single footballer on
their home, provided he is painted in their favourite team's strip or even
made to represent a particular player. Hence the Norwich canary,
complete with sponsor's jersey advertising Foster's lager, in Skedge
Way, Blofield, Norfolk (*12.1*). But there is no quantity of football
weathervanes to match the religious fervour of its followers, unless they
are all very obscurely placed.

Other team games are also sparsely represented. The only hockey
vane we found was at Lower Eggleton, Hereford & Worcester. With
hair secured in businesslike bunches, the swerving figure from the local
women's club badge was an appropriate choice for a county player. The
vane was made by Cyril Ashley.

Those sports in which individual performance is readily perceived
within corporate effort encourage more weathervanes than full team
games. Thus many of the club-houses and pavilions of the cricketers,
tennis and bowls players fly weathervanes. Some of these sports also use
specialized   equipment   whose   shapes   can   create   interesting

weathervanes even without players, an advantage not shared by a football. Sailing clubs, with their reliance on wind information, often display only simple arrows, the informative dials being inside the clubhouse. Because some of these sports are socially advantageous – especially golf, in which election to the club denotes more than just golfing prowess – associated weathervanes are generally held to give something of an air to private homes too.

Sports in which participants perform as individuals lend themselves to weathervanes copied from photographs. These days of popular heroes and 'champs' might be expected to produce numerous portrait vanes of sporting gods. But they fall from grace so soon that this is one kind of weathervane that would prove too durable. A thoroughly idiosyncratic stance on a weathervane is therefore more likely to be that of the owner than of some star. Occasionally, as in the boxer with red shorts and gloves, formerly at West Hoathly, Sussex, it may refer to both; it belongs to the British, European and World middleweight champion of the 1970s, Alan Minter.

As well as the semi-explicable paucity of soccer vanes and portrait vanes there are other surprising gaps. Archery, for instance, among Britain's oldest sports, is notable by its absence. The exciting potential of athletics images is ignored. Swimmers and divers are not depicted, though a stylized diving figure logo on several swimming-pools would make a stylish weathervane. Such omissions undermine the expectation of weathervanes presenting the newer sports of parachute jumping, hang-gliding and wind-surfing, all doubly appropriate as subjects from their own reliance on wind power.

The absence of indoor sporting activities on weathervanes is less remarkable, though one farmer at Croglin, Cumbria, does recall youthful

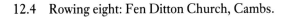

12.4   Rowing eight: Fen Ditton Church, Cambs.

darts matches in a flying dart. What marvellously graceful gymnastics weathervanes there could be! Of course, somewhere in Britain someone will have erected weathervanes that are exceptions to all these generalizations. The point is the thin scattering of weathervanes illustrating quite widely enjoyed activities.

Certain major sports, however, are more than adequately represented. When cricket devotees devour ball-by-ball commentaries from the Antipodes at 3 a.m., small wonder that their enthusiasm also manifests itself aloft.

Even to many who know nothing of the game, cricket is inseparable from Father Time (*2.10*). This well-loved figure, upon whose bowed shoulders so many layers of meaning have been draped that he seems as ancient as time itself, is only just approaching pensionable age. Apart from a spell during the war, after he was hooked off by a barrage balloon cable, he has stood on MCC's grandstand at Lord's in St John's Wood, Greater London, since Sir Herbert Baker presented him in 1926. Aided no doubt by TV, he has penetrated British consciousness so deeply that he is nearly as widely available, in mail-order imitations, as a cock. Thus village cricketers at clubs such as Kibworth Beauchamp, Leics., can now also claim to play under the eye of Father Time. In Sussex, Arundel Cricket Club's home-made version is lively rather than dignified; almost any imitation or variation – and they are many – suffers by comparison, though Brandeston Forge's design has dignity.

Wishful thinking dictates most cricketing weathervanes, however. On club grounds as rural as Cromer, Herts., and as urban as Broadwater, Worthing, Sussex, founded in 1771, a batsman lofts a mighty six. Two designs, the Rural Development Commission's and a more energetic mass-produced one, hog the field. John Allen's naturalistic adaptation for Brentor Cricket Club, Devon, adds wickets at each end. On the Town House pub – formerly the Cricketers – at Tower Ramparts, Ipswich, Suffolk, since the 1930s a wicket-keeper has crouched behind the batsman in a most convincing grouping (*12.2*). Behind the wicket at Lurgashall, Sussex, stands not Father Time but an umpire, hand raised in a dismissive gesture. His mainly wood and hardboard construction will make him particularly vulnerable to the ivy that has already smothered all the elaborate decoration and arms.

Various items of cricketing equipment can be used effectively on weathervanes. The cricket club at Stoke Bruerne, Northants, tops its plain white arrow with a scarlet cricket ball as finial. Enthusiasts at Withersden Mill, Stonegate, Sussex, arrange a bat horizontally as pointer, the ball lying on it as finial, and stumps impaled vertically on it to provide windage. Even more imaginative, however, is the equipment plus the stylized team of twelve men incorporated into the arms (*12.3*). This was designed by the cricketing owner, made in the unlikely setting of London's Edgware Road, conveyed into Hampshire by commuter train and finally retired to Cricketers, Hindon, Wilts.

Depicting whole teams is easier if they are compact, a rowing eight, for instance. This singularly uneccelesiastical subject on Fen Ditton Church, Cambs., (*12.4*), recalls how over fifty years ago the clergyman reprimanded noisy crews for disturbing his Sunday services. Urged on that occasion to join the congregation, Town and University crews have assembled annually for a service ever since. Their blades remain permanently in this 'Oarsmen's Church'. After several mock-ups to establish a convincing perspective, Lister's made the vane in copper and wrought iron, and painted it in a local rowing club's colours. A keen rowing family presented it in the 1970s.

Sports contested in pairs or small groups but relying on individual performance are favourite weathervane subjects. Top of the list for number and variety is golf, though there is no Rural Development Commission pattern. Its fashionable, well-heeled image prompts vanes on homes as well as on clubhouses. Realism is usually a goal, and there are flashes of humour. Despite the game's antiquity and the plethora of golf courses in Scotland, golfing weathervanes are not noticeably more numerous there.

12.5 *Left:* Portrait of John Panton, Ryder Cup golfer and 'pro' at Glenbervie Golf Club, Grampians. 12.6 *Right:* The final strokes: on Angmering Golf Course, Sussex.

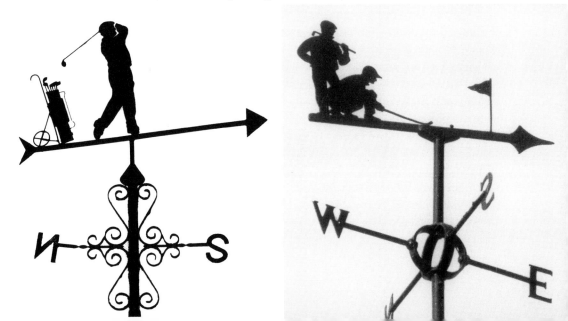

That golfing mecca, the Royal and Ancient Golf Club at St Andrews, Fife, has the simplest arrow weathervane, its interest in the proud club badge as finial. Many other clubs display their initials in an arrow, but there is as strong a predilection for pictorial weathervanes on clubhouses as on homes. Occasionally an irrelevant cock is used; the swan that decorates Longniddry Golf Club, Lothian, turns out to be the crest of the landowners, the Wemyss family. And despite the useful function weathervanes still fulfil at golf courses, no one at Piltdown Golf Club, Sussex, actually noticed when their pictorial weathervane went missing, presumed stolen.

Representations of players (by implication, this is exclusively a man's world), adjuncts to the game and associated ideas, alone or in combination, illustrate all the main aspects of a day's golf.

Walking jauntily out with his trolley is the figure erected on Aberdyfi Golf Club, Dyfed, to celebrate their centenary in 1986. It was presented by Edgbaston Golf Club, a sign of the two clubs' long association. Thirty years of annual matches between them have seen many Birmingham players retire to Aberdyfi and change allegiance. The figure looks irrepressibly like Lee Trevino in his peaked cap, but the press gave him another nickname – 'Sevvy Weather'.

An unfettered drive is a moment many golfers like to perpetuate in their weathervane. The ball is about to whizz down the fairway from Pepys Hollow, Castle Rising, Norfolk, while in Ramsey Road, St Ives, Cambs., county players with handicaps of two and six crowned their home with a mass-produced representation of the follow-through. This is also the moment captured at the Sussex clubs of Camber and Worthing, and at Yelverton, Devon. Each is slightly different, distinctive swings perhaps suggesting particular members. Yelverton's vane, an Erme Wood Forge product, is further 'personalized' by showing the player driving through a hazard of their course, two grazing Dartmoor ponies. There is scope in this idea for some entertaining combinations. Graham Walker's lithe golfer, with a good collection of clubs in his trolley, drives off from Strubby Grange, Lincs., named in an arch of iron letters beneath him.

Photographs obviously provide good models. At Eastfield Farm, Hough-on-the-Hill, Lincs., the vigorous action of Argentinian Vicente Fernandez appears. With the head of the club accidentally welded onto the back of the shaft, the results of his swing should be interesting ... A remarkable likeness of John Panton, Glenbervie's popular pro-fessional since 1946, makes an excellent weathervane on their

12.7   Bowls players; with interesting lettering:
Broadwell Bowls club, Glos.

Grampians clubhouse (*12.5*). Although he now plays little competitive golf, this permanent record of his style provides members with a constant spur to strive for comparable Ryder Cup and international successes.

Having struggled out of the bunkers their inaccurate driving landed them in – and apparently even this humiliation has been perpetuated in a weathervane – golfers reach the last, tense strokes on the green, most popular of all golfing representations. Clubs at Drayton, Norfolk, and Rhosneigr, Anglesey, are among many with single putting figures. The straddling Henry VIII-type putter on North Berwick's course, Lothian, is less typical in attitude. Looking entirely comfortable on their new home almost on Angmering golf course, Sussex, are a 1938 couple in aluminium, then a newish weathervane material. One crouches lining up the hole with his club; his partner watches, club propped casually over his shoulder (*12.6*). Equally naturalistic are two players on Alderley Edge Club, Ches., one concentrating hard while his companion holds the pin. On Merseyside, the period appeal of Royal Birkdale Club's gentleman golfer, watched by his caddie, lies in his shapeless, discreetly long plus-fours over his spindly shanks. And the owners of Barwonheads, Camber, Sussex, can watch two players and two caddies, all in highly characterful attitudes, apparently quite undismayed by the wild gyrations of their garden mast.

12.8   Early days of tennis: Falmouth Club,
Corn.

Should a day's play be less than successful, the '19th hole' beckons encouragingly. Can its influence be responsible for the putter at Park Golf Club, Southport, Merseyside, standing in profile from where he will have to scoop his ball croquet-fashion through the figure 19 to reach the flag-marked hole on the pointer?

Members of the club at Maesteg, Glam., made a vane dispensing with players altogether. The motif is a golf club, its head weighting the pointer; an outsize tee supporting a ball emblazoned '19' constitutes the tail, perhaps enticing the players to consolation after weaving through the sheep on their course. The single cardinal arm, shaped like an arrow and set on the east-west axis, is puzzling. Silloth and Solway Club, Cumbria, uses golf equipment with greater sobriety. From the tail half of the golf club motif is suspended horizontally a bag of golf clubs, and between the two the club's initials. All are green and white with a white golfball finial.

Close runners-up numerically, but certainly not in variety, are weathervanes depicting bowls. Their presence on countless pavilions, though bowls is one of the less wind-conscious sports, has been attributed to a leisured, retired bowling fraternity with money to spare. The argument is somewhat invalidated by the almost total lack of bowls vanes on private homes.

Nine-tenths of bowls vanes show a single stooping male figure, bowl either in hand or just released, often towards a jack on the pointer. The norm is the Rural Development Commission's pattern, soundly realistic with his wrinkled trousers and panama; he is on a garage in Lelant, Corn., in Station Road, Scalby, Yorks., and on clubs everywhere. He is more upright on Ambleside Bowls Club, Cumbria, hatless and rubbery-limbed at Thorpe Bay, Essex, disproportionately long-limbed too at Penryn, Corn. On the pavilion at Clacton, Essex, he advances on tiptoe like a stage villain, stiff-armed and apparently bowling the jack at the wood. At New Romney, Kent, he could be mistaken for a fielding cricketer, and he almost overbalances in his eagerness at Crieff, Tayside. At Kirkcudbright, Dumfries & Galloway, his white suit, goatee beard and round black hat seem likely to picture a particular member, contemporary with the 1913 clubhouse. As in golf, ladies' participation in the sport is little noted, and the lady has to wait her turn as the man bowls at Pershore Bowls Club, Hereford & Worcester.

To diversify our spot-the-difference absorption in motifs, there are sudden reminders of complementary interest elsewhere on the vane. Thus in addition to its two players, one alert, one portly, the weathervane on the pavilion at Broadwell, Glos., has compatible

12.9 Norfolk Dinghy class:
The Grange, Blofield, Norfolk.

cardinal letters, each circular as though carved from a wood (*12.7*).

Especially in municipal parks, pavilions are likely to host several sporting activities. Beech House Park, Worthing, Sussex, home to world bowls championships and with spanking new clubrooms, nonetheless still serves general players. On the clock tower of the old café and changing-rooms, set between bowling-greens and tennis courts, the bowls player with his wood has been watched since at least 1932 by a tennis player with his racquet, in arbitrary but equitable conjunction.

The lithe figures and dynamic attitudes of tennis, together with the size of the sport's following, ought to stimulate tennis weathervanes as numerous as those of cricket and golf, but there are few. Unlike its cricket and rugger counterparts at Lord's and Twickenham, the All-England Lawn Tennis Club's vane at Wimbledon, Greater London, is a straightforward representation and not particularly well known. On a surface no groundsman would acknowledge, a player has his knees flexed and racquet back, ready to stretch for a sizzling ace. The half-pointer projecting at a lower level and outwardly sloping cardinal letters are standard beneath many other motifs, and intimate fairly recent manufacture. The graceful and athletic possibilities of typical service, forehand and backhand shots have yet to be fully exploited in weathervanes.

How much the game has changed since it was played as in *12.8*. The genteel costume, racquet shape and vicarage-garden net support all suggest that the vane was placed on Falmouth Club, Corn., when it was built in 1904.

12.10   Mountaineering: School Lane, Storrington, Sussex.

Of the enormous numbers of Britons whose obsession is to be afloat, quite a proportion race for sport as distinct from leisurely cruising. For practical reasons of cost and accessibility, this means dinghy and small boat racing. Although some sailing clubs may fly weathervanes of vessels quite unrelated to those they sail (presumably the Royal Norfolk and Suffolk Yacht Club at Lowestoft, Suffolk, is not sailing medieval cogs these days), many do reproduce classes raced there. Hence the Sharpie at Wells Sailing Club, Norfolk, the Zenith dinghy with a former commodore's sail number at Denver, Norfolk, and the Royal Corinthian one-design, cleverly angled to suggest it is heeling in a stiff breeze, placed on the clubhouse of the same name at Burnham on Crouch, Essex, on its completion in 1931.

Racing dinghies can become as much members of the family as animals. So they are reproduced with loving accuracy on private homes. The Norfolk Dinghy, for instance, which has sailed above the Grange, Blofield, Norfolk, for nearly twenty-five years portrays the class prototype, though numbered 2, as numbers were arbitrarily allocated after the first half-dozen of the class had been built in 1931 (*12.9*). With a second-hand Norfolk Dinghy now fetching over £2,000, it hardly bears contemplation that they then cost just £65 each.

These dinghy weathervanes share one very odd feature. Either they have ghost crews or they are on automatic pilot. Perhaps they are regarded as dinghy portraits rather than racing scenes, for the Rural Development Commission dinghy pattern shows that the figures of helmsman and crew can be successfully introduced.

Mountaineering is more of a continental activity, but Britain can produce some testing climbs. The late John Rhoden was a mountaineer of some note, with a first ascent recorded in his name in Snowdonia. All the beautiful detail on his weathervane (*12.10*) in School Lane, Storrington, Sussex – the ice-axe pointer and three roped figures with packs and pompom hats – is thoroughly enjoyable at single-storey height.

Striking weathervanes can emerge from any sport. One of the oldest is falconry, known in Britain before the Conquest and common for centuries, but now among the country's more esoteric sports. The falconer David Harvey created for a customer in St Brelade's Avenue, Parkstone, Dorset, is casting off the hawk from the gauntlet, with a pointer ready to flush the quarry. Very unexpectedly, the falconer is a lady (*12.11*) – and the lady who ordered the vane, a falconer.

Bird-control of a different kind is practised by pigeon racers. A beautifully painted pigeon weathervane on a loft at Stone, Bucks., and a simpler one behind Ribby Road, Wrea Green, Lancs., may help to attract homing birds. A vane at Craven Arms, Shropshire, revives memories for a pigeon-fancier forced to give up through illness. Against the unlikely background of roaring traffic behind Valley Side, Chingford, Greater London, a painted David Harvey weathervane shows the owner kneeling to release his birds for their flight home of anything up to 500 miles.

12.11 Lady Falconer:
St Brelade's Avenue,
Parkstone, Dorset.

Modern transport has made organizing the pigeons' thrice-weekly training flights much easier, but some sports could not function at all without mechanical or technical equipment. The stylized hot-air balloon on an outbuilding of the Black Horse at Great Missenden, Bucks., marks where a balloonist made a chance landing, later forming a club which meets regularly and holds Easter ballooning rallies here.

Various sporting motor cyclists appear. A cheerful Michelin-type figure, cut from tin, joins numerous other home-made novelties in the garden of The Hollies, Market Drayton, Shropshire. Graham Walker's speedway rider at Theddlethorpe All Saints, Lincs., has earned the '1' in the kind of gearwheel beneath him by flashing past the marshal, though the flag is still raised. David Harvey's motocross enthusiast rides on his rear wheel, at present across the flowerbed, in Mardle Road, Leighton Buzzard, Beds.

Motor racing's exciting, sometimes outlandish car shapes do not seem to have attracted weathervane owners, and the record-breaking 'Golden Arrow', visible thirty years ago in King Henry Road, Lewes, Sussex, is no longer evident.

Some people, however, can attain considerable speed without motorized assistance. The Rural Development Commission skier has not come to light, but in Downham Road, Outwell, Norfolk, the characteristic action of speed skaters – effort before grace, warmth before fashion – is portrayed (*12.12*). On the frozen Well Creek bordered by the road and on the flooded washes they whizz along, rejoicing in conditions that shrivel the less robust. The weathervane spurs its owner towards a third winning of the Fen speed-skating trophy.

Certain old sports have, thank goodness, died out or been made

12.12 Fen speed-skater: Outwell, Norfolk.

illegal. So-called 'fighting cocks' on weathervanes are not the small-headed, huge-spurred genuine article so much as ordinary cocks in aggressive mood. The ugly thrills of both bear and bull baiting were outlawed in this country in 1835. It gives a shock, therefore, to find a bull, already speared several times by a matador with flying cloak, at Etchingham, Sussex. Both the vane subject and the house name, Buena Vista, date from the 1950s, when a Spanish Embassy official brought his sick wife here to benefit from the English country air.

Finally, something rather different in the form of an arrow weathervane, its arms decorated with lively representations of a cricketer, footballer, athlete and tennis player. It was erected in the playground of Horsted Parva primary school, Sussex, as a memorial to a child killed in a car crash. What a touching comment on the importance of sport in young lives today.

13 Wildlife

In learning how to hunt particularly tasty or particularly pernicious living creatures and how to domesticate them or enjoy their companionship, our forebears' chief weapon was the understanding that grew out of observation and close contact. Human and animal experience was closely akin, and interpreting eagles, lions or fish in terms of majesty, courage and agility a very ancient approach. Such creatures were therefore early incorporated into heraldry. Their first appearance on weathervanes is with the non-realistic anatomy of the heraldic style and period. But particularly in the last 150 years, scientific studies have demanded greater physical accuracy and fostered increasingly naturalistic representations alongside the heraldic. Today we still accept bird, animal and fish weathervanes in all three modes. The symbolic and heraldic have been looked at; this chapter focuses more on the representational.

Birds are far the most popular wildlife weathervanes, though with fewer examples in Scotland, Wales and parts of the English Midlands. Most of the Rural Development Commission's ten designs are widely reproduced. Game birds appear everywhere; waterbirds and wildfowl congregate more in appropriate habitats; small garden birds, mostly so difficult to differentiate, nearly always have some personal or local relevance. 'Twitchers' should quickly be able to notch up over thirty weathervane species.

Birds would seem made for weathervanes. They are in their natural element, aerodynamically already correctly 'designed' for three-dimensional representation. There are problems, however, in representing in vertical silhouette something which is basically T-shaped and moving in a horizontal plane. Moreover their flying forms have to be anchored. Too flimsy a tether quickly snaps; too obvious and heavy breaks the illusion of free flight. This is perhaps why many designers sacrifice the excitement of flight for birds standing, rising or alighting, when the 'anchor' reflects gravitational pull and is visually less intrusive.

Makers may introduce some elements of habitat or naturalistic twiggy perches. They may rely on exaggerated silhouettes or colour for recognition. Full-bodied birds especially can have beautifully feathered effects, but the technique is not extensively practised. Delightful effects can be arrived at beyond realism, however. Three gulls, linked by wing-tip, tail and beak on Sidney Dye Home for the Elderly, King's Lynn, Norfolk, though irrefutably gulls, have become a single decorative form; pattern and rhythm have taken precedence over naturalism (*13.1*).

No county appears to lack the Rural Development Commission's pheasant, silhouetted on a grassy bank. Pheasants are also the only species frequently modelled in the round. One, of copper with feather-marked tail, is believed to have identified a shooting estate at West Hoathly, Sussex, since about 1790. Another feathered-textured bird, on Shoreham House, Kent, was made about 1912. The style, therefore, gives little clue to the date.

Tails up or down, crouching or stretching, heads smaller or larger, weathervanes reflect how different the pheasant's proportions appear as he struts and turns. The tail, it must be admitted, is often the identifying feature. Colour contributes too, though inaccuracy produces some strange pigeony hybrids, and solid colour without feather-mottling can look very crude. Pheasants are seldom shown in flight. The really handsome gilt and black pheasant in North Street, Chichester, Sussex, is flat-bodied but given three dimensions by wings sweeping sideways and down. All the jewelled markings of body and head feathers are textured, and wing feathers separately modelled. Once again, current occupants of a building find themselves in possession of a really beautiful object about whose history they know nothing.

The sportsmen's other favourite quarry, the tubby little partridge, is seldom found, despite a Rural Development Commission pattern. In an attractive group on Wotton Farm, Surrey, two adults, alertly presented by tiny pierced eyes, with three young, signify the owner's sporting proclivities.

The liking for wildfowl, however, spreads far beyond sportsmen. Once again, vertical impalement of flying wildfowl produces

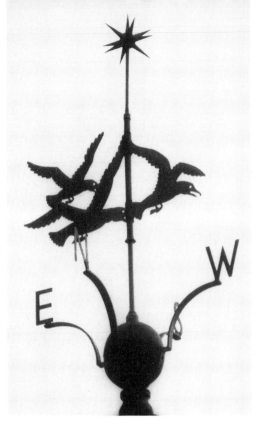

13.1 *Left:* Circling gulls – pattern from realism: King's Lynn, Norfolk.

13.2 *Below left:* Heron, cast and painted for convincing detail: South Walsham, Norfolk.

13.3 *Above opposite:* Avocet by Cley Marshes Reserve, Norfolk.

13.4 *Below right:* Osprey, with convincing painted detail: Aviemore, Highlands.

13.5 *Below:* Wren at her nest, a family compliment: Astwood Bank, Hereford & Worcester.

uncomfortable sensations. Horizontal impalement somehow looks less agonizing, as two ducks flying along an arrow show on Ubbanford Bank Cottage, Norham, Northd. Still better are birds obviously descending or rising, very effective both full-bodied and painted. The mast-head mallard overlooking the harbour on Mariner's Hill, Blakeney, Norfolk, swoops colourfully, calling as he descends. A duck rises by the Wye at Aberedw, Powys, showing the different three-dimensional effect of a flat body with wings spread laterally. The shrieking bird, dancing on one toe on Sudbrook Lodge, Ham Common, Greater London, does not know whether he is coming or going. In Brandeston Forge's popular cast design, a pair takes off downwind from the reeds, a technical compromise with realism.

Although particular species of geese may appear on weathervanes (David Harvey has reproduced the Nene geese so successfully rehabilitated by the Slimbridge Wildfowl Trust), most goose weathervanes use some or all of the Rural Development Commission's three geese, feeding in different attitudes. Two adjacent houses overlooking the river at Belaugh, Norfolk, complete the group between them.

Swans are now forbidden game, and it is their beauty that weathervanes celebrate. Their elegance proves elusive: the weathervane advertising the Swan pub at Kettleshulme, Ches., is very static compared with its lively painted sign. A cast swan-and-cygnet among reeds on Pond House, Wadhurst, Sussex, has a picture-book quality. Above the main street of Marlow, Bucks., a slightly arched neck gives the bird more grace, but weathervanes ignore the fluid Art Nouveau designs, preferring to formalize the swan's statuesque dignity. Thus several acquire gold crowns, and St Hugh's pet swan, full-bodied in copper on his church in Scunthorpe, Humberside, has angles and curves reminiscent of paper sculpture. The Rural Development Commission's dramatic swan rising into flight, exactly right on a riverside summerhouse at Horning, Norfolk, is naturalistic. But, like the King's Lynn gulls, flying swans make ideal material for the move from representation towards abstraction, an idea borne out by the attractive swan-cum-pennant on the corner of Buttermarket, Ipswich, Suffolk.

Seabird weathervanes are almost exclusively coastal. A full-bodied gull soaring above Domus, Western Esplanade, Broadstairs, Kent, is modelled with convincing realism, though its gilding has dulled since 1907. The owners of Stoptide Lodge, Corn., have cleverly painted their silhouette gull, landing with arched wings. But why the almost total neglect of the more slender, elegantly diving tern? An eighty-year-old

13.6　Eager fox near Brompton in Allerton, Yorks.

reptilian cormorant dives for his fish from a sandcastle of a house, Surf Point, Rhosneigr, Anglesey. He is still Palethorpe property, an earlier magnate of this meat-processing firm having arranged for him to be made, probably by his own workmen. Few weathervanes, surely, can claim to have emerged – so shapely too – from a sausage factory.

An instantly recognizable shape and waxwork poses make the heron an irresistible subject. By coasts north, south, east and west, by rivers and lakes he stalks. Most deceptively, cast with great surface detail and meticulously coloured, he stands by South Walsham Broad, Norfolk. The Broads Society, whose emblem is this 'harnser' painted for them by the noted bird artist Roland Green, presented it to their founder on the Society's twentieth anniversary (*13.2*).

Other inland fishing birds, such as grebes, create Broadland weathervanes but East Anglia has greater rarities. Billy Bishop, for thirty-eight years warden on Cley Marshes, Norfolk, was given a weathervane of a black-tailed godwit the year they first bred there. When it was blown down and bent, the friend repairing it thought he would paint it too. It caused much laughter: the up-bent bill had metamorphosed it into an avocet (*13.3*). But by another amusing twist Cley had by then attracted avocets too. So Billy called his retirement home Avocets, where the weathervane still stands as his memorial.

In lowland East Anglia, as in rugged uplands, the eagle exerts powerful fascination, even in the Rural Development Commission's rather muted pattern. Similarly static, although drawn from life at London Zoo, is the eagle placed on Hurstpierpoint College Chapel, Sussex, in 1930. However, by Chelmsford Road roundabout, Chipping Ongar, Essex, can be seen a thoroughly predatory silhouette, all spread talons and feathers, created by a lady experimenting at evening classes. Nothing matching the superbly modelled twelve-foot wing-span eagles commemorating the American Union of 1782 has surfaced in Britain, but a small eagle above Lord Street, Southport, Merseyside, adopts their stance with raised wings, on a sphere to show the feet realistically; an arrow actually indicates the wind. Supposedly made for a church which was never topped out, it was bought at a street market.

Another local speciality, the osprey, flies over a holiday complex at Aviemore, Highland, a fish grasped in its talons. Only at close quarters are the superb texturing and modelling revealed as nothing more than flecks and streaks of paint. Fine *trompe l'œuil* (*13.4*).

At the opposite extreme, pesky pigeons almost all claim to be doves. In shiny new copper on Dovecote House, Langford, Oxon., where the nest-holes remain incorporated into the garage wall, in white paint on Dovecote Garden turret, Fulford, Yorks., on Dove Antiques, Debenham, Suffolk, and similar locations the attribution is fair enough. One assumes that a bird above a zodiac-girdled globe at Ditchling, Sussex, signifies the dove of peace. Brandeston Forge's pretty, fluttering foursome has travelled to many counties.

Familiar and suitable bird shapes are not always used. A woodpecker is attractively set against a branch on Treetop Cottage, Hadlow Down, Sussex. But at Leiston, Suffolk, the bird is nonsensically hammering its tree-trunk on the point of the arrow, which therefore swings with its tail pointing to the wind. Rooks fare better. A silhouette rook curtseys jauntily to another with spread wings on Watton Road, Swaffham, Norfolk. The rook of Rook's Nest Farm, Walkern, Herts., guards a twiggy nest among bare branches, while a beady-eyed bird, epitomizing the village rookery, has perched on his curved branch on Harston Village Hall, Cambs., since 1923.

Little garden birds pose problems. The greater the enlargement, the less recognizable most species become. But for people named Robin or living at Lark Rise, Dippers or Kingfisher Cottage, they are inevitable choices. A plump, fringe-winged little flutterer at Finchwood, Marple Bridge, Greater Manchester, surmounts a summerhouse banded with coloured glass panels depicting finches of various kinds, all probably dating from the 1880s. As an image of domestic tenacity, refusing to budge from her eggs although her nest had to be moved during building-work, even the diminutive wren appears, on the house named Wren's Nest in her honour at Astwood Bank, Hereford & Worcester (*13.5*). Flying swift and swallow silhouette weathervanes are familiar, but the perching swallow at Bosham Hoe, Sussex, is unusual. An iron strap is curved to make the outline, which is partially infilled to give windage. The bird faces down-wind.

The peacock arouses somewhat ambivalent responses. Belief in its incorruptible flesh, symbol of the Resurrection, may have faded; both ridicule of its pride and wonder at its spectacular plumage persist. But the displayed tail, set across the bird as in reality, is impractical in three dimensions, and the challenge of perspective representation evidently too daunting. Trailing, solid tails look rather clumsy, stylized tails of wrought-iron swirls more attractive. The curvaceous bird on Felbrigg Hall's dovecote, Norfolk, restored in 1937, has his crest formalized into a coronet. Most unusual, however, is a sadly battered peacock on Bird Cage Cottage, Fleckney, Leics. – made of reeds.

Nine-tenths of weathervane birds, it is clear, aim to be representational. Owls, too, the most popular species after pheasants, can be pleasingly realistic. Convincing tawny owls alight in central Aldbourne, Wilts., and on the Owl Pottery, West Mersea, Essex, though both have vulnerably tenuous toe-contact with the arrow. A picture-book owl on a branch, silhouetted against the moon, watches Wivelsfield Road, Haywards Heath, Sussex. But owls lend themselves to anthropomorphism. In particular they wink; they leer. On a barn at South Lopham, Norfolk, a pair of owls is over-simplified into skittles; at Swymbridge, Devon, they resemble a pair of alert cats. An owlish trio, one winking and the largest

13.7   Dovecote guardian: Shilton, Oxon.

sporting a mortar-board, hold hands above the school at Kingston, Sussex – the design, apparently, of a ten-year-old pupil. The weathervane of Redbridge Library, Greater London, two adult owls scolding a youngster, is hardly serious enough to convey the wisdom of books. However, along Ide Hill, Kent, where no such symbolism is looked for, four wide-eyed owls, in shocked but gleeful gossip, are entirely delightful. In the USA very similar designs appeared in the 1920s.

Deeper probing would probably uncover heraldic origins for a few unidentified species. Some, like the full-bodied pelican-type bird raising his feathered wings above the old Liverpool Institute, are visually very exciting.

There are also a few exotic visitors. A tiny hoopoe gyrates rather wildly on his twig in Millbank, Tewkesbury, Glos., reminding his owner of happy times abroad. But a fitting finale is the world's largest species, the ostrich – in Scotland. About 1900 the owners of Candacraig House, near Strathdon, Grampian, bred ostriches in South America to satisfy obsessive fashion-mongers. So the deeply textured cast ostrich, source of their prosperity, was set to run across their roof.

Animal weathervanes are less of a self-sufficient group, people's appetite for them being partially satisfied by domestic animal, farm and hunting vanes. Even so, the two wild animals most popularly depicted are creatures of the chase, foxes and deer. Apart from these, the Rural Development Commission offers only a hare. Other wild mammals on weathervanes are very scattered. A second big difference from bird

13.8　Animal and heraldic crest: Mildenhall, Wilts.

vanes is in the proportion of native to foreign species. Nineteenth-century weathervanes in particular reflect the period's intense interest in exotic beasts, which formerly appeared mainly with heraldic or symbolic links.

Foxes rival cocks in their ubiquity, with a greater concentration in midland and fewer in coastal counties. Because they are a somewhat impersonal choice, practically none is documented. Foxes join horses and pennants as favourites on stables, farms and stately home outbuildings, Badminton House and Dyrham Park, Avon, and Callaly Castle, Northd., for instance. A slight *naïveté* suggests that many of these may well be contemporary with their buildings. Popularity ensures renewal, however: at Mayfield, Newtown, Powys, aircraft aluminium has replaced iron in an exact replica of the 1883 original.

Crowded urban settings seem congenial to the weathervane as to the real fox. He ignores dual carriageway traffic at Rotherham; he surmounts shops at Wakefield, a bank in Carlisle, a market cross at Newent, Glos., a clock-manufacturer's in Whitchurch, Shropshire, and, on a suitably lofty yacht mast, names his firm in Falmouth, Corn. He is not over-awed by the 'Ad Dei Gloriam 1859' on his home near Ramsley Moor, Derby., and even stands pertly on Berrynarbor church tower, Devon. He tops a turret on Rhyl Hospital, Clwyd, and looks very spry for all his 125 years in the middle of Hemswell, Lincs., – on a tall, striped maypole.

Why should the verminous fox be so popular? Beyond his obviously suitable shape, the answer must lie partly in sport. Hunting is no fun, no challenge, without a worthy adversary. Centuries of huntsmen, as well as cottagers defending their backyard poultry, have had to learn respect, however unwillingly, for the fox's wiliness. Today, with perverse ambiguity, he has even come to symbolize, for some owners, their conservational efforts. He permeates literature from the nursery upwards. In places he has become practically a weathervane cliché; Bicester, Oxon., for example, has five fox vanes within 200 yards of the market square.

Stable or coach-house foxes may resemble horses in similar positions – full-bodied, textured, impaled, gilded or painted white. The majority, however, are silhouettes, frequently gilded or painted, though blinding scarlet seems an unnecessarily extreme interpretation of rufous. Impalement is usually behind the front legs, but one eighty-year-old copper fox on the Old Stables, Harpenden, Herts., is stuck through the belly and so runs downwind. Only a few 'rocking-foxes', as at Badminton and Dyrham, have ground beneath their feet.

Variability is the keynote. Fox weathervanes often display such dubious anatomical verity that only the conspicuous brush differentiates them from dogs. They come seated, standing, loping, running and leaping at full stretch. The presence – and positioning – of an eye alters their entire demeanour.

Seated foxes are the rarest. A superbly poised animal with cut facial detail deserves better than just to be stuck into the barn thatch at Stone House, Whitchurch, Bucks. Elm House Farm, Saltfleetby St Clements, Lincs., displays a tiny but alert fox standing in grass atop a huge barn. Loping foxes are common; a dovecote at Bishopstone, Wilts., has a good example, though a fox does strike an incongruously predatory note in such a position. A well-painted running fox near Brompton in Allerton, Yorks., although it has a touch of the Disneys, gives a convincing display of slavering enthusiasm (*13.6*). The Rural Development Commission's emaciated leaping fox is everywhere. The fox's predatoriness seems accepted in identical lively scenes of a fox prowling after three anxious geese; Chawton, Hants, Walcot, Lincs., and Beechurst Park, Haywards Heath, Sussex, all share this 1920s design. Prompted by his six-year-old son, the farmer at Woodforde Farm, Weston Longville, Norfolk, set his fox in pursuit of a squawking cock. Apart from the motif itself, farm scrap was used, and sand-blasting and stove-enamelling virtually eliminated maintenance. Ripe, Sussex, provides an entertaining variant – a welcome bit of come-uppance as the goose says 'Boo' to the fox.

As earlier, more exclusive animals of the chase, and later the epitome of peaceful status in private pleasure grounds, deer might have been expected to match foxes in weathervane popularity. So large an animal has such an impact on the landscape that Scotland, for example, should be full of deer weathervanes. We actually found not one there, and everywhere the scattering is fairly thin. On inns in particular they carry symbolic or heraldic as well as decorative weight. A full-bodied animal with impressive antlers leaps over the former White Hart in Windsor, Berks. In 1983 metalwork students at Impington Village College made the white rampant stag of the Trust House Forte company, four feet six inches high and weighing over 100 lb, for the Post House Hotel, Histon, Cambs.

A decorative stag usually stands haughtily alone. At Yealand Redmayne, Lancs., Brackenthwaite Cottage's stag gains tremendously from his setting against tracts of open countryside. A school at Wearhead, Dur., provides a slightly simplified but dramatic stag bellowing on a hillock. A slightly sentimentalized stag guarding a seated hind is surprisingly infrequent. So is the Rural Development

13.9   Ornamented lion: Greene's Flour Mill,
Maldon, Essex.

Commission's very attractive scene of stag and hind feeding by a group
of fir trees. The gilt running stag on the College of Matrons, founded in
Salisbury Close, Wilts., in 1682, ignores naturalism. The supporting
horizontal with its triangular wind-catcher astern irresistibly recalls a
Christmas reindeer and sleigh. Its attitude is almost identical to that of
the Saxlingham Nethergate quarry-stag mentioned in Chapter 11 but,
although still naïve, the effect of three dimensions and no horizontal
there is markedly different. Setting the antlers to spring upwards and
outwards from a silhouette body can give the weathervane interest from
any angle.

Among other hunted creatures, hares, although in the nineteenth
century they were described as popular motifs, nowadays seldom appear
without some connection with a hunt. The example dashing across the
barn roof at Rottingdean, Sussex, indicates where a pack of beagles used
to be kept.

Of other traditional quarry, the boar has so nearly dropped out of
British consciousness that he is unexpected on a sports pavilion at Little
Eversden, Cambs. At Shilton, Oxon., the fierce, tusky beast of *13.7*
guards the Manor House dovecote, probably built by Cistercian monks
about 1300. The vane is prosaically attributed to a pig farmer, but on a

dovecote it has the air of a talisman against other predators. On Romans Halt, Mildenhall, Wilts., the badger (*13.8*) intriguingly reverses the normal sequence. Erme Wood Forge made it as the wild animal, with convincingly cut eye-stripes, but it was acquired by former Cabinet Minister Henry Brooke – since 'Brock' is his crest.

The smaller denizens of the British countryside make only occasional forays to the roof-tops. While less universally deplored than rats, the nuisance value of rabbits outweighs their attractiveness. The squirrel, however, by his bushy-tailed agility seduces many to turn a blind-eye to his destructiveness. Squirrel weathervanes occur quite often near Kent and Sussex woodlands – one expression of local colour that is not extended throughout the whole weathervane spectrum. As a craft-shop trade sign at Coltishall, Norfolk, the image is clearly of acquisitiveness, not the thrift that Americans associate with squirrels. Really small mammals on weathervanes run the same risk as small birds of appearing monstrous when created so much larger than life. Mouse's Corner Cottage, Newland, Herford & Worcester, has an obvious motive, but its mouse with flourishing tail would look livelier with an eye.

The reasons for exotic animals on weathervanes are diverse and sometimes unfathomable. Camelford's camel may be a rebus but across the Cornish peninsula in Wadebridge it is a less obvious decoration for a shopping precinct. Its bright yellow paint has unfortunately caught the eye of vandals who have, if not broken its back, twice bent it beyond recognition. The beaver above Bishopsgate, City of London, represents the old Hudson's Bay Company. This relatively small animal is made large – it weighs eighty pounds – to suit its lofty position. Even loftier is the Jumbo water tower in Colchester, Essex. The name supposedly originates from a clergyman's scathing complaint about this elephantine structure being built in his parish. Barnum's circus Jumbo being then all the rage, the water authority's retort, in a typically British blend of insubordination and amusement, was an elephant weathervane. Perhaps they intended only a small irritant: Jumbo's massiveness has been rendered almost toy-like. Whatever its altitude, an animal itself large, bulky and powerful loses its dignity if made too small, like the bear on a garage at Docklow, Hereford & Worcester.

The same applies to lions, heraldic or otherwise. Sixteenth-century Brighton must have found Deryck Carver's monumental Black Lion of Flanders quite awesome (*2.4*). It still impresses, with its gilt mane, tail and leg-fringes. In deference to this Flemish refugee who, although burned at the stake in 1555, had introduced important new brewing techniques at the Black Lion Brewery, the building is now the Deryck Carver pub and its vane carefully maintained.

Naturalism really goes by the board when the folk-art habit more popular in the USA than in Britain is adopted, of cutting out of the vane's flat surface shapes quite unrelated to its subject. The 1895 lion on Greene's flour mill in Maldon, Essex (*13.9*), looks as though a child had jabbed at it with a biscuit-cutter, decreasing its efficiency and structural strength but making it more fanciful.

When science no longer rules, perhaps it is unreasonable to be curious about one or two strange pairings, a squirrel and frog at Stewkeley, Bucks., and a rabbit and duck in the unlikely setting of residential Totteridge, Greater London. But it really would be fascinating to discover the story behind the monkey taunting a cockatoo on Tollgate Cottage, Hailsham, Sussex ....

Fish have an inherently well-proportioned, sleek form and double-finned tail which make them ideal weathervane subjects. Silhouette fish usually have fins projecting in a vertical plane; a few are further enhanced by cut gills. Occasionally silhouettes have fins projecting sideways like stabilizers or are stylized into almost abstract designs. Huge numbers are full-bodied. Their surfaces range from the smoothest gilt to the most scrupulous rendering of individual scales, with no loss of efficiency as decoration is increased. Their natural streamlining resists wind damage and, although there is seldom confirmation, some fish weathervanes, especially on churches, may claim considerable longevity.

In their concentration on Christian symbolism, many churches mount unspecified 'fish' – primitive silhouettes at Glamis, Tayside, and Boscastle, Corn.; sleek and solid on Abernethy's eleventh-century round tower, Tayside; plump with projecting fins at Crimond, Grampian; with a curiously appliquéd head and top jaw at Holyhead, Anglesey. The same imagination is discernible in the parroty grins of fish on churches at Torver, Cumbria, and Morecambe, Lancs., and in the curvaceous dolphins at Dolphinholme, Lancs., and Flookburgh, Cumbria. Solid tails but outline heads are adopted at Morpeth, Northd., and on the astonishing privately built church above Loch Awe, Strathclyde.

On such buildings as watermills, the lifeboat museum at Lytham, Lancs., and where netmakers of Musselburgh, Lothian, hammered out a primitive riveted fish for their factory in 1865, fish weathervanes probably stem from the watered-down symbolism that accounts them 'lucky'. Perhaps they also brought prosperity to Coln St Aldwyns

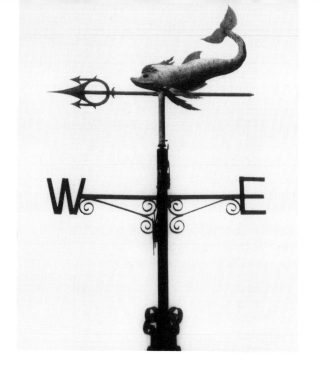

13.10   Decorative *repoussé* dolphin designed by Edward Seago (*left*):
The Dutch House, Ludham, Norfolk.   13.11   Salmon taking
fly (*right*): Finstall, Hereford & Worcester.

corn-mill, Glos., and Eardisland dovecote, Hereford & Worcester – and academic success through Great Yarmouth Education Office, Norfolk. Pisces weathervanes are not evident, however: the double fish on Tetbury Town Hall, Glos., both face the same way and appear to be heraldic dolphins.

The oddest physical combinations acquire 'dolphinism' from lively postures and cheeky, knowing expressions. On weathervanes, including church weathervanes, they are often used indistinguishably from 'fish', though sometimes genuine heraldic connotations are suggested by crown finials, as at Powderham, Devon. A dolphin sometimes symbolizes Christ. A full-bodied copper dolphin, therefore, pierced with a spear, on St Andrew's Church, Croydon, Greater London, probably since 1872, while possibly referring to St Andrew as a fisherman, is thought may represent the Crucifixion. However, a closely related design on Worthing Museum, Sussex, opened as the library in 1908, cannot carry the same meaning. Dolphins on the village hall at Goring, Oxon., and the old town hall, Minehead, Som., suggest they had become fashionable on public buildings. Schools at Brighton, Sussex, Flitcham, Norfolk, and Saltburn by-the-Sea, Cleveland, are a logical extension. However, private premises have very few. An enchanting little brass silhouette with looped tail dances over a coach-house at Worlington, Suffolk, but perhaps the dolphin's heraldic associations make it seem too pretentious on modern estates.

The most splendid private fish/dolphin was designed by artist Edward Seago for his home in Sardinia, and superbly executed in copper *repoussé* by Eric Stevenson, the only smith for whom the Worshipful Company of Blacksmiths has struck a gold medal. It breasts its way along a trident pointer. After the artist's death it returned to the Dutch House, Ludham, Norfolk, but its original mounting with Greek lettering was left behind and the ironwork now beneath it suffers by contrast with its high quality (*13.10*).

Real dolphins, recognizably Delphinidae, are scarcely acknowledged, though the Dolphin Hotel by St Ives Bridge, Cambs., re-opened in 1985 with a new weathervane, a dolphin arched above neat wave-crests.

Other 'real' fish tend to be recognizable as members of a family rather than accurate to the last fin. Perhaps a carp-type fish on Cubley church, Derby., stemmed from some parishioner's interest in the species; the supposed herring on St John's Church, Great Yarmouth, Norfolk, and the salmon-type on St Andrew's Church, Tweedmouth, Northd., now straining for its estuary view over intervening warehouses, are locally important species. Another Tweed salmon fittingly crowns the old town cross, Norham, Northd., but primarily the salmon is a subject for private house weathervanes.

Salmon or trout are not sufficiently significant in regional economies

13.12   Carved wooden fish with metal tail: Kingsbridge, Devon.

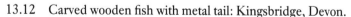

to influence the distribution noticeably, though some salmon vanes certainly find appropriate settings – for example, alongside the Wye at Llyswen, Powys. The salmon on Little Barn, Grimston, Norfolk, is a deliberate teasing reminder to the owner that his wife would like one in the freezer. In fact, the occurrence of salmon vanes from Inverness to Ilfracombe suggests a strong element of the lucky mascot for hopeful fishermen. Depicting the fish in mid-leap is popular but when anchored only by its tail it can bounce alarmingly in high winds. The salmon with delicately cut fins on Combe Cottage, Finstall, Hereford & Worcester, is half under, half above the water as it swirls to take its fly (*13.11*). Norfolk provides something rather unexpected: an actual trout portrait. The splendid six-pounder on Ham House, New Buckenham, provided great sport in the Test. He was reverently drawn round, complete with the notch out of his tail, for the weathervane, before providing still further enjoyment – smoked.

Other than salmon and trout, non-fishermen could probably name a pike. Several effectively predatory pike weathervanes, on a rebuilt mill at Sharnbrook, Beds., on the old cider mill at Combe Corner, Hereford & Worcester, and in Lucastes Avenue, Haywards Heath, Sussex, have virtually no known history.

Other species have scattered representatives. The fish on a barn at Gooderstone, Norfolk, peppered over sixty years ago by the youthful denizens of Oxburgh Rectory, resembles a gurnard. Another at Drayton, Oxon., rather like a tuna, with interesting projecting wire fins and jagged little waves on the pointer and the north cardinal, was designed and made by the owners. Yet another owner is an authority on bass, so this species, prized for both sport and commerce, graces Old Farm, Trebetherick, Corn. An unusual wooden fish with a metal tail, behind Embankment Road, Kingsbridge, Devon, may represent the locally important red mullet. Its carved eye and gill and scales still bear traces of colour. Wood weathers to look old quite quickly, especially in Devon's moist climate, and despite its primitive design this is probably less old than it looks (*13.12*). In contrast, Bradford on Avon, Wilts., has a fish weathervane which may be sixteenth-century. It surmounts the tiny chapel on the bridge, which later became a lock-up where offenders – John Wesley among them – cooled their heels 'over the water but under the fish'. The copper-gilt model, known as a Bradford gudgeon, is apparently actually a ruffe (*2.5*).

The four weathervanes placed on London's Natural History Museum in South Kensington on its completion in 1880 lack the accuracy and fine detailing of creatures in the building's carvings. However, they

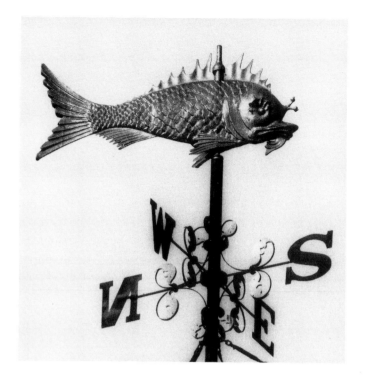

13.13   Fibreglass replica on Billingsgate Fishmarket,
City of London.

continue its dual theme; two existing species, a sculpin and a four-winged flying fish, balance two extinct species, a fossil form of lungfish and some kind of primitive spiny shark. Visually far more dominant, at eight feet long and on low, plain roofs, are the two Billingsgate vanes (*13.13*), no particular species but symbolic of all those sold at this City of London fish-market. These 1981 fibreglass replicas were made when the century-old cast-metal ones had to be left behind on the market's former listed premises.

A flying fish, scaly, full-bodied and painted bright yellow, on Newton Manor, Swanage, Dorset, was erroneously imagined to be one of the Billingsgate fish, sent down to Swanage in a ballast load of iron bollards etc in exchange for stone. It is striking where it is but would make no impression on Billingsgate's acres of roof. At Rollesby, Norfolk, a garage sheltering a Barracuda car, used at displays, has what is claimed to be the appropriate weathervane, but it is clearly a swordfish.

The Sussex coast is not exactly awash with sharks, but both St John's, Lewes, and Alciston churches have fish vanes, recently professionally identified as basking sharks. St Nicholas's church, Brighton, also had one, but perhaps others fought shy of using this shark pattern after the *Brighton Weekly* printed the following rather sour little verse in 1796:

Say why on Brighton's church we see
   A golden shark displayed
But that 'twas aptly meant to be
   An emblem of its trade.
Nor could the thing so well be told
   In any other way –
The town's a shark that lives on gold,
   The company its prey.

The copper thresher shark silhouette overlooking the Severn at Etloe, near Blakeney, Glos., evolved from the pooled resources of two brothers, a TV properties master and a pilot. Technical perfection – tested in a wind tunnel – complements the dramatic tail fin, cut gills and eye, and the imaginative concept of upturned and downturned arms to signify sunrise and sunset (*13.14*).

In contrast to sharks, there are some jolly little sea-horses on weathervanes. The silhouette on the old Market Building at Lytham, Lancs., perches upright on his arrow-tail. The charming little one on the Maltings, Writtle, Essex, balancing at an angle on his middle, was made in 1934 by a gifted young Cleminson from the family crest as a holiday task. His greeny-copper three-dimensional surface is carefully detailed, and he has great character. On Sea Point, Kingston Gorse, Sussex, a skeletal seahorse finial quite dwarfs its tiny arrow motif.

Finally, Bergerie Farmhouse, Beaulieu, Hants, provides the biggest surprise of all. The vane presents a creature of the most unsuitable square-fronted shape. It came from the USA, where economic importance outweighed its disadvantage of shape. It travelled to Britain alongside its owner on Concorde. It is an enormous whale.

Naturalists whose interests centre on insects, reptiles or plants will find

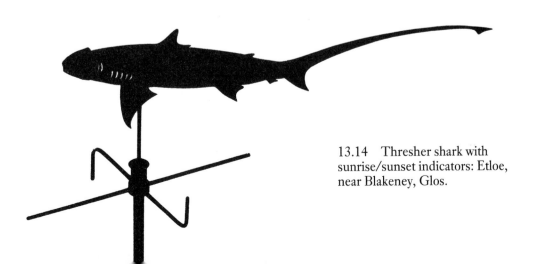

13.14   Thresher shark with sunrise/sunset indicators: Etloe, near Blakeney, Glos.

13.15   Gilded rose spray: Alciston, Sussex.

very thin weathervane pickings. Owners seem to choose these subjects only if they have a symbolic or other significance. So the toad, snail and bees appear in Chapter 7, the grasshopper in 17. Snakes, which Americans use on weathervanes both naturalistically and symbolically, have not captured the British imagination.

The aerial butterfly would seem natural weathervane material. It was a favourite Art Nouveau design, and silhouettes with delicately pierced wings appear in most nineteenth-century American catalogues. Some apparently even had wings that moved. We have found not one. Perhaps, now that butterfly 'parks' are proliferating, they will appear as trade-signs.

Botanical weathervanes are also uncommon. The Old Poultry Yard at Welbeck Abbey, Notts., has oak leaves cut into a banner, but even during botany's Victorian heyday plant shapes were more often formalized into patterns than used naturalistically. Perhaps plants sprouting from the roof smacked more of a building in decay than of prosperity. Today a few simple tree shapes identify Mulberry House or Elm Lodge, but the weight of flower heads tends to snap long, slender stems. So four tulips in bulb country, on Bank House Farm, Moulton Common, Lincs., sway with only short stems rising from a solid clump of foliage. More delicate is a swirl of rose leaves, with half-opened bloom and bud (*13.15*). Although this pretty gilded decoration dates only from 1970, marking the conversion of Candlemas House, Alciston, Sussex, no one can recall the design's origins.

The concentration of plant forms, however, is into mounts and decoration. Quantity castings are by no means to be despised, but the outstanding wrought-iron rose and thistle at Ogle, Northd., (*16.5*), recalls the ornament in early screens, and reminds us how rich, yet refined, ironwork can be.

14 Machinery and Transport

Man is puny and lazy but paradoxically loves power and speed. He very early began a love-affair with the horse, which, with the aid of the wheel and other ingenuities, enabled him to satisfy these passions. Then he transferred his devotion to the powerful machines and speedy vehicles he invented to supersede the horse.

Many vehicle weathervanes encapsulate these ideas of power and speed. They may also be advertisements or attract like-minded enthusiasts. However, streamlining has reduced characteristic outlines to such sameness that up-to-date cars or trains do not offer such interesting possibilities as older ones. And practically no owners choose to look at weathervanes of machines or vehicles associated exclusively with war.

Some designs which emphasize the job performed, rather than the machine or vehicle, may surface elsewhere, notably the ploughman in Chapter 8. But several other Rural Development Commission designs show working scenes in which the vehicle is as important as the man. Two designs are frequently found: a farmer driving either a pony from the back of a small two-wheeled cart, or two horses from the front of a farm waggon. Two others, of horses bolting with a waggon or hauling timber, are not favoured. In an apparently new motif on Cliftonville seafront, Kent, the horses lead their waggon downwind. What a pity the scrolling, made thoroughly tatty by salty gales, was not also renewed, for the motif is well detailed even though there is no driver. A version cast in aluminium at Baughton Forge has even more detail, with harness, wheels etc standing proud, and texture to the mane and hayload.

Horse-drawn vehicles on weathervanes, however, are primarily those for transporting people. What one might call the public sector is represented by the mail- or stage-coach ('It has no provision for outside passengers, yet has an open window') on Ersham Farm, Hailsham, Sussex. One does not suspect a trade-sign in such a weathervane, but many local brides have travelled in one of the horse-drawn vehicles collected here by an enthusiast. Highwaymen hold up stage-coaches with one, two or four horses, with or without alarmed passengers. The design sits oddly on the headquarters of the Royal Life-Saving Society at Studley, War., but it was left behind from Manor House days. Made cheaply and flimsily, this design can look like a cartoon, but Erme Wood Forge's good workmanship, in the large gilded example on Meadows Riversdale, Bourne End, Bucks., gives it a sturdy energy (*14.1*).

Rural Development Commission also offers two men in wide-brimmed hats driving light carriages. The side view showing only two wheels is on Little Plumstead school, Norfolk. A three-quarter view showing all four wheels is rarely found in all its detail, probably because it is fiddly and therefore costly. Both designs are good silhouette versions of the kind nineteenth-century American firms produced in three dimensions. A cruder silhouette with a high-stepping horse and uncomfortable-looking driving-seat on two solid wheels has spread to Norfolk, Hertfordshire, Sussex and Yorkshire, sometimes highly coloured and always with the same scrolling and curly-ended letters and arrowhead. Adding a small cab fits it for the Coach House, Goldhanger, Essex. At Leckhamsted, Berks., the owners of a version with two extremely prancing horses, cast in bronze at their own foundry, brought

14.1   The Rural Development Commission's highwayman scene: Bourne End, Bucks.

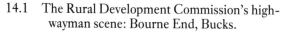

it to their new home to discover that what they had bought under another name had always been known locally as 'the Coach House'. A suitable finial for a stable at West Hanningfield, Essex, consists of a standing horse, harnessed to an empty buggy. Although several smiths have made the Rural Development Commission's attractive donkey cart carrying two girls, with dachshund escort, it has proved very elusive.

It was a big step from horse-power to the often enormous steam-driven engines that replaced it. The big names in the development of steam engines – Newcomen, Watt, Stephenson – were British. Perhaps that is why, although more efficient methods have supervened, Britons have such a passion for anything steam-driven. Self-propelled steam traction engines, driving much larger and heavier machinery than horses could, changed the face of farm work. In ploughing, first one engine with an arrangement of pulleys pulled the plough across the field, then later an engine at each end. Traction engines powered all sorts of farm and fairground equipment before moving into transport.

Weathervanes often re-create these traction engines with fanatical detail, but as silhouettes, not in the model form American manufacturers

14.2 Traction engine, patiently made: Wells-next-the-Sea, Norfolk.

favoured. Even so, it is the details – chains with links, wheelspokes, belts, levers etc – which mark out the vane of an enthusiast. The Rural Development Commission's popular example is found diversely from a Dyfed forge at Templeton to a Lincolnshire farm at Pinchbeck, where it is most lovingly painted.

A slightly different engine was painstakingly detailed with a fretsaw by Sam Parsons of Wells-next-the-Sea, Norfolk, a prime example of amateur patience and time balancing professional skills (*14.2*). Ironfounder Charles Wicksteed cannot have foreseen, when he gave Kettering, Northants, land for what is now Wicksteed Park, that, affectionately dubbed 'great-uncle Charlie in his ploughing engine', he would preside permanently over its public lavatories. He has a characterful stance, and his dog has turned to encourage him from the pointer. A steam thresher of the kind made by Burrell from *c.*1900 to 1935 was placed on the electricity pole at Springwell Farm, Little

Chesterford, Essex. 'It looked so bare when the barn was demolished,' explained the owner, 'and we had one in the yard for the chap to copy.'

A superb silhouette weathervane, accurate to every detail of a trade catalogue photograph, is another Burrell engine on Cranmer House, Fakenham. Designed by H. Neal, the county architect responsible for other fine weathervanes on Norfolk's Homes for the Elderly, it was made by Eric Stevenson in copper and weighs a hundredweight. The plaque reads: 'Norfolk-built Burrell tractor of 1903 designed specifically for farming. Single crank compound Devonshire-type 6NHP engine ...'. Another steam thresher, an arm-motif on Garrett's weathervane at Leiston, Suffolk (*7.10*), represents one of the firm's earlier products. A different Rural Development Commission design with a flat top attracts people more interested in showmen's engines, though we have found none decorated with miniature fairy lights or otherwise coloured.

On farms, steam-engines have been supplanted by tractors with internal combustion engines which, particularly in the last forty years, have revolutionized agriculture. Retired farm workers especially like to recall in their weathervanes the tractors that so dramatically eased their physical labour after World War II. 'That's my Marshall,' says one at Holme Hale, Norfolk. 'Those were our farm colours,' says another of a scarlet and blue weathervane at Hopton, Norfolk. Cook's Farm,

14.3   Tractor and combine harvester, now Rural Development Commission patterns: Rockland St Peter, Norfolk.

Pinchbeck, Lincs., shows how cleverly the bright and dark green livery of the farm's Deuz-Fahr tractor can be copied to give an illusion of detail that the simple silhouette actually lacks. The winner of a Young Farmer's Club welding competition, however, painted 'Huddersfield Agricultural Services' on his tractor and trailer weathervane, not the expected Fairfield Farm, Flinton, Humberside.

Harrows, rollers, fertilizer-distributors, drills, planters, hoes – all can be shown with tractors. The most vivid silhouette is probably with raised plough-shares, big and dramatic on a huge barn at Hindringham, Norfolk. Plantation Farm, Rockland St Peter, Norfolk, has a six-foot-eight-inch weathervane depicting the caterpillar crawler tractor and Class combine harvester which, as the first in the area, were their owner's delight. The Rural Development Commission made working drawings for Overton's, the local forge (*14.3*). The designs have subsequently become widely popular, though elsewhere the two machines appear separately. Bill Cordaroy made an interesting farm sprayer for a house at Happisburgh, Norfolk, a silhouette body but with arms projecting sideways, aeroplane-wise.

After the limited capacity of stage-coaches, the carriage-loads of passengers that could be harnessed to steam-engines saw in those engines a symbol of freedom. Now they need no longer take whatever job offered within walking distance; on rare days off they could travel speedily to somewhere enjoyable. How much this perception subconsciously underlies the continuing popularity of steam-locomotive weathervanes is impossible to assess, but they persist despite the phasing-out of steam during the 1960s. The response to modern trains is decidedly cool.

Usually an engine silhouette stands either alone, or on an arrow. An ex-railwayman at Brough, Cumbria, has added a slotted metal strip (a DIY shelving track?) to simulate the track quite effectively. An enthusiast at Lavendon, Bucks., has utilized the thickened arrow tail as the engine's body, with cab and steam rising above it and wheels projecting below. A loco is not, apparently, a design people envisage cut into a banner.

Railway stations, the most obvious sites for locomotive weathervanes, rarely have them. In 'railway towns', locomotive vanes achieve municipal building status, but elsewhere they largely express personal taste. Generally they represent classes rather than particular engines, though inevitably the latter are more interesting. A note on the architect's 1963 drawings for Sidney House Home for the Elderly, Stalham, Norfolk, is as precise as the weathervane itself: '4-4-2 tank locomotive which travelled on the North Walsham/Stalham/Gt Yarmouth line. Built 1909, scrapped 1942. One of a series of three only locos to be entirely built in Norfolk, in the Midland and Great Northern Railway Works at Melton Constable. Line closed 1959' (*14.4*). Yet an engine of the greatest historical significance, *Locomotion I*, which opened the Stockton & Darlington Railway in 1825, is very simply represented in Stockton-on-Tees Market Square, Cleveland. British Rail's headquarters in York carries a steaming locomotive, said to be a B13 type and not the former tank engine, on an arrow seven feet six inches in length. It is a pity that an ugly strengthening rod introduces awkwardly into the design on one side, but pleasing to see the NER plaques still encircling the spherical mount. An enthusiastic owner at Dower Cottage, North Curry, Som., who made a 4-4-2 engine 'of the kind used on the Brighton line' must have been familiar with the York weathervane, for the smoke shape and cut-outs within it are identical.

For the apogee of loco weathervanes go, appropriately enough, to Crewe, Ches. Stephenson's *Rocket*, having won the Rainhill Trials in 1829, ensured that steam locos were used on the Liverpool/Manchester railway. A whole national rail network was stimulated, and Crewe was born. After seventy-five years its proud new municipal buildings honoured Stephenson's invention in a superb weathervane (*14.5*). Astonishingly, it is quite undocumented. Its exquisite scale-model details would be less remarkable on an American railroad station: here, it is an exciting novelty. Three cheers for binoculars and telephoto lenses.

14.4   Local loco: home for the elderly, Stalham, Norfolk.

14.5 Model of
Stephenson's *Rocket*:
municipal buildings,
Crewe, Ches.

On the roads it seems incredible that already in 1829, the same year as Stephenson's *Rocket*, a steam carriage could drive at a steady 15mph. Telford and McAdam had improved road surfaces beyond recognition, and with internal combustion engines being developed by the 1860s, mechanized road transport should have leapt ahead. But resentful stage-coach and, later, railway owners contrived punitive tolls on steam-driven road carriages, and the speed limits on any private mechanical road vehicle were screwed down from 10 to 4 mph, in apparently direct relation to their increasing efficiency and numbers. So the initiative passed to the Continent. The British car's escort with his red flag became a joke. Sadly, we could not find a weathervane depicting this scene, though one is known to have existed at Clun, Shropshire.

From this virtually standing start, the internal combustion engine has accelerated through dream and status to necessity. How extraordinary then that on weathervanes the horseless carriage should still be so vastly outnumbered by the carriageless horse.

Car weathervanes, chiefly silhouettes though a few have surface detail, swing mainly above private homes, not always on the garage, and flaunt their owners' love-affairs. Weathervane representations tend to stop at about World War II. Individual makes, even models, then still had distinctive outlines, increasingly smoothed out since in the interests of aerodynamics. Inevitably, there are also a few nondescript representations that no manufacturer would willingly acknowledge.

Theoretically, any car weathervane could be as old as the car it

14.6   Road hog: Rugely, Staffs.

14.7   Morgan; an unusual view: Cradley, Hereford & Worcester.

14.8　Service-station vane:
　　　　Brundall, Norfolk.

14.9　Playing its part in testing brake-linings: Sherburn in Elmet,
　　　　Yorks.

14.10 Fire crew, 1934: Norwich Fire Station, Norfolk.

depicts. In practice, those of veteran or vintage cars emerge as another nostalgic group. 1930s cars may either be nostalgic or a contemporary announcement of status achieved. Post-war models are likely to be family pets.

Early cars, themselves full of character, acquire even more from their drivers. On one of several owner-made weathervanes at Lyncroft, Batesway, Rugeley, Staffs., a veteran vehicle is propelled by a delightfully moustachioed old boy, patently an early road-hog (*14.6*). Above a modern bungalow in Wendlebury, Oxon., drives a small open tourer with a passenger seated behind the driver, both in attitudes suggesting dizzy speed. Variations on an amusing episode in which a policeman halts a car, sometimes looking at his watch to indicate he has caught it speeding, sometimes apparently allowing a wandering dog priority, were popular in the 1930s. Perhaps they were not sturdily made, for they all seem to have vanished.

Car weathervanes which seek to create some illusion of a setting by a signpost on the pointer really should carry through the idea by giving the car a driver. Few do: the owners are more concerned with their car as portrait. Instructions are often most precise. Hubbard's made for a garden mast behind Christchurch Road, Norwich, Norfolk, 'a blue-grey Jaguar Mk7'. Blue-grey dissolves into the sky, however, so a cheerful red Jaguar now heads along a green road towards the signpost.

Car portraits are legion. David Harvey produced a 1934 Lagonda

Rapier for an owner in Nup End Lane, Wingrave, Bucks. Morgans arouse passionate devotion, with an especially enthusiastic club in Malvern, Hereford & Worcester, where they were made. On Nethergreen Farm at nearby Cradley, the Morgan three-wheeler weathervane was won in a club event. It is interesting in being the only weathervane we found with the car shown head-on instead of in profile. This view, as seen by any approaching Morgan devotee, is quite unmistakable and announces clearly that here he will find congenial conversation (*14.7*).

With owners such sticklers for accuracy, it is amusing to find the Rural Development Commission's vintage car claimed variously as a Renault, a Bullnose Morris and an Austin! This design responds well to colour, yellow with black hood at Barroway Drove, Norfolk, crimson at Donington, Lincs. Here it does duty as a trade sign on Burdall's Service Station. A cast open tourer with some surface detailing performs the same function at Stanton, Suffolk. Brundall Garage, Norfolk, has a saloon car, the driver crouched over the wheel, willing its empty tank to carry it the last few inches to the petrol pump, all 1947 vintage (*14.8*). Another Jaguar type, at Sherburn in Elmet, Yorks., is among the interesting few weathervanes on active service. Brake-linings are tested on this site, and the wind's known direction and strength contribute to evaluating how heat-sensitive or rapidly cooled by airflow a material is. One of the staff made the weathervane, of a ¾-inch thick asbestos-type brake-lining substance (*14.9*).

Weathervanes depicting public cabs and trams were either not made or have not survived. Nor are trolley-buses, for example, made now as objects of nostalgia, even though so many people used them in Britain from 1911 right up to 1955. The old bus station in Ardrossan, Strathclyde, now a factory, has recently replicated its late-1920s coach vane, but the modern touring coach at Bourton on the Water, Glos., despite its use as a trade-sign, is too plain a rectangle to be successful. The Ardrossan coach, like most cars, is lightened by cut-out windows. The Bourton example's painted windows are visible only at close range, and even then it appears to be travelling at night with all the blinds down.

Lorries too have stark outlines, and as weathervane choices they are restricted to those whose living they supply. They range from a little pick-up truck at Witchford, Cambs., to huge articulated haulage trucks. At Chawton, Hants, this strikes a rather strident note next to Jane Austen's quiet garden. At Kniveton, Derby., the Foden lorry wears the firm's red and grey colours; green and yellow are those of a haulage contractor at Oving, Bucks., whose eight-wheeled flat-bed lorry dominates his garage. A break-down truck with a Mini hooked to its crane was made by a friend for a farm at Rayne, Essex. Had the silhouette, like the rest of the vane, been made of wood, one might have suspected he whittled it while he waited.... Heavy machinery has usually only specialized appeal. Thus an employee made the weathervane of a ten-ton Burrell steam road roller for the Essex Highways' depot at Thorrington, and a garden centre at Clacton, Essex, flies an antiquated digger above its 300-year-old-barn.

Professional accuracy can be assumed in weathervanes of such specialized vehicles as fire appliances. A Bacton Close home in South Wootton, Norfolk, displays one presented by colleagues as a wedding gift. The Denis RS series engine is beautifully painted with Norfolk Fire Service colours and insignia. Its number plate, PJB 1 Y, proclaims that PJB experienced a once-in-a-lifetime occasion in that year of Y registration. Fire stations often lack weathervanes, but Norwich, Norfolk, has a delightful one (*14.10*). The architect Stanley Livock created for the new 1934 building a real Trumpton crew, one ringing an alarm bell as their Merryweather engine chugs towards a fire, guided by a lad in school uniform. Later the trailer pump was added to increase the vane's efficiency. The boy, not surprisingly since he had been temporarily taped on with sticky tape, bit the dust in the 1987 hurricane. Now he is properly secured again. Gold paint has replaced the scarlet, black and white, returning the vane to some semblance of its original appearance, genuine gold leaf being beyond the voluntary contributions of the station officers.

Up till the last war, using the roads for pleasure meant cycling. A cycle is not an easy weathervane subject: it has little solidity and too much weight forward, especially in the favourite pennyfarthing. An arrow-tail helps efficiency. The clever 'old ordinary' made by an engineering lecturer and cycle enthusiast at Elder Cottage, Chattisham, Suffolk, is a tiny scale model, spokes correctly arranged, the rider's legs straddling the machine and separate arms holding each handlebar. Another enthusiast marked his collection on Crow Hall Estate, Denver, Norfolk, with an aluminium silhouette of a lady-front tandem of about 1898 (*14.11*). This machine required a measure of agreement. Nominally the lady steered, but a rod coupling both handlebars enabled the gentleman to out-manoeuvre her with his superior strength. However, the only brake was in the hands of the lady.

Today's pleasure-seekers on the roads are probably caravanners. They do not erect on their houses weathervanes of cars towing caravans, rightly fearing that these might be misinterpreted as camp-site signs. The

14.11   Lady-front tandem: Denver, Norfolk.

romantic horse-drawn Romany van, on Ivy Cottage, Walcot, Humberside, a reminder of one formerly owned, is used to advertise modern caravan sites at Hockley, Essex, and Wells-next-the-Sea, Norfolk. In contrast, the sign for a caravan site at Point Clear, Essex, is bang up-to-date, a static van, uncompromisingly rectangular and given windage only by its arrow, which therefore points downwind.

All the weathervane vehicles considered so far have been built for journeying on land. Enormous distances challenge and extensive water barriers defeat them. The old solution to the latter, to build ships, has produced so many weathervanes – Britain is an island, after all – that they have their own chapter (15). The other, specifically twentieth-century answer is the aeroplane.

Aeroplanes are as 'natural' for an airborne position as birds, yet while so many bird weathervanes are flat, a great many aeroplanes are modelled; indeed, children's cast-off toys perched on garden poles as bird-scarers are distractingly common. Weathervanes span the whole history of aeroplanes, for once giving equal weight to the romance of early designs and the striking shapes of contemporary machines.

The Red Baron's 'air circus', commanded by Goering after Richthofen's death, flew over Sussex in the First World War, which accounts for a wooden Fokker biplane at Carter's Farm, Gun Hill. But The Briery, Troutbeck, Cumbria, a fine Edwardian mansion now converted into apartments, has the most fascinating plane weathervane. It reproduces in surprisingly accurate detail a 1909 Blériot Type XI machine (*14.12*). The original owner must surely have been personally involved with the considerable aviation activity in the Windermere area at that period. One longs for some documentary enlightenment. The Troutbeck weathervane challenges the supposed uniqueness of the one on the spa-house in Poland Springs, Maine, USA, erected to celebrate Blériot's visit with his plane, and his successes in local air-races there.

The American tradition of making three-dimensional weathervanes persists: Gary Powers was presented with a weathervane model of the U-2 aircraft shot down in 1958 over the USSR. In Britain, later aeroplanes are more likely to be silhouettes. Through Hodgson's Dakota and David Harvey's Jet Ranger and other helicopters to John Allen's Concorde, the story is brought up to the present.

14.12   Blériot's plane, 1909; vane probably contemporary: The Briery, Troutbeck, Cumbria.

15 Ships

Salt still courses strongly in the island blood of the British, if ship weathervanes are anything to go by. This group encompasses the greatest number of really spectacular weathervanes, executed with a loving skill beyond the mere tug of purse-strings, so expressive of the makers' deep satisfaction that our own is stirred in response. Ships are beloved.

No landlocked county resists them entirely, but the finest ship weathervanes do tend not to have sailed too far inland. The east and west coasts of Scotland and parts of Wales, none too flush with any weathervanes, enjoy several excellent examples.

The variety of ships depicted is apparently endless, most of them north European, although deepest Sussex has been invaded by a Mediterranean war galley and Chinese junk. There are Viking longships and Roman galleys, with oars to supplement sail-power and to steer. There are medieval cogs with mast and single sail planted amidships in their walnut-shell hulls, looking as though they have sailed straight off a medieval seal. There are sailing warships and merchantmen of the fifteenth to the nineteenth century. The earlier styles are in the south, later ones further north, reflecting the northward move of shipbuilding as wood gave place to iron and steel. There are supposed portraits of famous historical ships, and sleek modern racing craft, powered fishing vessels and twentieth-century warships. Especially among smaller vessels intended for coastal or inland rather than ocean work, there are regional craft, though it may require local knowledge to recognize them for what they are. Even symbolic church ships tend to re-create vessels the craftsmen were familiar with. And since to be waterborne constitutes many a Briton's idea of heaven, there are countless loving, if not always successful, representations of the family cruiser or dayboat.

These are broad categories, however, and any assumption that one could absorb the history of British shipping from weathervanes would be most unwise. Of course, many designers and makers, especially those with seafaring knowledge, will have laboured to record as accurately as possible the hull shape, the height and disposition of masts, the size and set of sails, the rigging that controls them, and myriad smaller details. But real accuracy would be against all the odds. Even a three-dimensional 'scale model' will seethe with compromises: for the sake of the strength to withstand aerial strains, proper balance and functioning, adjustments to perspective, and practical constructional considerations.

In particular, any square-rigged ship – that is, almost all until the nineteenth century – is problematical in three-dimensional form under full sail. If it points its bow into the wind in the conventional way, its sails, billowing forwards as square sails do, will be contradictorily implying a wind from almost behind. Moreover, they will constantly try to turn the vane away from the wind and set up great strains. One answer is to turn the ship and let it run downwind, sail off the back of the arrow, with its sails filled. This looks more authentic, but it creates terrific windage and a real danger of the spindle snapping completely. A three-dimensional ship is also so eye-catching that the observer is likely to miss the arrow pointing in the opposite direction.

15.1   Sails half turned on South Shields
Town Hall, Tyne and Wear.

A better solution more frequently adopted is to show the ship as though manoeuvring in harbour, with sails furled to the yards and only a mizzen set. This fore and aft sail at the stern becomes the vane's natural tail. Even then, pennants often stream contrarily forwards from the mast-heads as though to a stern gale, destroying the carefully contrived authenticity.

A constructional compromise that can show square-rigged ships under full canvas is a three-dimensional hull, but with sails cut from flat sheet, their three dimensions implied by sharply curved outlines. A gilt ship of this kind on Liverpool parish church now appears as a finial, but it must surely have been a weathervane: there is no logic to its thick tubular mainmast except as a spindle socket.

Other failures of authenticity may stem from guesswork about underwater lines or from nautical ignorance. Fewer and fewer men, even sailors, now have any experience of how the complicated rigging on these large sailing-vessels worked. Repaired rigging may therefore owe more to imagination than to history.

All these problems are less acute in three-dimensional weathervanes if they depict fore-and-aft rigged schooners, sloops, ketches, yawls, yachts. These can head into the wind carrying all their canvas with less loss of realism.

Whichever kind of ship it depicts, a flat weathervane is an exercise in illusion. The best excellently simulate three dimensions. Others make no pretence and exaggerate, using impossibly raked masts and blousy sails with unashamedly decorative emphasis. Sailors in any case have to accept that ship weathervanes point *directly* into the wind as no ship can be made to do.

Assessing weathervane ships is further complicated by the fact that ships themselves are difficult to date within 400 years or so. North European ships of about the year 1400 had acquired the squared stern and rudder but still carried one more or less central mast and one square sail. Within only fifty years they had adopted three masts and five or six sails, plus a lateen mizzen. Give or take the occasional extra mast or a taller mast for an extra sail, this remained the norm for merchant shipping for the next 400 years. Similarly, warships developed high 'castles' for fighting, then gunports between the castles to accommodate the heaviest guns, all by the year 1600. Then they too remained basically unchanged for 250 years. No sailing warships were built after about 1840, but highly successful and competitive clippers continued trading. Within this whole period, therefore, and especially between 1600 and about 1850, changes were so gradual as to be scarcely discernible by the layman.

15.2 *Santa Maria*, safe with only her mizzen set: Victoria Embankment, London.

15.3 Sir Arthur Mee's *Golden Hind*, vulnerable with all sails set: Beeston, Nottingham.

Add problems of recognizing ships to problems of presenting them, and it becomes clear why even maritime experts prefer to describe a weathervane ship as 'of sixteenth-century style' or 'having an eighteenth-century look', even when it purports to be a particular ship. The style of the ship is in any case no guide to the age of the weathervane. As ever, the overwhelming majority date from within the last 150 years.

More ship weathervanes are three-dimensional, and spectacular for it, than any other group except perhaps cocks. They form a distinct sub-group, demanding extended consideration independently of silhouette ships. It is interesting that two notable early ones are Scottish. 'Att Kirkcudbright the sexteine day of Ayprill 1646', run the old town council minutes, 'the bailzies and counsall convenit for the tyme have givine full powar and commissioun to George Meik merchand ... to bring home ane ship maid of bras for putting upone the top of the steipill'. There is still a ship, believed to be the original, on the old Tolbooth of this town in Dumfries and Galloway.

In Glasgow, on the seventeenth-century Merchants' Steeple, a splendid lookout for merchants awaiting their ships returning up the Clyde, the gilt ship retains its 'beak' and little circular castle on the bowsprit, but a missing mast needs replacing. The vane's historical interest warrants it.

Apart from a very occasional suggestion of stylized waves, these large 'models' are not presented as if floating on water. Their huge bulk sails through the clouds apparently unsupported. The ship on South Shields town hall, Tyne & Wear (*15.1*), with its overall length of six feet six inches and height from keel to masthead of over seven feet, is by no means exceptional even in Britain and is frequently exceeded in the USA. Such a vane is likely to have been hammered from malleable copper sheet, rigged with sixty or seventy yards of copper or bronze wire rope, and probably took over 200 skilled man-hours to produce. Ballasted with lead, it is a formidable object to balance on a vertical rod. (Imagine manoeuvring an unconscious ten-stone man in such circumstances ...) It needs a twenty-foot steel axle in a stone casing to support it. Clearly any interference with such a weathervane's free rotation will quickly bring down individual sails, if not the whole vane. Worn sails and rigging, removed to make way for a new set, can seldom have suffered such indignity, however, as those of South Shields in 1921, which were refashioned into souvenir toasting-forks.

Even in 1910 this South Shields weathervane cost £108 – near enough £5,500 in 1988 terms. It is an exception among weathervanes of this quality in being allowed to appear in its underwear – usually they were dressed in expensive gold leaf. The increasing cost of re-gilding means that many of these ships have now acquired the blue-green copper patina that is more in tune with contemporary taste.

The household budgets of mere ordinary mortals could seldom stretch to weathervanes of this calibre, but some beautiful three-dimensional ships adorn various aristocratic residences. In Norfolk, York Cottage, now Sandringham Estate Offices, has a small, beautifully executed gilded carrack. Was it erected by King Edward VII to welcome his visitors there? Or by King George V, while York Cottage was his beloved private retreat? No answers are known. On London's Victoria Embankment Lord Astor placed another superb example on his town house, later the Accountants' Hall and now home to Messrs Smith & Nephew. He commissioned it from J. Starkie Gardner, eminent ironworker and author of standard works on wrought iron. It portrays the caravel *Santa Maria* in which Columbus discovered America (*15.2*).

The fine model of a seventeenth-century ship on Anmer Hall, Norfolk, was a gift to Captain (later Admiral) Sir Frederick Hamilton on his retirement from the Naval Gunnery School at Portsmouth. Even in 1908 it must have been an unusually lavish presentation. The vessel is unnamed but appears to have a carved wooden hull supported by iron straps. Sturdy but delicate ratlines, coiled wire rigging and a huge ensign give it real presence on the small tower built especially for it. It must surely still give great pleasure to the present owners, the Duke and Duchess of Kent.

The no-expense-spared air of an elaborate three-dimensional ship weathervane naturally arouses curiosity on more ordinary dwellings. Which came first, the copper galleon on an attractive dovecote turret or the name 'Galleon Cottage', Aldbury, Herts.? Why should a full-rigged nineteenth-century merchantman, presumably originally with sails, have adorned a farm building at Acton Lodge, Acton Bridge, Ches., since the turn of the century? And so on.

The ship weathervane on a garden mast in Rydal Drive, Beeston, Notts. (*15.3*), is better documented. Originally it soared above the Darenth valley in Kent on the gazebo of Eynsford Hill. Here from 1913 lived Arthur Mee, famed for his editorship of the *Children's Encyclopedia* and *Children's Newspaper*, among other things. Mee himself explained that Hyder's Forge copied a silver model of Drake's *Golden Hind*, given to him by Queen Elizabeth I. He also described the little 'treasure chest' on the deck. Made of Roman lead lined with Saxon oak, it contained a bullet from the Spanish Armada, a sliver of stone from Drake's home, and an English shilling which had touched Drake's Drum. The beautiful weathervane, restored to its pristine white and gold glory, with painted Tudor roses on its pennants, is back in Mee's home town and remains in the family. The little chest still contains its 'treasures'. But why? Where did they come from? Such tantalizing gaps.

Over ninety per cent of three-dimensional ships, however, grace public buildings of various kinds. They look particularly well on churches, although *The Antiquary* commented in 1888 that, ' ... a kind of fatality has attended the churches employing ship vanes', citing four London churches, all destroyed or demolished. Portsmouth, however, is undismayed: hence the careful preservation and replacement of its symbolic 'Golden Barque', mentioned before, after gale damage in 1954. Several City of London churches retain once fine weathervanes, particularly of nineteenth-century ships, but inevitably they are of less significance to the non-Anglican communities the churches now serve, and their obvious disrepair is ominous. The weathervane vessel on the 1834 Barony Church of Scotland in Ardrossan, Strathclyde, looks contemporary with its building, while that on nearby Fairlie parish church has sleeker, almost racing lines. In complete contrast, the architect of Our Lady of Ransom, a 1901 church at Eastbourne, Sussex, opted for a medieval cog of copper.

Christian piety overflowed into schools, orphanages, almshouses etc, often also generously surmounted with three-dimensional ship weathervanes. The Ogilvie School, part of the Ogilvie Trust transferred to Clacton, Essex, in 1913 as a school for delicate children, has a three-masted gilded Tudor galleon with flying sails. Essex County

15.4　Medieval cog: Morecambe College of Further Education, Lancs.

Council now keep it in excellent repair. Not so, alas, the weathervane on the Heritage Craft School, Chailey, Sussex, originally in the philanthropy of 'The Guild of Brave Poor Things', a description of crippled children not to our present taste. The weathervane, with four masts but no sails or rigging, is scarcely recognizable as Henry VIII's *Great Harry*, England's first double-decker warship, resplendent with all sails drawing and pennants flying, as it was erected in 1932 and still recorded forty years ago. It illustrates with sad clarity both the damage sustainable by square-rigged ships sailing downwind and the difficulty of meeting hideous repair costs.

In 1933 a tea-planter, grateful for the safe convoy of his ships during World War I, left his entire fortune to the Admiralty. It enabled them to move their thousand-pupil school, the Great Hospital for the Sons of Seamen, founded in 1712 with a mere twelve lads, from Greenwich to Holbrook, Suffolk. An impressive copper *Victory* tops Nelson House, part of the original complex, built by men who walked the eight miles from Ipswich on the off-chance of obtaining work. Its two hundredweight is perilously overweight for its cupola in this exposed location, but the workmanship is superb.

An attractive medieval cog, white-painted and with its hull interestingly ribbed to suggest the planking, tops what is now Morecambe College of Further Education, Lancs. (*15.4*). The Ship Institute, built at Newlyn, Corn., by the Bolitho family in 1911 for

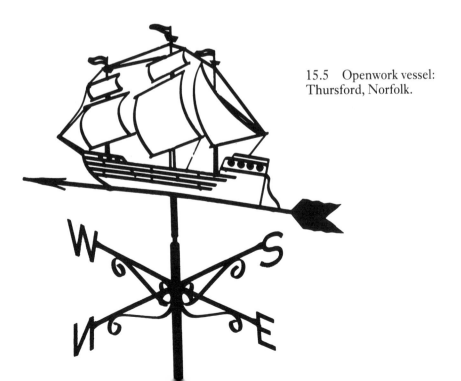

15.5   Openwork vessel: Thursford, Norfolk.

working seamen, carries a beautiful representation of an eighteenth-century ship of the line made, appropriately enough, in Newlyn copper. Great Yarmouth's Fishermen's Hospital, was to accommodate 'twenty decayed fishermen' according to its founders in 1702. The kind of herring buss they would have worked at that date forms its gilded weathervane, though illustrations suggest it was erected some years after the foundation. It shared in recent refurbishment paid for by a public appeal which has ensured the Hospital's continuance as retirement accommodation for those who made their living from the sea.

Great Yarmouth is also one of many places with three-dimensional ship weathervanes on their town halls. This one is a gilded nineteenth-century herring lugger of the kind which operated out of the harbour the Victorian Town Hall overlooks. The Court House weathervane at Irvine, Strathclyde, also represents a nineteenth-century vessel. For twelve years it lay in a yard, and while it is good to see it repainted white and re-erected, its top-hamper looks incomplete.

Some authorities deliberately contrast their modern buildings with an old craft. County Hall in Exeter has a gilded medieval cog weathervane known as 'the Devon ship', as seen on Westward TV. In the past, civic authorities have preferred near-contemporary vessels. In 1780 Rochester Guildhall, Kent, replaced its hundred-year-old pennant – which had cost all of £5 – with a gilded warship six feet long. Tradition long claimed it as Admiral of the Fleet Sir Cloudesley Shovell's *Association*, commissioned in weathervane form by the town council to commemorate him. The present authorities avoid any positive attribution but have bestowed some recent restoration work on what is a considerable civic asset, whatever its identity. Whitby, Yorks, sites its commemorative weathervane model of the *Resolution* not on a civic building but on a mast at West Cliff, near the statue of its captain, the navigator Captain Cook.

Institutions or corporate bodies with watery connections also naturally favour three-dimensional ship weathervanes. On the City of London's Trinity House, Britain's principal lighthouse and pilotage authority, the vane appears to depict a galleon of the sixteenth century, when its charter was granted by Henry VIII. Aberdeen Harbour Board's assumption that its schooner-type weathervane is contemporary with the 1885 building is supported by the style of the arms and lettering, but sadly they know nothing more about it. A particularly beautiful Tudor vessel above the offices to Lloyd's Register of Shipping in Fenchurch Street, City of London, must lift many City spirits. It closely resembles the one at Sandringham, with the interesting additional feature of the

15.6   Ancient Mediterranean galley: Hadlow Down, Sussex.

iron basket for a beacon light mounted on the stern.

On commercial premises with no obvious shipping connections, a costly three-dimensional weathervane tacitly acknowledges how fundamentally trade underpins prosperity. Businesses are concerned less with the style of the vessel than with making some topical or regional statement, while conferring dignity on the building and indirectly on themselves. The Rural Development Commission's Viking ship on a riverside tea-room at Hoveton, Norfolk, recalls Viking penetration of these East Anglian waters in the ninth century. Metropole Court on Minehead seafront, Som., has an attractive early Tudor vessel with an emblem cut into its square sail, canvas stitching lines on the mizzen, and an anchor. It is thought to date from when the building was a hotel, rather than from its earlier days as a maharajah's palace. The medieval cog on Lloyds Bank's Oxford branch was probably inherited from former occupants. NatWest's weathervane at Dartmouth, Devon, is a later barque, interestingly lit from below.

Famous individual stores have chosen ship weathervanes too. Opened in 1925, Liberty of London's Great Marlborough Street frontage in Westminster is Tudor in style, resembling a row of intimate shops rather than a department store. Its teak and oak came from two old men-of-war, HMS *Hindustan* and HMS *Impregnable*. (Over 3,000 hundred-year-old oaks had gone into the *Impregnable*.) A faithful gilded copper model of the *Mayflower* above the main entrance at once sustained the building's period air and hinted at the spirit of enterprise which brought quality merchandise from distant lands to Liberty's.

The Bristol & West Building Society is among the select few firms to patronize work of this kind today. It crowned its early 1980s building on Broad Quay, Bristol, with a splendid weathervane reproducing explorer John Cabot's flagship, sails elegantly furled, apart from a graceful mizzen. Richard Quinnell's forge made it in copper and bronze, finished with gold leaf. It turns with a grace that belies its weight of several hundredweight. Across hurtling traffic it faces an interesting comparison, a gilded barque set above former dockside warehouses, now the Watershed Arts Centre. With bare yard-arms, this is altogether simpler, but balanced by fancier lettering and some delicate scrolling. On the pleasant new Lion and Lamb precinct, Long Garden Walk, Farnham, Surrey, the developers Arundell Securities required a weathervane to correspond to the 1930s *Golden Hind* on the town hall, also their responsibility. The development coincided with the raising of the *Mary Rose*, so they commissioned her in three-dimensional gilt, flying downwind, from David Gillespie of Dippenhall Hall nearby. Would that more companies shared this enlightened policy of incorporating artwork into new buildings and developments.

Smaller, more modern yachts rarely rise to costly three-dimensional construction. Apart from a pleasant yacht on a boathouse at Rippling Waters, Marlow, Bucks., which looks Edwardian but about which no information is available, the most interesting sounding one was made by Hyder's. To commemorate Sir Francis Chichester's circumnavigation of 1966–7, it enclosed a model of *Gipsy Moth* in a hollow globe, but its whereabouts have not been traced.

Inevitably, silhouette ships are far less spectacular. But they do suit more ordinary premises – and pockets – than the three-dimensional aristocrats, as the Rural Development Commission's eight silhouette to two three-dimensional patterns suggest. Silhouettes too cover the entire historical range from Roman onwards, and are more suited to the illustration of inland and coastal boats. Technical variations include what is effectively an open-work line drawing, on Rose Cottage, Thursford, Norfolk (*15.5*). Only the arrowtail offers much functional surface. Few silhouettes are gilded; some are coloured. Many are home-made, with the range of quality that that implies.

Some silhouette ships have sailed well inland. A perverse sense of humour adorned a pub with an oared galley weathervane and named it 'The Sea Around us' – at Loughborough, Leics., just about as far from the sea as possible. How doubly perverse to render the joke pointless by changing the name to 'Junction 23'. Also well inland, on Anne's, Hadlow Down, Sussex, is an ancient Mediterranean ship propelled by oars and sails together and bristling with spears and tridents (*15.6*). Circumstantial evidence suggests that the Edwardian owner of nearby Buxted House may have provided it when he enlarged and beautified Anne's for his mother. As a founder of the Shell Oil Company, he might naturally have been expected to be interested in the eastern Mediterranean. The vane was probably made in this area of Sussex, where ironwork is still a speciality. Still more startling is a Chinese junk, made to remind previous owners of Appletrees, Northiam, Sussex, of their sojourn in Hong Kong.

Most inland ship weathervanes are less exotic and often merely impressionistic. Gainford church, Dur., and a farm at Stockerston, Leics., are typical, with vaguely sixteenth- and seventeenth-century vessels respectively, both designs duplicated elsewhere. Less usual is a fifteenth-century-type craft with 'striped' cut sails, oddly placed above Whitestone reservoir in Hampstead, Greater London (*6.1*). At Wotter, Devon, black hull and scarlet sails on a powder-blue mast with brilliant yellow letters jolly the rainiest Dartmoor days. In contrast a sailing-barge on a mast at Ivy House Farm near Leek, Staffs., is soberly convincing with tanned sails.

Just how arbitrary the term 'inland' is in Britain, laced with waterways easily navigated by the smaller craft of earlier centuries, is indicated by the Roman galley atop a Home for the Elderly at Brundall, Norfolk. A Roman repair depot on the River Yare near here served their camp at Caistor St Edmunds. Eric Stevenson perforated vessel and sails to create the most masterly *trompe-l'œil* effect, and the dramatic mounting – a double circlet supporting a stack of Roman spears – reminds us sharply that civilization was not always benign (*15.7*).

For a glimpse of the breadth of choice in silhouette sailing-ships, a few random landfalls from a clockwise whizz round the coastline must suffice.

South-west – Sevententh-century type ships are popular, e.g. Sennen Road, Land's End, where it helps the owner plan excursions for his sea-bird studies. An elegant topsail cutter on Rodmoor House garage, Portishead, Som., and simpler cutters surmounting each apartment

15.7   Roman galley: Brundall, Norfolk.

15.8   Viking ship: Broadstairs,
Kent.

block of the new development around Bristol docks.

Wales and Merseyside – Gwynedd: bigger nineteenth-century schooners and fully rigged four-masters, preferably in colour. Notable examples are on a mast along Llanbedrog's main road and across the peninsula, where Nefyn once boasted 200 master mariners among its 2,000 inhabitants. A three-foot-long brig such as was built here to carry slate last century was painstakingly fretsawed from sheet steel by parishioners just after the war, replicating the corroded 1880s original. Its black hull, white sails and red pennants contrast strikingly with the grey stone church. Merseyside: curvaceous but unidentifiable craft above curving fleur-de-lys decoration have topped a low garage in Park Road West, Southport, for over sixty years. Across the Ribble, in Lancashire, Lytham St Anne's pier weathervane hints at a pilot boat.

Scotland – Girvan, Strathclyde, decorates its 'stumpy Steeple' (ex-tolbooth, ex-prison cells) with a stylized ship which, with the encouraging motto 'Always sailing, never sinking', forms the town's arms. Silhouette ships often sail on water, but Girvan's rippling waves and slightly waved north pointer are unusually attractive. Another pilot boat, its gold-painted sail cut with a crown and 1986, tops a retirement home on Dunbar shore, in Lothian.

East Coast – Cleveland: Redcar's Victorian-looking clock tower has a stylized medieval copper cog. Norfolk: Wells-next-the-Sea church

15.9   Decorative *Golden Hind*:
Chapel of HMS *Raleigh*, Torpoint,
Corn.

flies a painted seventeenth-century merchantman. The nineteenth-century clipper surmounting Cromer's former council offices is said to have replaced a punning crow weathervane: local fishermen complained that this bird of ill omen was jinxing their catches. Mundesley's seventeenth-century warship, supported by leaping fish (probably cod here) instead of scrolls, is mounted on a seafront mast. Suffolk: a Walberswick house enjoys a copper war lugger.

Kent – One of the jolliest Viking ships imaginable finishes off an amazingly ornate sea-front shelter in Broadstairs. Its cheerful dragon figurehead, red and yellow striped sail and row of multi-coloured shields make a brave show against stormclouds and blue sky alike (*15.8*). Early this century Fordwich church appropriately replaced its cock weathervane with the lion-prowed medieval cog from the Cinque Ports seal.

South coast – A white-painted seventeenth-century warship swings above the mirrored sphere on Brighton's Palace Pier. The Rural Development Commission's still-popular design of a seventeenth-century-type ship with dolphins rollicks above a modern home at Bosham, Sussex. By Bosham harbour another earlier ship, gilded and primly vertical, was placed pre-war on a sewage pump-house masquerading as a summerhouse.

The whistle-stop tour ends back in Cornwall with the grand-daddy of all silhouette ship vanes, on the chapel to HMS *Raleigh* at Torpoint – eleven feet two inches of *Golden Hind*, waves, globe and arrow, with letters curved and pointed to match (*15.9*). It aims unabashed at decorative effect, rather than the nautical accuracy the location might have dictated. Erme Wood Forge designed and made the vane. The ebullient Jim Bailey graphically relates the horrified disbelief with which he watched the three-hundredweight vane swinging beneath a helicopter, suspended by just a tiny ring, which he had welded on only as a temporary means of moving the vane about the forge. It held. A moment to savour – afterwards.

This catalogue has taken no account of the private sailing-cruisers and fishing-boats, half-deckers and dinghies with which would-be salts dot the entire landscape. These range from a sleek raciness to a squat disproportion whose very ability to float must be in question. But criticizing them touches doting owners on the raw.

Neither has the survey indicated any regional specialities. East Anglia's weathervanes, for instance, illustrate, in Essex, a barge (Point Clear) and oyster-smack (Tollesbury Church); in Suffolk, a sail drifter (Southwold Church); in Norfolk a herring lugger (Great Yarmouth

Town Hall) and lugsail crab-boat (Sheringham). Great Yarmouth's restored ice-house beside Haven Bridge has a Norfolk wherry. These nineteenth-century river traders, with huge single tanned sails, loaded ice while they were frozen in, bringing it downstream on the thaw for the use of the Yarmouth fishing fleet. *Albion*, the only surviving true wherry, is picturesquely presented in a waterfront pub-sign at Acle (*15.10*). Norfolk Dinghies, Broads One-Designs and other local racing classes appear as weathervanes all over the Broads. Other regions could probably compile comparable lists.

No matter how shapely and fitly designed, powered craft are obviously felt to be less inherently decorative than those under sail. The few on weathervanes tend to have specialist owners. Commercial fishing-boats predominate; in Suffolk, lovingly reproduced steam drifters correct in every detail of deck gear, paintwork and registration represent Lowestoft's fishing fleet. Grand Avenue, Pakefield, Lowestoft, has several, and the 'fishermen's beach' to which it leads yet another. A retired Scottish fisherman, Andrew Ritchie, makes distinctive motor drifters. Their plywood hulls, woven nylon strapping for rubbing strakes, dowel spars etc gleam under several coats of marine varnish. Rigging of terylene line and a swinging steadying sail of plasticized sailcloth are realistic finishing touches. Two smart examples have gone to Seahouses, Northd., one to his fisherman son's home (*15.11*), the other to the Old Ship pub by the lifeboat slipway.

Simplified renderings such as a coaster at the Old Bakery, Redgrave, Suffolk, and a cheerful tug on Rake House, Burton, Ches., suggest

15.10 Trading wherry *Albion* in pictorial setting: Acle, Norfolk.

15.11   Leith fishing boat: Seahouses, Northd.

amateur efforts to recapture some image of a personal past. Ignoring its *Onedin Line* association, Charlestown, Corn., has put what looks like the harbourmaster's little motor-sailer on the harbour office.

Powered river craft are few indeed. A boathouse on Hickling Broad, Norfolk, declares its owner's enthusiasm for early 1900s steam-launches, but the canal narrow boats and smart motor cruisers that throng the waterways are virtually ignored.

So are warships. The destroyer at Valetta, Long Hanborough, Oxon., was made by the owner to match his well-known topiary hedge, trained and trimmed as the destroyer *Verity* on which he served throughout the war. The hedge looks particularly well 'dressed overall' with Christmas lights. Even the model battery-operated lighthouse outside on the grass verge has its own minute swivelling destroyer weathervane. A cruiser weathervane curiously surmounts the entrance pillar to Fairfield Close, a private road in Exmouth, Devon. But apparently no battleships, aircraft-carriers, submarines.

Lifeboats too are without honour in their own country. We found just one, a silhouette of a modern lifeboat running down its launching-ramp from the boathouse. Sam Parsons made it for Wells-next-the-Sea hospital, Norfolk, in memory of a doctor who had been lifeboat secretary.

This very sketchy survey of one of the largest weathervane groups suggests two contrasting conclusions. One is that fine three-dimensional ship models must be carefully preserved, for despite a few honourable exceptions we shall not see many of their like again. The high initial outlay, their susceptibility to damage and high repair costs make them an endangered species. The other is that the British are still such a web-footed race that, in silhouette form at least, the popularity of the subject, from dug-out canoe to America's Cup challenger, is unusually secure.

16 History and Imagination

By 'historical weathervanes', we mean those whose significance lies in some event or character of the past. In one sense, obviously, anything past is historical, but our response is often to a Viking ship or a wheelwright at work rather than to the moment they represent. Similarly, countless weathervanes stir the imaginations of both creator and viewer. But there is a recognizable group which actually originates in the imagination. The primary stimulus is not a physical horse or car or building activity but an idea, though the frontiers between real and imaginary are hazily drawn.

The simplest form of historical reference is the date, which may be associated with virtually any kind of motif. The nation overflows with loyal commemorations of coronations and jubilees – 1837, 1887, 1897 and 1953 being the most numerous. Still more frequently, dated weathervanes record some event of less worldshaking significance. Observers are therefore advised that 1887 may have been Queen Victoria's golden jubilee, but an 1887 weathervane could well be announcing a bit of church restoration accomplished, new business premises opened or the arrival of the squire's son and heir.

Aggressively dominant dates may shrink to tiny figures, even trailing in a little shape behind the main motif, as on St Thomas a' Becket Church, Lewes, Sussex. Here, '1756' records the time when, after five years of selling scrap metal, including the old vane, and exacting shilling contributions, £4.5.0 was finally raised for the new vane. Wivelsfield Road, Haywards Heath, Sussex, shows another unusual treatment, in which the date 1961 is both turned into a decorative pattern and reads correctly from either side – a kind of numerical palindrome.

A date does not guarantee the vane's age. Banners dated 1564 and 1577, on Manwood House, Sandwich, Kent, and Bedales, Scaynes Hill, Sussex, announce the dates at which the houses were built, but are stylistically later than that. At Stourbridge School, West Midlands, a 1667 banner records its foundation date on a later building in a modern replica. Then there is the curious case of Old Place, Lindfield, Sussex. Thirty years ago, its banner said 1888, a restoration date. Now it says 1891. Why? It still has the same pointer and scrolling, though now damaged.

Nowadays, when national dates are no longer learned by rote and local memories are shorter, *aides-mémoire* to weathervane dates come into their own. Crowns, particularly, define royal dates, like the oversized gilt crown with '1953' on Ranworth Church, Norfolk. Baylham Church, Suffolk, goes one better: its 1887 banner and crown also shout the actual word 'JUBILEE', lest we forget. An interesting cock weathervane now in St Peter Hungate ecclesiastical museum, Norwich, Norfolk, was pierced with both the date 1713 and the word 'PAX' to commemorate the signing of the Treaty of Utrecht.

But initials occur more often than complete words. Rye Church, Sussex, was given a well-proportioned banner pierced with 'AR' and '1703' to mark Queen Anne's coronation, while the point of Daventry Moot Hall's 37-38 pennant is made by a VR finial (*16.1*). Initials on church weathervanes are likely to be those of church wardens at the date stated; later generations sometimes confusingly add their own, at odd angles or back to front. The initials on Great Yarmouth's 1680 oval banner are those of this Norfolk town's bailiffs at that date (*1.3*).

16.1 Dated and initialled commemorative vane: Daventry Moot Hall, Northants.

16.2   Local and national history; Henry VIII with Anne Boleyn: home for the elderly, Aylsham, Norfolk.

Sometimes the initials are those of a local landowner, identifiable from estate cottages.

Pictorial images may also support the date. The Paston School weathervane in North Walsham, Norfolk, combines the date 1805 with Nelson's *Victory* in silhouette, to commemorate its most famous old boy's most famous exploit.

Even without dates, initials or images can still speak of events or personages. Royal initials, as on St Giles's, Northampton, for instance, still communicate successfully enough. A charming Royal Wedding

16.3   Gladstone and the British Lion: Whiston, Northants.

conception of John Allen's at Churchtown Villas, Buckland Mona-chorum, Devon, flanks the Prince of Wales feathers by the initials C and D; the pointer is weighted by a diminutive dome of St Paul's suspending a wedding bell.

But memories fade. At Great Yarmouth, Norfolk, it is the name Sewell House rather than the initials-and-horse weathervane which proclaims the birthplace of *Black Beauty*'s author, Anna Sewell. The banner on Long Alley Almshouses, Abingdon, Oxon., shows the stepped cross of the Guild of the Holy Cross, who built the almshouses in 1466, with 'RE6' identifying King Edward VI, who granted the charter to Christ's Hospital which replaced the Guild in 1533. Even supposing such references were still understood when the weathervane was erected in the early eighteenth century, they hardly leap into our minds today. There must be hundreds of examples elsewhere whose historical significance is simply no longer recognized.

Human figures are less subject to oversight or misinterpretation. Some typify a group: a possibly 300-year-old Roman centurion on Hedenham Hall, Norfolk; an undocumented engraved brass crusader in the heart of England next to Meriden Church, West Midlands; a Norman soldier, set in 1985 to swing on an arrow whose circular tail contains the harmoniously interlocking curves of the Chinese Yin and Yang symbols, adopted by some peace organizations, and so seen by some as paradoxical above Colchester's fortified castle, in Essex.

Other weathervanes portray individuals, seizing delightedly on striking physical characteristics. Henry VIII is a gift. Above an old people's home at Aylsham, Norfolk, he swaggers alongside his queen – presumably Anne Boleyn from Blickling nearby – with a Tudor greyhound (*16.2*). Boudicca, the first-century British queen who resisted the Romans so fiercely, dashes along in her chariot on Oakley, Quidenham, Norfolk, as she does on the village sign. At Whiston near Northampton, the squire/parson so loathed Prime Minister Gladstone's vacillating policies that, having vented the most unclerical desire to run him through, he created a derisive weathervane for his stables in which the unfortunate bewhiskered politician is flung about by the tail of the British lion, patently not in command (*16.3*). The Duke of Wellington charges across Wellington Place, Lewes, Sussex; Lord Nelson is in Derby; Pope Paul in Southwell, Notts. – and so on.

Figures familiar to residents often puzzle strangers. Who, they ask, is the Red Indian lass kneeling with bow and arrow above the old people's home at Heacham, Norfolk? Princess Pocahontas is the reply (*16.4*). After several times saving white settlers from her father's braves, in 1614

16.4 *Left:* Pocahontas, Indian princess: home for the elderly, Heacham, Norfolk.

16.5 *Right:* Baron Ogle in his deer park: Ogle, Northd.

she married John Rolfe of Heacham, then a Virginian colonist. When they returned to England with their young son, 'La Belle Sauvage', though somewhat more civilized than she is here rendered, was well received at Court but succumbed to the English climate and died at Gravesend, all by the age of twenty-two. On Middle Holding, Ogle, Northd., ' ... the weathervane', wrote its designer Edward Reed, 'follows a print depicting one of the Barons Ogle deer hunting in his park....' With the Royalist William Cavendish, 'barons Ogle' became Dukes of Newcastle at the Restoration, so another long memory is required here (*16.5*).

Not only the aristocratic or nationally famous are immortalized. In 1780 George Jackson founded, with the Adam brothers, a firm to make the architectural ornament associated with Adam designs. An international who's who of buildings bears witness to the firm's continuing skills and worldwide reputation. George Jackson himself, resplendent in tan breeches, grey coat, scarlet waistcoat and black hat, gazes confidently from a boathouse at Bosham, Sussex. His cut wooden figure, above very refined ironwork fashioned by George Mason of Bourne, Lincs., recalls his owner's years as the firm's managing director.

More parochial is Dr Herbert Schofield, who visited America so often that his Loughborough College students dubbed him 'the Peripatetic Principal'. The 1938 weathervane on Hazelrigg Hall shows him in his stetson running with his suitcase to board the *Queen Mary*. His students wave farewell, implore his swift return or, quite overcome, turn away to grieve into a handkerchief (*16.6*). On an Institute of Technology this ought to be one of the weathervanes whose physical future is secure.

Historical *aides-mémoire* need not be limited to figures. First World War troops made a church weathervane to recall Hingham's seventeenth-century sons who sailed from Norfolk to the New World (including one Samuel Lincoln with a descendant not entirely unknown ...). Its 1980 replacement, though more modern in style, retains the same basic design: a cross surmounted by an emigrant ship, sailing along a five-foot-six-inch arrow.

Ripon, Yorks., has a 'Wakeman's Horn' which has set the watch nightly for over a thousand years and still figures in civic pageantry. It joins a rowel symbolizing the city's manufacture of spurs to crown Britain's

16.6   The Peripatetic Principal: Loughborough College of Technology, Leics.

oldest obelisk, built in 1702, with eleven feet of dramatic bronze (*16.7*). At its restoration in 1985, councillors found the horn to contain 1889 council minutes, calling-cards and the account for repairs to the obelisk – £49, a depressing contrast to their current bill of £13,000. They hope the expenditure will keep their 1985 time-capsule undisturbed for another hundred years.

16.7   The Wakeman's Horn and rowel spur: Ripon market place, Yorks.

The confused shadowy area between historical fact and fiction is the natural refuge of saints and angels, irrefutable fact to some, sheer fantasy to others. Not all saints are represented by their symbols; figures and scenes are popular.

The combination of archangel and saint on a 1935 weathervane at Thundersley, Essex, somehow implies a rivalry persisting after more than 700 years. On the pointer, St Michael brandishes his sword above what was his church – until 1220. After that, it was rededicated to St Peter, in control on the weathervane tail, holding his key. At Chipping Ongar, Essex, a lively scene shows St Martin riding past a kneeling beggar; his raised sword appears threatening, but he gave the beggar his cloak, afterwards seeing it in a vision around Christ's shoulders. Such piety accords incongruously with the weathervane's reputed appearance, at its installation in the 1920s, in the *Daily Mirror*. On Newbold on Avon Church, Wark., St Botolph, a patron of travellers, with a Cross as staff, leads his donkey along an unusual aeroplane-like arrow, its horizontal 'wings' held by struts.

Churches have no monopoly of saints, however. St George slays his dragon above St George's, Great Yarmouth, Norfolk, now a theatre, but also beside St George's Hill golfcourse, Weybridge, Surrey. Eden Fowler made the rather confusing Rural Development Commission version for George Stores in Bisley, Glos. An exciting battle with a long, sinewy dragon whose tail becomes the pointer is conducted above St George's School, Windsor, Berks. In contrast, St Francis has stepped straight from the Giotto fresco in Assisi to bend tenderly towards fluttering birds in a garden at Ditchling, Sussex. St Felix's companions were otters, said to have led his seventh-century boat to Flitcham, Norfolk, 'Felix ham', where, as at 'Felix-stowe' he founded Christian settlements. Hirondelle House, formerly Flitcham Vicarage, shows his sculpted figure standing with bishop's crook sailing downwind in a tiny dragon boat. Elaborate ironwork suggests this lovely weathervane is early twentieth-century, when royal encouragement beautified all the Sandringham parishes (*16.8*).

Less well known is St Francis of Sales. An early seventeenth-century Bishop of Geneva noted for devotional work, his portrayal on Pear Tree Cottage, Henfield, Sussex, with Cross and sword, suggests rather the Church Militant. St Blaise and St Dunstan, in identical poses, marked the Queen's silver jubilee by their arrival on Guildford Old People's Centre, Surrey. St Blaise holds the woolcomb of his grisly martyrdom, St Dunstan the tongs with which he seized the Devil by the nose. Their arrowtails, a woolpack and Saxon coin respectively, symbolize the town's past.

In a most exciting 1963 weathervane designed by David Carr, a seven-foot-six-inch St Bryce scans the scene from Kirkcaldy's Town House, Fife (*16.9*). Around his feet is a symbolic tree from the arms of the former borough of Dysart. He was made by Haddons Ironworks of steel, copper and iron, a blend which some blacksmiths would see as incompatible.

Often, it is only wings that elevate the saint to the angel. Gilded spread wings and raised sword mark the Archangel Michael on Brantham Church, Suffolk. Here he found a new home when his Laudian church at Manningtree, Essex, had to be demolished. Such physical transference is rare, but saints and angels do sometimes find themselves presiding over something less dignified than formerly. A graceful five-foot winged figure, raising a wreath like a classical goddess (*2.8*), gleams on the eye from every uphill approach road to Burslem Town Hall, Staffs. It is now a recreation centre.

On the shrine of Our Lady of Walsingham, Norfolk, the Angel Gabriel's identity is declared by a pennant bearing the salutation 'Ave' ('Hail'). His wing feathers and robe folds are indicated in black on the gilding, and the arrow point bears a star. He was almost certainly devised by the man who restored the whole shrine in 1938, Alfred Hope Patten.

On American weathervanes, angels usually fly horizontally, often blowing a trumpet, in clear affinity with medieval European altar-pieces. One famous Gabriel, reproduced on the 1965 American Christmas stamp, aroused fierce controversy by its manifestly feminine form; peace

16.8   St Felix arrives at Flitcham, Norfolk.

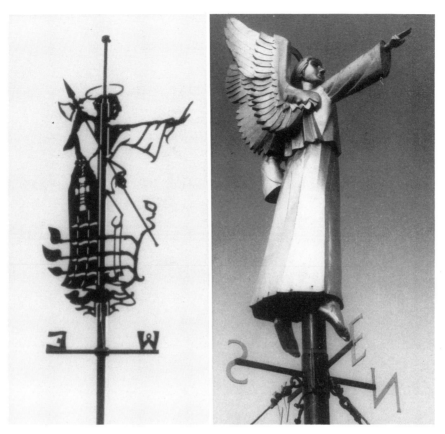

16.9   St Bryce, 1963, on Kirkcaldy Town House, Fife (*left*); fifteen foot angel, 1961, on Guildford Cathedral, Surrey (*right*).

16.10   Seventeenth-century continental angel: Beccles, Suffolk.

16.11   Eve takes the forbidden fruit: another Rural
Development Commission pattern.

was restored only by declaring angels sexless. An angel in this pose by
the River Waveney at Beccles, Suffolk (*16.10*), came from Belgium
between the wars. The solid brass figure with three-dimensional
trumpet was once painted. Experts at the Victoria & Albert Museum
suggest it may be as early as 1680, though the ironwork beneath is
modern.

But the *pièce de résistance* is the angel on Guildford's commanding and
beautiful new cathedral, consecrated in 1961. This gilded copper figure
was so designed by William Pickford that however it turns some felicities
of its strong lineaments, wing feathers, sheaf of lilies etc, will be
revealed, others hidden. 'Front' and 'back' become inappropriate terms.
The pose is remarkably similar to Kirkcaldy's St Bryce, the treatment
remarkably different (*16.9*). It is the largest British weathervane we
know of, the actual figure being fifteen feet tall and weighing almost a
ton. The drama of leaving the cathedral in darkness and floodlighting
the angel is quite breathtaking.

The fallen angel Satan's influence on the world is acknowledged in an
extremely decorative Rural Development Commission pattern showing
Eve picking the forbidden fruit, an appropriate embellishment on a fruit

farm at Surfleet, Lincs. Elsewhere, at Ivy Bridge, Devon, Erme Wood Forge's favourite plain knob pointer suits the design particularly well (*16.11*).

The Eve weathervane shows no sign of the lurking serpent. However, his direct descendant the dragon rivals the ship in weathervane popularity. Whatever motive placed dragons on churches, public buildings or homes, what come through most strongly are the unfettered imagination and sheer relish of their creators. Clearly, no dragon is intended to glorify Satan and sin. Church dragons were usually the instruments of saintly glory which symbolically delivered the world from the jaws of hell. So the grisly beast with such well-developed teeth at Orleton, Hereford & Worcester, was slain by St George. Another, now humbled inside Upton Church, Norfolk, for damaging the tower, tried to swallow St Margaret, but the cross she wore grew so large in his throat that she emerged unscathed. St Michael's ultimate victory over evil is doubly stressed at Sittingbourne, Kent, for both the 1834 dragon and its replacement have been brought low. Despite their defeats, they all look singularly cheerful.

St Mary-le-Bow's dragon, in London (*2.6*), and Welsh dragons have their heraldic impetus. A heraldic origin is also claimed for the 'Wessex' dragon, though the creature so designated is as variable in the south-west quarter of England as everywhere else. Spotters may enjoy the puppyish crouching of a four-legged dragon on Christchurch, Bristol; the wide-jawed, straight-tailed legless creature on Compton Dando Church, Avon; the cheeky, upturned tongue of the two-legged Tollsey House dragon at Wotton-under-Edge, Glos., with his spread wings; the double-looped tail flourished by another legless masthead dragon in Exeter, Devon, on the site of the old north gate – but all *Wessex*?

Even freer poses may owe more to the dragons of Eastern culture. Though not wingless, as they are, there is good muscular tension and vigour in the full-bodied copper dragon on the University College of Wales, Cardiff (*16.12*), probably dating from 1907.

Another sizeable group lives in Scotland, though no common heraldic origin seems to be claimed here. That on the obelisk-like steeple of St Andrew's, Dundee, Tayside, is sadly enmeshed in high-level roads. A black and gold crocodilian species on Kirriemuir Parish Church, Tayside, achieves three-dimensional effect by flecked markings. His lack of wings is functionally compensated for by the most enormous tail point. Another wingless dragon, stylized and serpentine, gesticulates above Edinburgh's High Street. The appearance of a full-bodied gilt dragon with big upward loop to his drooping tail, on Anderson's Institution, Forres, Grampian, is beginning, like the school, to look over sixty years old.

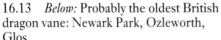

16.12   *Right:* Dragon, *c.* 1907: University College, Cardiff, Glam.

16.13   *Below:* Probably the oldest British dragon vane: Newark Park, Ozleworth, Glos.

Local integration can be very complete. In Haddenham, Bucks., the Green Dragon pub is opposite a lane called Dragon Tail, with Dragon Cottage on the corner, its weathervane a lively dragon with claws spread. (An identical creature, though known to the owner as a griffin, overlooks Shamley Green, Surrey.) Local history surfaces again in the dragon on St Mary-at-Latton, Harlow, Essex, incongruously situated by the pounding New Town dual carriageway. It bears the legend 'J1696A', tentatively attributed to James Altham, resident at that date at Mark Hall nearby, and one of a family known to have been church benefactors.

Dragons have always appealed to children. An illustration in Brian Wildsmith's *Mother Goose* inspired the 'Happy Dragon' Frank Foley made for a family near Wakefield, Yorks. Unmistakably friendly, he is absolutely guaranteed not to alarm the most nervous child. A crouched gilt dragon, body dwarfed by spread wings, hollow-eared and wide-eyed on a school in Leatherhead, Surrey, looks almost gloating by comparison. The authorities assume it to have been chosen to appeal to the children's imagination. And imagination they must have, for this is the Royal School for the Blind.

Above all other reasons, however, dragon weathervanes are chosen for their decorative shapes. The Victorians loved them, and one design is particularly popular. Its wings show membranes, and its sinuous body the surface decorativeness achievable in cast manufacture. The illusion of three dimensions is most convincing. It still adorns hotels in Porlock, Som., and Bideford, Devon; a pub in St John's Wood, London; a private house in Broadstairs, Kent; shops in Rugby, War.; a clubhouse in The Mumbles, Glam., etc, and must be the most mass-produced dragon ever.

Other decorative dragons range from an embarrassingly portly copper creature above the Washington Hotel on Llandudno seafront, Gwynedd, to a flat gilt one on York Cottage Stable, Sandringham, Norfolk, so highly stylized that it has been taken for a banner. Another form of stylization is that on Chelmsford Cathedral, Essex, where the body is a sphere, the tail and dorsal 'wing' look like pleated paper, and only the pointer has the serpentine neck and head. Dragon or serpent pointers are also frequently added to BAPs.

Wren's dragon on St Mary-le-Bow, City of London (*2.6*), described in Chapter 4, is so famous that many others claim to be copies of it. Clearly some of the copiers suffered from short memories or short sight. But the palm for the oldest dragon weathervane goes, so far as we know, to the sixteenth-century one on Newark Park, Ozleworth, Glos. Once again, 'early' does not mean 'primitive': this is detailed, sophisticated craftsmanship, serrating the necessary joins in the copper into a spiny

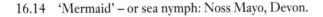

16.14 'Mermaid' – or sea nymph: Noss Mayo, Devon.

tail and marking the entire body with scales. Just over three feet six inches long, he stands stiffly on four legs, his claws spread horizontally, almost as though he once stood on a flat surface (*16.13*). The National Trust property, formerly a hunting lodge, has been lovingly rescued from dereliction by its American tenant. This splendid dragon has now been regilded to crown his achievement.

If these infinitely variable creatures, stiff and stout or long and wriggly, with or without wings, with four, two or no legs, are all dragons, it is hard to see why the three-dimensional gilded weathervane on Sir William Turner's Hospital, Kirkleatham, Cleveland, should always be singled out as a wyvern. Even if, like the chapel, he is almost 250 years old, it is also unusual to find over-cautious makers adding tie-rods *between* wings and tail, and wings and head, relying on his height to render them invisible.

Griffins, their lions' bodies topped by eagles' heads, are usually easier to distinguish. A most striking half-round example with elaborately pierced eye, ear and teeth, surmounts East and Old Parish Church, Forfar, Tayside. Church or church-hall griffins, as on Market Rasen Church, Lincs., and Evelyn Hall, Abinger Common, Surrey, may well come from the arms of local landowners or benefactors. Rebuses also occur: Erme Wood Forge made the example on Bosham Quay, Sussex, for a Mr Griffin. The Griffin Brewery at Chiswick, Greater London, uses the device, including in weathervane form on its sports pavilion. At the National Trust's Snowshill manor, Glos., the gilded griffin on the barn was actually collected in Germany as an inn sign.

Identification is not always simple, however. A rather charming little fellow flying with spread, cut-through wings above Lawrence Sheriff School, Rugby, War., is supposedly the emblem of this sixteenth-century grocer, guarding his treasures from the East – a griffin. Indeed, the school magazine is so named. But the head is not an eagle's.

Of the other half-and-half creatures, dolphins and seahorses have largely been absorbed into heraldry. High Wycombe's eighteenth-century Guildhall, Bucks., has a characterful centaur, or Sagittarius, but why and whether he pre-dated the 1920 refurbishment of the Guildhall, have not come to light. There are clear signs that his tail has been lengthened to increase his efficiency. A similar figure, but with one foreleg raised and more orthodox bow, was originally made for The Lodge, West Grinstead, Sussex, the home of a keen archer related to the novelist John Galsworthy. Some years after The Lodge was demolished in the 1960s, the weathervane was found in pieces in the garage of Lodge Cottage, where it now stands.

The ancient lure of mermaids is poorly represented in weathervanes, especially considering they are such close relatives of that original Tower of the Winds Triton, in the first century BC. A silhouette swimming mermaid with trailing hair advertises the Mermaid public house at Hedenham, Norfolk. The buxom seated mermaid on the 1838 clock tower at Hoddesdon, Herts., was chosen during a special trip to London by the powers that were, simply because they liked her. From wand to tail tip, she is over four feet six inches long. Centrally pivoted, she needs an odd extra 'tail' for windage. A replica now does the work while the original takes a well-earned rest in Lowewood Museum.

Once in this fantasy world, who shall constrain a designer within rules? Thus at Crow's Nest, Noss Mayo, Devon, the owers designed and made a 'mermaid' but gave her indisputable feet. She must be a sea nymph. Speed is vividly rendered in the exaggerated backswept dolphin fins, echoed by body, flying hair and sharply angled arms (*16.14*). The feet may be a departure from the norm, but they do not arise from weak draughtsmanship, as the Liver Bird did.

Legends are full of fantastic or larger-than-life creatures that look entirely at ease flying across the sky. A phoenix rises from Phoenix, or King Charles's, Tower on Chester city wall. This emblem of the Painters', Glaziers', Embroiderers' and Stationers' Company recalls that they met in the tower regularly in the seventeenth century, not that from here King Charles watched his army's defeat. It now houses a Civil War Museum.

The unicorn's associations with the Virgin Mary, Christ's purity, wisdom and peace are perhaps dauntingly powerful, for there are few unicorn weathervanes and they are usually heraldic or reduced to the status of lucky charms. On Paul Mead Barn, Bisley, Glos., the unicorn's neighbourliness with the lion (*4.14*) inevitably gives him patriotic overtones. Only about eighteen inches overall, his long horn elegantly balances the flying tail of the strong rampant form. This half-round gilded unicorn by Eden Fowler has great grace and beauty (*4.15*).

The grace of Pegasus, the winged horse of Greek legend, seems difficult to capture. On the gatehouse to Fergustie Gardens, Elderslie, Glasgow, Pegasus appears to be a standard Victorian moulded horse with wings stuck on. Wings may be set at different angles – for example, on a modern Pegasus at Great Alne, War., and a 1930s brown one with green wings on a barn near Bloxwich, West Midlands – but most look irretrievably like afterthoughts. Wings and body are far better integrated in Brandeston Forge's cast product, and the full-bodied gilt Pegasus on

16.15   Peter Pan: St Christopher's school, Langford, Oxon.

Foston Hall Prison, near Sudbury, Derby., has wings more convincingly and pleasingly spread.

Pegasus, ridden by Bellerophon, spear poised for hurling, is a more successful design, full of pace and vigour. It adorns Her Majesty's stableyard at Sandringham, Norfolk, homes near Cooden Beach, Sussex, and on the A 11 at Thetford, Norfolk, and Queens Park clock tower, Caterham, Surrey. Ironwork is identical; only the lettering differs. The helmet and spear suggest equally strongly the Teutonic Valkyries.

Mercury, or Hermes, has no need of a flying steed. The Rugby Football Union ground at Twickenham, Greater London, seizes on his ability to show anyone a clean pair of heels (*2.10*). In Perth, Tayside, both his associations, as messenger of the gods and patron of business, suit his downwind flight above the Victorian Station Hotel, ignoring the irony that he is also the pagan god of pickpockets and thieves.

Imaginary figures, such as Father Time and Britannia, are used symbolically, but still more weathervane figures originate in the stories which live in our affections, often from childhood. A cow jumps over a crescent moon on a garage in Somerville Road, Sutton Coldfield, West Midlands, while at Bryngwen, Trewent, Dyfed, the cow was copied from a magazine picture, a plastic whirligig figure rides it, and a full moon forms the arrow tail. Adhesive DIY letters complete this ingenious concoction.

Fairytales are represented by a pretty bonneted goosegirl with three geese, a popular between-the-wars design. Brook Cottage, Slaugham, Sussex, and Balmoral Avenue, Great Yarmouth, Norfolk, are among widely distributed examples.

The notion of the Pied Piper enticing the children of the surrounding villages to St Christopher's Primary School, Langford, Oxon., is attractive, and its weathervane is usually known by this name. However, the designer's concern was clearly rather with youthfulness, for the weathervane is closely derived from the Kensington Gardens statue of the most successful embodiment of perpetual youth, J.M. Barrie's Peter Pan.

Even more beloved than Peter Pan is Alice, and it is on another primary school, at Daresbury, Ches., that she appears in her blue frock, sharing an arrow-tail with the White Rabbit. Facing them from the pointer is the Mad Hatter, and as a finial a plump Cheshire Cat grins down. When The Smithy House, Daresbury, was sold in 1966, local pride in the village as the birthplace of Lewis Carroll made its 'Alice' weathervane a much coveted object. However, the owner refused all

16.16 Harald Hardrader's raven from the Sagas:
Lower Bentham, Yorks.

tempting offers, and gave it to the school to mark his long association
with it as chairman of the managers. Its gaily painted figures give much
pleasure to children and passers-by alike.

The folk-figure of Robin Hood marks a woodland caravan park at
Golden Cross, Sussex, and is also one of a successful mass-produced
range. Lower Raydon, Suffolk, offers a scarecrow reminiscent of Worzel
Gummidge, and the Rural Development Commission highwayman
scene (*14.1*) is typical of many an adventure tale. Christopher Robin, in
waterproof hat and wellies, plays a fish half his size on Whistlebrook
Cottage, Ivinghoe, Bucks. This was one of David Harvey's early efforts,
with spindly ironwork on which he later improved. Somewhere, surely,
must be Pooh and Piglet. Charles Schultz's cartoon character, Snoopy,
lies in characteristic ease on his kennel roof in Fairlands, Angmering on
Sea, Sussex. He is small, but bright red, black and white paint makes
him noticeable.

From adult fiction comes a romantically cloaked figure hastening past
a signpost to 'Wuthering Heights' – the house name of a Yorkshire
woman exiled to Adams Road, Swaffham Prior, Cambs. Devotees of
Sherlock Holmes must somewhere have translated one of his
characteristic attitudes into a weathervane.

The raven on the Jubilee Hall of Lower Bentham, on the
Lancs./Yorks. borders, inhabits the Sagas. Embroidered on Harald

Hardrader's banner by his daughter, the raven flew out whenever success was imminent. The weathervane raven actually flew out of a locked house when the contractor broke a window in his enthusiasm to reach and erect him. His smart Teflon coat has already received the predictable initiation by airgun peppering (*16.16*).

A more familiar figure surmounts part of the complex catering for winter holidaymakers at Aviemore, Highlands, rather unsubtly tempting younger visitors. Above the entrance to 'Santa Claus Land' he drives his russet reindeer with their gift-laden sleigh, reduced to little more than an advertisement.

Santa Claus may be the victor in the commercial stakes, but far outstripping him in appeal to the imagination of the weathervane-buying public is the witch, apparently entirely immune to the superstition that a witch on the chimney brings bad luck. Witches, like dragons, come large or small, flat or textured, of wood, metal or plastics, plain or painted – but not gilded, black being their natural hue. Apart from one at Cleasby, Yorks., who rides a cow (surely hagstones guarded against witches borrowing horses, not cows?), they all ride brooms. These may be simple triangles, realistic besoms or even, as on Moze Cross Cottage, Great Oakley, Essex, an extended clear plastic one like a vapour trail. On the ex-Plymouth Brethren Meeting House in Rudgwick, Sussex, the familiar is a goose; in Links View, Frinton, Essex, a rat. But cats predominate, sometimes before but usually behind the witch, on the broom itself. They look a little silly crouching comfortably, better when balancing against the rush of air.

To patients arriving in Southgate Road, Potters Bar, Herts., for dental treatment, the witch may be amusing but harldly encouraging. Children enjoy them on schools, as at Ticehurst. Sussex. But Warboys, Cambs., commemorates some rather nasty witch-hunting both in several vanes and on the school badge. Here, in 1593, in a bizarre episode very similar to the later Salem witch-hunts in Massachusetts, a few hysterical children condemned Alice and John Samuel and their daughter, Agnes. A contemporary pamphlet writes with horrified relish of, 'The most strange and admirable discoverie of the three witches of Warboys, arraigned, convicted and executed at the last Assizes at Huntingdon for the bewitching of the five daughters of Robt Throgmorton Esq, and divers other persons, with sundrie grievous and divellish torments. And also for the bewitching to death of the Lady Cromwell, the like hath not been heard of in this age.' The story deserves a finer witch weathervane than the town clock-tower boasts at present.

Few of these witch weathervanes are unique, but the most widespread

16.17 Zestful Rural Development Commission witch: Gwalchmai, Anglesey.

is also the best: the Rural Development Commission pattern. Slender and grinning, she oozes energy, flying with her streaming hair and tensely balancing cat. Customers at Shipton-under-Wychwood, Oxon., and Gwalchmai, Anglesey (16.17), are among many to have demanded that she wear the typical hat. Flying above the roof on a windy, moonlit night, she has been known to induce instant sobriety.

17 British Legends

Under the weight of mass canned entertainment, it is easy to lose sight of the potency of folk-tales, but there are some weathervanes wholly attributable to their inspiration.

Witches may no longer be feared, but the Devil is less lightly dismissed. One of his favourite manifestations all over Britain is as a Black Dog 'as big as a calf' with glaring eyes – or eye; or, yet more unnervingly, headless. Each community names him differently, but his East Anglian name, 'Shuck', is said to derive from the Anglo-Saxon for 'devil'. The creature himself claims descent from the Norse war-dog, the Hound of Odin. To meet him means death within the year, though many youthful sightings appear to be related in old age.

Shuck had a particularly busy day in Suffolk on Sunday 4 August 1577. At Blythburgh he interrupted the Second Lesson with 'a strange and terrible tempest' which tore down the bells, flung the spire through the roof and smashed the font, killing two parishioners. His hot breath blasted the congregation as he dashed for the north door, which bears the scratch-marks of his claws 'unto this verie day'. In no time he had loped the fifteen miles to Bungay. Here, according to one Abraham Fleming,

This Black Dog or the Divel in such a likeness (God hee knoweth all who worketh all) running all along down the Church with great swiftness and incredible haste among the people, in a visible form and shape, passed between two persons as they were kneeling on their knees and occupied in prayer as it seemed, wrung the necks of them bothe at one instant clene backward, insomuch that even in a moment where they kneeled they strangely died. Then the Black Dog gave another worshipper such a gripe in

17.1   Black Shuck: Bungay, Suffolk.

the back that therewithal he was presently drawn togither and shrunk up, as it were a piece of lether schorched in a hot fire; or as the mouth of a purse or bag drawn togither with a string.

Shuck's predilection for ancillary lightning is noted in the weathervane on a decorative lamp standard where Bungay town pump once stood. In 1933 the town reeve organized a children's competition of which the graphic vane in *17.1*, probably refined by the local artist Hugh de Poix, was the winner.

If sinister dogs lope through folk-history, how much more are the tales occupied with that archetypal image of evil, the serpent or dragon. St Michael and St George, the one a religious, the other a more political figure, confront their dragons on weathervanes, providing potent symbols of good and evil together. Variations on their exploits, in which less exalted heroes release a community from thraldom by outwitting hitherto invincible monsters, often with some supernatural aid, are seen in the stories of the Lambton Worm and the Wherwell Cockatrice.

It was entirely in character that young John Lambton, growing up in medieval Durham, defied his parents' churchgoing custom and went fishing that Sunday. All day he sat by the Wear, untroubled but catching nothing. Only as twilight deepened did he feel a strong tug on his line. But when he finally landed his catch, he recoiled in shocked disbelief.

This was no fine salmon but a slimy, disgusting, writhing worm of unmatched hideousness. 'It's the Devil himself!' he gasped, and hurled it into the well. He stumbled home, pursued by a triumphant cackle that made his hair stand on end. For weeks his nightmares crawled with worms and rang with the ghastly laughter. At last, realizing that his very soul was endangered, he joined one of the Crusades.

But the Worm grew and grew. Out of the well it came, snatching sheep and cattle and children. Brave men might cut it through, but its severed parts rejoined with apparently increased strength, coiling and crushing the life from them.

After seven long years, John Lambton returned to save his family and neighbours from the evil he had loosed. Humbly, he consulted the local witch.

'You must fight the Worm in the river, not on land,' she counselled, 'and in armour fitted with spikes. If you succeed in slaying it, you must promise to sacrifice the first living thing you meet on your return. Otherwise "For nine generations by and by, No Lambton in his bed shall die." '

A few days later, when he challenged the serpent at the river's edge, he acknowledged the witch's wisdom. For, as the Worm tried to crush him, his spiky armour pierced it until the waters ran red. And each time he hacked off a limb, the current swept it away before it could join again. So by evening the Lambton Worm was slain.

17.2   The Lambton Worm: Washington, Tyne and Wear.

John Lambton blew three weary but triumphant blasts on his horn, the signal for his father to release his greyhound for the sacrifice. But his delighted father himself ran out to meet his son. John Lambton stood aghast. Then, without a word, he slew the greyhound. But the curse he had defied fell on him, and Lambton after Lambton died a violent death.

The legend is still well known in a Northumbrian music-hall song. In *17.2*, John Lambton, complete with spiky armour, battles with his worm in Lambton village centre, among smart modern buildings, for Washington New Town, Tyne & Wear, has absorbed Lambton. One wonders what lesson children pedalling rumbustiously around may derive from it.

The Wherwell Cockatrice weathervane, formerly on its Hampshire church, has vanished into the bowels of Andover Museum. The victor over this monster, offspring of a duck and a toad, was a forester called Green who confronted it with a mirror. Maddened by its own reflection, the cockatrice battled with it ceaselessly for a full week, after which it fell senseless and was effortlessly despatched. Nearby, in Harewood Forest, is 'Green's four acres'. What a paltry reward.

Dragons and their relatives epitomize evil in their monstrous forms. But as evidence of the superstitious terror the most commonplace creatures can arouse in the ignorant, we have, in verse, 'a full and particular account of a sea monster, seen on Badbury Down, October 12 1706'.

A shepherd lad walking along a Dorset lane at Badbury Down came across a giant crab. It had probably fallen from the cart of a fisherman taking his catch to market. But the shepherd, terrified by this many-legged monster that nipped him so sharply, fled in panic to the village. Everyone ran to his defence, brandishing their pitchforks and rakes, one pushing grandpa in the wheelbarrow, the dog barking encouragement. Confronted by the crab, however, their bravado evaporated. The dog yelped, his nose nipped. The leading labourer fell back in shock, all looked at each other with a wild surmise, and grandpa's hair stood on end. 'Wheel I off, wheel I round, wheel I back to Shapwick Town,' he cried, 'or we be all dead men.' They needed little urging: all rushed back to the village and barricaded their doors. From that time, Shapwick men have allegedly been known as 'wheeloffs'.

The weathervane was erected on – where else? – Crab Farm, Shapwick, Dorset, in 1865, quite early for a story vane. After a century's corrosion, it crashed through the barn roof, and an aluminium replacement was made. Earlier illustrations show an extra figure, with either a wooden leg or a crutch, between grandpa and the spindle, finer detail in the two- and three-tined forks, less stocky figures with greater vitality and pierced eyes imparting genuinely startled expressions. Nonetheless, the replacement (*17.3*) keeps the legend of Shapwick alive. The weathervane, though not the farm, belongs to the National Trust and is a nice illustration of their concern with an artefact which, while not in itself old or valuable, is a manifestation of local rural culture.

More sinister by far is the evil that comes from a source, especially a human one, from which good is expected. Wicked uncles and hapless children are epitomized in *The Children in the Wood, or the Norfolk Gentleman's last Will and Testament*, a ballad first published in 1595. Tradition associates the episode with Watton, Norfolk.

'A gentleman of good account', said to be the owner of Merton Hall, at death's door commended his small son and daughter to the care of his brother. Their mother, also dying, promised that God would reward him according to how he tended the children. Less than 'a twelve month and a day' passed before he plotted to acquire their considerable fortunes. Allaying wifely suspicions and childish fears with promises of a London education, 'He bargained with two ruffians strong' to bear them from his home at Griston Hall into Wayland Wood, there to murder them. The children's winning ways made the ruffians regret their errand. One, however, determined to carry out the murder, 'Because the wretch that hired him Had paid him very large'. In the ensuing quarrel he was killed by his kinder fellow, who was, however, too fearful to bring the babes food and abandoned them in the wood. Blackberries alone could not sustain them, and they died, lying unburied, 'Till Robin Redbreast piously Did

17.3   The Shapwick Monster:
        Shapwick, Dorset.

cover them with leaves'. Then their mother's prophecy took shape. Nameless terrors haunted the wicked uncle's conscience. His barns were fired, his lands and business and cattle all failed, his two sons were drowned on a voyage to Portugal. After seven years he was thrown into prison for debt. Later the ruffian, condemned to death for another robbery, confessed his part in the affair, but the wicked uncle was beyond further punishment: he had died in Norwich gaol.

The weathervane (*17.4*), on Linden Court, Watton, was designed by H. Neal in 1959. It is another of his outstanding series that includes the Brundall Roman galley, Stalham and Fakenham engines, Aylsham Henry VIII, Attleborough turkeys, Heacham Pocahontas, Lynn gulls and South Wootton dancer – all on Homes for the Elderly. The copper vane cleverly shows the Babes in perforation. Wat, part of the town sign, flees in terror, but down below on the W, with a leaf in his bill, waits Robin Redbreast.

17.4   Babes in the Wood: home for the elderly, Watton, Norfolk.

At about the same time the Babes were wandering in the wood, a member of another Norfolk family was busy proving to queen and country that not all men used their position of influence for evil ends. The universally accepted trading symbol of the grasshopper, doubly founded in legend and heraldry, is our reminder of Sir Thomas Gresham.

Two versions of the grasshopper legend are told. In one, an old Norfolk woman, investigating the insistent rasping of grasshoppers, found they were guarding an abandoned baby. He grew to manhood in her care and became the founder of the illustrious Gresham line. A variant of the story tells that it was Thomas, born about 1519 to Sir Richard Gresham, Lord Mayor of London, who was lost as a child and found through the grasshoppers' commotion. His safe recovery had a profound effect on the nation, for as a thrusting merchant and financier he was ambitious to make London rather than Antwerp the commercial centre of the world. When at his instigation the first Royal Exchange was founded, Queen Elizabeth I opened it in 1568. Grasshoppers ornamented every pinnacle, and the grasshopper weathervane dominated them all. Although the idea that it was to recall his origins is charming, a *Gras-Heimchen* (field cricket), a rebus on his name, had already become the family crest.

If the full-bodied grasshopper, eleven feet long, still swinging above the City's bustle, is genuinely the original one, as is claimed, it has witnessed scenes of astonishing contrast: empty, grass-grown streets during the summer of the Great Plague of 1665, when over 50,000 Londoners died; 50,000 modern Londoners rejoicing in the proclamation of a new monarch from the Exchange steps. The grasshopper vane is claimed to have risen phoenix-like from the ashes of both the Great Fire of 1666 and the Exchange fire of 1838. When Queen Victoria opened the third, present, building in 1844, there was the grasshopper apparently unscathed. Prudently, its survival potential was not put to the test of the 1940–41 Blitz.

The charmed life of this grasshopper seems to have been equalled by its equivalent across the Atlantic in Boston. Here, in 1742, Peter Faneuil built a great trading hall. America's most famous early weathervane-maker, Shem Drowne, crowned it with a fifty-two-inch grasshopper which imitates the Royal Exchange grasshopper, but not slavishly. The Faneuil Hall grasshopper, too, is a survivor. Fire and earthquake have toppled but not destroyed it. In 1974 it suffered the indignity of being kidnapped – by helicopter – and held for ransom. But it has returned, its green glass eyes observing modern Boston as calmly as they watched the Boston Tea Party.

The original rag-to-riches Gresham story made the transatlantic crossing too, only to be transferred to the vane's maker, Shem Drowne. He, it is said, was woken from a nap in a field by a boy chasing a grasshopper. The boy's wealthy parents became his patrons. Well might he share the ancient faith in the grasshopper as a bringer of good luck.

The sixteenth-century prophetess Mother Shipton, however, used it in one of her doomladen verse prophecies. Should the grasshopper on the Royal Exchange and the dragon on Bow Church ever meet, she foretold, the streets of London would run with blood. After the 1838 Exchange fire, the grasshopper was sent for repair, and by chance to the same workshop that was repairing the Bow dragon. Nothing happened. What Mother Shipton had apparently failed to foresee was that her bluff would be called.

Despite this long-standing association of the grasshopper with trade, there are few grasshopper weathervanes. The Royal Exchange grasshopper's most direct descendant is not a trade vane at all. At Holt, Norfolk, a silhouette grasshopper surmounts a boarding-house at Gresham's School. This dazzlingly gilded modern realization of the school crest shows the Gresham grasshopper, this time with backswept antennae, standing on a wreath and holding a key, part of the arms of 'The Warden and Commonalty of the Mistery of Fishmongers of London' who have run the school's finances for over 400 years (*17.5*). There is also a fine, full-bodied copper grasshopper perched on a turret above shops in Earlham Road, Norwich, Norfolk. The figures 1896 ornament the arms but the present tenants know nothing about it. Even in 1896 such a vane would have been costly, and quality, full-bodied vanes are much to be prized nowadays. But who will prize this one?

High birth is not the only road to success: folk-tales abound with stories of the humble who make good. The unusual weathervane on Great Ponton Church, Lincs., combines two such tales.

About 1500 Anthony Ellys, lord of the manor and a wool merchant, sent home from Calais casks marked 'Calais Sand'. His wife, puzzled but dutiful, had them stored in the cellar. Proudly and delightedly, he took from them on his return the treasure he had sent home in this way for safety. His wealth assured, in 1519 he built the grand Perpendicular tower to the church, inscribing his motto 'Thynke and Thanke God of all' on it.

Generations later, in this same district, an itinerant fiddler literally scraped a living through the kindness of the villagers paying him odd pence to fiddle at weddings and fairs. But no one missed him much when he disappeared, and he soon passed out of mind. With the years, Anthony Ellys's thank-offering tower needed repairs, but the villagers could not raise the money. They were delighted when a stranger offered to pay for the church to be repaired – and surprised when he insisted that the weathercock on the pinnacle be replaced by a weathervane of a fiddle. It was the poor musician who, having saved from the villagers' odd pence enough to take him to America, had made his fortune there and returned, as Anthony Ellys had done, to make public affirmation of his gratitude.

Travellers rushing down the A1 must not allow this unusual weathervane to distract them. Several replacements have been made, the present one revolving on an old gingerbeer-bottle marble. The silhouette is simple, almost crude: its interest is in the legends.

Irresistibly drawn by the ruins, every summer hundreds of holiday makers on the Norfolk Broads moor their boats and squelch across the marsh to examine what remains of St Benet's Abbey. Only part of the arched gateway from the eleventh-century abbey stands, with a brick windmill tower like a sandcastle that was built onto it in the eighteenth century. But re-create in imagination the dormitories and infirmary, cloister and guest hall, kitchens, brewery, bakehouse and barn, stockyard

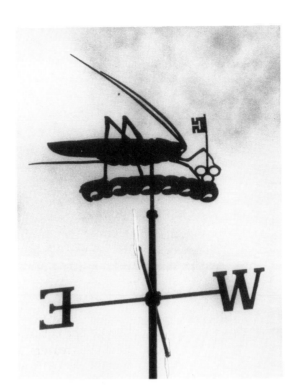

17.5   The Gresham grasshopper: Gresham's School,
Holt, Norfolk.

and fishponds and swanpit. Above all, imagine a great church, some 340 feet long and 100 feet wide. All these once stood there. Small wonder that such an impressive place in so wild and lonely a location has a legacy of ghost stories, some less than savoury.

One charming legend, however, is commemorated in a weathervane at Ranworth. At one time, St Benet's Abbey was home to a monk known for his gentleness as Brother Pacificus. Because of his skills, he was called upon to repaint part of the beautiful rood screen in the church at Ranworth, on the other side of the River Bure. Daily, he rowed the two miles up the river, along the cut and across the Broad to Ranworth Church, accompanied by his little dog, Caesar. All day, while his master worked devotedly at the screen, the dog would wait patiently in the boat, to greet him affectionately and stand again as figurehead on the long row home.

One sad night Brother Pacificus found his abbey sacked and burned, his fellow monks killed or fled. For the rest of his days he wandered disconsolately among the ruins until, at his death, the villagers brought him back across the river to Ranworth and buried him beside the church he loved.

Still, it is said, he can be seen rowing soundlessly across the Broad, and sometimes kneeling by the screen he worked at so lovingly. If spoken to, he will raise his hand in benediction before dissolving into nothingness, leaving behind him only a sense of ineffable tranquillity.

The Ranworth weathervane (*17.6*) records this legend. Behind the monk is the abbey silhouette, though as it is seen by twentieth-century holidaymakers, not as he would have known it. Artistic licence also allows him to pole rather than row his boat – and with some vigour, for Caesar leans into the wind with backswept ears. Ranworth Church with its lofty tower stands on the bank before him, awaiting his ministrations.

However, history as well as legend is incorporated into this weathervane. The Broads, it is now known, are man-made lakes originating in medieval turf ponds or peat-cuttings that flooded when the sea-level rose. The cottage this weathervane graces stands by what is thought to be one of the earliest of these diggings. The spindle of the vane has been made in the rounded form of a Norfolk peat-cutter, long-bladed and with a sharp, right-angled flange to cut and lift a turf. Instead of scrolls, the decoration is the round pokers of reedmace which still grow in the marshy borders to the pool. The vane was made in the workshop of Bill Cordaroy, at East Ruston, Norfolk, to the design of the owners. Close reference of this kind to local matters makes a vane uniquely suitable for its site.

17.6   Brother Pacificus: Ranworth, Norfolk.

18 Miscellaneous

A few weathervane leftovers do not fit comfortably into any of the preceding chapters. Nonetheless, some which cluster together interestingly, form a distinct subject group, were devised for specific purposes, combine with other meteorological instruments or are out-and-out toys should not be dismissed.

Four banners or pennants, undistinguished individually, together can achieve visual impact. Initials or dates can focus the interest, though placing separate figures on each vane gives no clue as to the order in which they are meant to be read. The four tiny banners on St David's Cathedral, Dyfed, Wales, show how slight shaping can echo the building's architectural details. In the sixteenth century St Nicholas's church, Newcastle upon Tyne, later the cathedral, flaunted no fewer than thirteen gilded weathervanes, then no doubt more glitteringly impressive and less hemmed in than now.

The four simple banners on St Sampson's, Cricklade, Wilts., were replaced earlier this century by more deliberate symbols. The cock of denial, the ship of the Church, and the lamb sacrificed joined one copy of the earlier banners, cut with a fleur-de-lys for St Sampson's French origins. None of them is exceptional, but the combination is unique. Similarly, the two-foot nine-inch cock on St Mary's and All Saints' Church, Chesterfield, Derby., is in itself visually unexciting. At close quarters its head, body and tail all prove unusually well endowed with over twenty inscribed names and dates, covering 100 years. But more remarkable is the way it rises from what for over 200 years has been known as 'the crooked spire'. This is so warped and twisted that its 228-foot-high tip is over nine feet out of true – a fact emphasized by the

18.1   Dovecote in the garden: The Dove House, Haddenham, Bucks.

weathervane's protruding apparently at an angle. In fact, it is held impeccably vertical, in order to swivel freely by a kind of tilted boss, which has to be readjusted at intervals, for the spire can still move several millimetres a year. At over six-foot-six tall, with eleven-inch cardinal letters and braced arms, this is a heavy vane, turning on a race of twelve half-inch phosphor-bronze balls. The overall result is a highly idiosyncratic feature of the skyline.

The outlines of less distinctive buildings can also make noteworthy motifs. A few generalized 'houses' occur, such as a fairy-tale thatched cottage with fenced garden on Chantry Cottage, Woodmancote, Sussex. It is a stainless steel replica of a weathervane the owners found *in situ*. Individually recognizable buildings are more interesting. 'Self-portraits' are popular. Casa Capella, an ex-methodist chapel and schoolroom at Crowton, Ches., appears on its own roof, complete with the well in the garden. The house windows have been cut out and infilled with coloured perspex, and its spherical mount spent its youth as a Belisha beacon.

On the garage to The Dove House, Haddenham, Bucks., is a portrait of the sixteenth-century circular dovecote that stands in the garden, its conical roof complete with vented cap, and with charmingly out-of-scale dove and trees (*18.1*). A dovecote was a concession the lord of the

18.2   (*opposite*) Mill-cap ornament: Tiptree, Essex.

manor granted his favourites, but much resented by the peasants whose crops fattened the doves. The weathervane probably dates from the 1925 conversion of the farmhouse to a private residence. House portraits like these would lose their point if moved elsewhere, though one of The Court House, Aldbourne, Wilts., has at least stayed in the same village.

Thame church silhouette appears on a weathervane on Thame Old Grammar School, Oxon. – relevant, but a dull substitute for its predecessor, which also showed Thame's seventeenth-century politician John Hampden speechifying in front of it. A glance at Brentor church, Devon, on its rocky outcrop, identifies the building in the weathervane advertising the Brentor Inn.

A number of Mill Roads have seized on the idea of immortalizing in weathervane form a building formerly of the greatest importance to every rural community. Whether most of the originals bore any resemblance to the post-, tower- or smock-mills shown with or without galleries is debatable. Three mills together are on one vane in Clappers Lane, Fulking, Sussex. The Rural Development Commission's pattern is attractive, though less so when simplified, without pierced sails and windows. One of the most agreeable mill weathervanes is a post-mill at Cross in Hand, Sussex, well made with twists in the arms and a twisted S-scroll placed on, instead of beneath the arrow.

A mill stump may wear a conventional weathervane: that at Blundeston, Suffolk, shows a windmill, though not a self-portrait. In contrast, some mills still with caps and sails sport a half-vane, half-finial adornment; it is operated by the wind but at one remove, being fixed itself but turning with the mill-cap. Cocks are the usual form, but a delightful nursery-frieze huntsman in a top hat rides startled and

stiff-legged on the mill-cap at Tiptree, Essex (*18.2*), while the post-mill at Six Mile Bottom, Cambs., has a hare.

The operative part of a mill-cap was really the fantail, which held the sails at the best angle to the wind to provide the power for milling or drainage. Similarly on oast-houses, particularly associated with hop-drying in Kent, Sussex and parts of Hereford & Worcester, the actual vane is the big tail. Most are left completely plain or just shaped at the extreme end. But quite a few ornaments stand on the tails. There are good rampant horses, a Kentish emblem and probably the most popular ornament in the south, at High Halden, Kent. But the apparently six-legged animals at Pickhill Farm, Small Hythe, Kent, show the visual hazards of adding extra supports. Surprisingly there are many of these Kentish horses in Sussex. Decorations on Two Knights Oast at Brede and on an oast at Hartfield, both in Sussex, make visual puns. Other designs include a squirrel, witch, Viking ship, barn flanked by trees, and the inevitable fox. They look particularly effective in echelon, none more so than the oast hunt scene described in Chapter 11. Oast bonnets and ornaments are now available in fibreglass, so their future as a genre seems assured.

Further west, an oast-house at Aldbourne, Wilts, progressed from being a malthouse, to a theatre once attended by Bernard Shaw, to a barn. On it stands a maltman with his shovel. This four-foot decoration is a 1960s replica of the wooden original, but the pipe he smoked had proved such a temptation to catapultists that it was deliberately omitted (*18.3*). Against all likelihood, the oast-type building on the shore at Sandhaven, Grampian, was not a fish smoke-house but cured bacon; its pig is of a size to swing the cowl. A complete miniature oast cowl with a tiny rising sun on the tail makes an ingenious weathervane, inserted into the hedge arched over a gateway on a main hill into Rye, Sussex.

There is no reason why any other form of wind-aligned ventilator should not also be decorated. The Italians adopted a kind of collar fitted round the top of industrial ventilating chimneys in Treviso, with ornamental vanes that swivelled with the whole top section. But can any other building match the enthusiasm of Wilkie's jute factory in Kirriemuir, Tayside? The roofscape of the two adjacent works is much animated by turreted roof-vents, still operated by white-painted arrows and banners – over 120 of them.

Another idea of impeccable ancestry, right back to Varro, a contemporary of Julius Caesar's, makes a weathervane operate not a ventilator but a dial. At Longleat, Wilts., the dial replaces a clock face on the turret; at Ripley Castle, Yorks., it is on a courtyard wall, while it is

18.3   Maltman, past and present: Aldbourne, Wilts.

painted on the gable of an 1877 agricultural building at Robertsbridge, Sussex (*18.4*).

More usefully, the weathervane may be geared to operate an interior dial. For his forge at Lower Swell, Glos., A.V. Nicholls adapted the idea of incorporating a dial with a map into the overmantel. His external arrow operates the gears which swing a pointer over a coloured map inside on the wall, to indicate the wind-direction on a gilded compass ring. The whole is set against a dark blue background within a gilt picture-frame. Dials may be set in ceilings, too: Thomas Jefferson installed one in his Virginia home about 1800. The 1840s example at Longmeads, Writtle, Essex, now a community centre, is unusually decorated with a flying heron or stork (*18.5*). Familiarity would doubtless overcome some initial puzzlement caused by the bird's head pointing with, not into the wind. Electric dials are eye-catching. They have no moving pointer but lights triggered by the vane mechanism activating contacts. They are, apparently, quite easy to contrive.

The fact that interior dials are fitted in such establishments as Greenwich Observatory and shore lighthouses confirms that the information transmitted to them, usually by a plain arrow or slab-tailed motif, is regarded as of serious use. Knowing wind-direction alone is inadequate, however. Many organizations – London Gliding Club below Dunstable

Downs, for instance – need to know its strength too and fit anemometers to record this.

Not that all anemometers are scientific instruments. Don Bales's elaborate ironwork includes twirling anemometer cups, not calibrated but as part of a clever decorative scheme where continuous movement, different in kind from that of the fluctuating motif, becomes an additional eye-catcher (*18.6*). Dual movement is hardly new. *The Antiquary* speaks in 1888 of ' ... a lady with an umbrella, which she elevated in token of rain whenever the wind blew from the south; and again, at Peckham, about a hundred years ago, the automatic wind-indicator, representing at certain conditions of the wind, a cat catching a rat'. Shaw's Corner, at Ayot St Lawrence, Herts., still has, on a subsidiary building, a copper pheasant of this type, its body hinged to a laterally arched tail; as the wind increases in strength the tail rises. The bird is believed to have been there during George Bernard Shaw's occupation, and may well have been erected at his behest.

Playing with the wind like this is probably even older than using it for any serious business, except possibly to propel boats. Little wind-jangled toys were known in Ancient China, and something very like modern seaside pinwheels developed as a toy in medieval Europe. So did carved and jointed wooden dolls. The two ideas combined first into figures with loosely fixed flattened arms which the wind could rotate, and later into figures which held in their hands devices, e.g. flags, which caught the wind. Often carved by fathers to amuse their youngsters, particularly on restrictive Sundays, these 'whirligigs' seldom lasted long. Survivors tend to be in toy collections; the gregarious groups in gardens – at Breedon, Leics. for example – are usually quite recent, even if still of painted wood. Their descendants, vivid plastic sawyers, water-drawers, cyclists and see-saws, proliferate at garden centres, cheerful but charmless.

Quite complex scenes were sometimes contrived. A propeller could work a linked mechanism controlling several movements, preferably repetitive. A wooden scene on Laurel Bungalow, Acton, Suffolk, activated two men sawing a log by sails turning on a windmill; sadly the sails are unlikely to be replaced now the maker has died. Little figures semaphoring used to be popular, and two model yachts on horizontal arms whose sails, swinging from side to side to simulate tacking, propelled them round and round. Designs like this featured in between-wars DIY magazines. In the National Trust collection at Snowshill, Glos., is a very complicated affair which one longs to carry out into the breeze – a large post-mill swarming with twenty-eight redcoats, arranged in sets of four to a spindle. How strong a wind would

18.4   *Left:* Wall dial operated by harvesting motif: Robertsbridge, Sussex.

it take to work that system of gears and pulleys? Do all the figures wave their arms vertically as well as rotating horizontally?

This kind of construction is beyond most amateurs – and the whirligig character is essentially amateur. Many stop short at a grouping of pinwheels or a whirling propeller attached to a static motif, more interesting if in the form of rotating wings on a bee or goose. Many an aeroplane, shooting scene and Mickey Mouse figure is, judging by the placing, intended as a bird-scarer. With quite the opposite intention, great ingenuity is used at Old Weston, Cambs., in combining weathervanes made of scrap with bird-boxes, all mounted on masts. Full marks to the blue-tits, who, after only one false start in attempting to fly in through the painted window, when they returned to find the vane had swung, blithely followed their peripatetic front door and successfully reared their brood (*18.7*).

A few aberrations remain, generally the sign of a failure to grasp the basic principle of a weathervane, or deliberate disregard of it. There is the absolutely symmetrical motif, which cannot possibly work, no matter how hard the cardinal arms try to convince us it is a weathervane – an intricately modelled thistle head, for example, above a shopping complex at King's Heath, Birmingham. There is an apparently conventional arrow on Hutton Grammar School, Lancs., but it actually incorporates the N/S letters. There are arrows which surely must indicate the direction of something (but since they appear to be fixed, it cannot be the wind) piercing some highly ornamented standards along pavements in Bideford, Devon. A resident near Arbroath, Tayside, has perpetuated the old jibe about Scots parsimony by using his cardinal arms to support a TV aerial instead of an ornamental motif. Conversely at Bodle Green, Sussex, the TV aerial supports a cow weathervane, cardinal arms and all. Bruntsfield Place, Edinburgh, offers Victorian cardinal arms and a finial, with no sign of there ever having been a motif. Similarly there seems never to have been a motif on a little thatched dovecote whose four arms project from its roof. A letter 'T' marks the north point. The whole rebus 'WEST' over 'cot' won a competition run in 1920 to design a village sign for Westcott, Surrey. One bright lass seized on its topicality to win another prize with it, as a fancy dress at a jazz dance, but the story that thereby she jumped the gun for the announcement of the winner seems to be apocryphal.

Lastly there are the puzzles. Devices no longer generally recognizable today may turn out to be heraldic, like the Meux family's 'two wings inverted and indorsed, and conjoined by a cord with tassels' on the guildhall at Wootton Bassett, Wilts. Others are simply unidentifiable:

18.5 Interior ceiling dial with heron pointer:
community centre, Writtle, Essex.

200 years of argument have not settled whether St Luke's, in Old Street, Islington, Greater London, wears a comet, a dragon or both, or whether the church really was known as 'Lousy St Luke's' because the maker expressed contempt for his scanty payment by a weathervane in the form of a louse. Puzzles increase as time and decay take their toll.

Without considerable on-the-spot investigation, it would be foolish to try to evaluate British weathervanes in the wider context of weathervanes in Europe and the USA. What is observable, however, is a genuine revival of interest in weathervanes in several countries. This century's wars, decay and redevelopment, responsible for the disappearance of many hitherto disregarded artefacts, have focused attention on them. Weathervanes, not hitherto considered a vital element in the appearance of fine buildings, even when the most notable architects designed them, are sharing in this awareness.

The common themes uniting recent studies of French, German,

Italian and American weathervanes are that weathervanes have historic interest, on both social and artistic grounds, that as long as design and workmanship are maintained their impact is pleasurable and that they should not be under-valued. In the USA the emphasis is on private and museum collecting, with the attendant fears about faking that Europe does not apparently share. Treviso is concerned with preserving its specialized chimney ventilator vanes. In Britain, museum collections hold some weathervanes, but single examples haphazardly disposed, in Maidstone, Middlesborough or Merseyside, make study and evaluation difficult. The stimulus of comparison is rare.

Another concern common to European and American writers is the quality of mass-produced weathervanes. The high standards of the weathervanes dispersed throughout nineteenth-century America through the catalogues of such firms as Westervelt, Fiske and Cushing, and the best of Britain's cast-iron products, are not matched today, banished, like so much else, by the economics of modern production. In order for vanes to be made and sold at a reasonable price, materials have to be cheap and corners cut at every stage of manufacture and finishing. Thus the very mass-production techniques that allow ordinary people to buy and enjoy weathervanes are in some sense counter-productive. They tempt buyers to accept the second best through ignorance of the best, and to be unadventurous.

There is no doubt that Britain has excellent iron-workers, capable of both bold and refined workmanship, and the artist-designers too. But the world of weathervanes is not yet one where they work extensively together. The British Artist Blacksmith Association (BABA), founded in 1978, will surely encourage what would be a significant step forward. The real difference between contemporary work in Britain and in, say, Germany, seems to be in artistic emancipation. German designers recognize that, while moderate efficiency lends its own beauty, science has freed twentieth-century weathervanes to concentrarte on artistry. Wonderful interpretations of mermaids, drunkards, angels – particularly angels – satisfy completely in their imaginative response to the demands of balance and proportion; genuinely beautiful, yet unequivocally contemporary, they underscore the high reputation of German ironwork.

By comparison British weathervane design, with a few notable and honourable exceptions, is static, stressing the nostalgic and representational. Except on this superficial level it has lost touch with the lives of the people. Contemporary aspirations, ideals, ideas, tastes even, find insufficient outlet. Imaginative creations in a modern idiom (as distinct from tricksy novelty) must move in harness with the essential

18.6   Complex ironwork, with spinning anemometer
cups and balls: Outwell, Norfolk.

preservation of past work.

The public are interested, but something has to sharpen their vague perception that the weathervane, although it can never be 'cost-effective' or 'bring a return', can make a considerable and lasting contribution to their lives in subtler ways. Presenting them with exciting new designs, of sufficient artistry to give enduring satisfaction, is surely one way to prevent the weathervane fly from becoming too deeply embedded in its amber.

18.7   (*overleaf*) Bird-box vane: Old Weston, Cambs.

Suggested Reading

Chapman, Brigid, *The Weathervanes of Sussex* (Temple House Books, Lewes, Sussex, 1987)

Messent, Claude, *The Weathervanes of Norfolk and Norwich* (Fletcher & Son, Norwich, Norfolk, 1937)

Needham, Albert, *English Weathervanes* (Charles Clarke, Haywards Heath, Sussex, 1953)

Pagdin, W.E. *The Story of the Weathercock* (Edward Appleby Ltd, Stockton-on-Tees, 1949)

Bishop, Robert, and Coblentz, Patricia, *A Gallery of American Weathervanes and Whirligigs* (Bonanza Books, New York, 1981)

Fitzgerald, Ken, *Weathervanes and Whirligigs* (Clarkson N. Potter, New York, 1967)

Kaye, Myrna, *Yankee Weathervanes* (E.P. Dutton & Co, New York, 1975)

Klamkin, Charles, *Weathervanes: the History, Manufacture and Design of an American Folk Art* (Hawthorn Books, New York, 1973)

Fiske, J.W., *Copper Weathervanes* (facsimile of 1893 catalogue, Wallace-Homestead Books, Des Moines, Iowa, 1971)

Comte, Marie-France, *Girouettes* (Laurence Olivier Four, Caen, 1981)

Pötz, Clemens, *Wetterfahnen* (Callwey, Munich, 1983)

Gardner, J. Starkie, *English Ironwork* (Victoria & Albert Museum, London, 1922-30)

Lister, Raymond, *Decorative Wrought Ironwork in Great Britain* (Bell & Sons, London, 1957)

Lister, Raymond, *Decorative Cast Ironwork in Great Britain* (Bell & Sons, London, 1960)

Lister, Raymond, *The Craftsman in Metal* (Bell & Sons, London, 1966)

There are numerous other books on metalwork. Those mentioned suit the general student: readers capable of benefiting from more technical studies are probably already familiar with them.

As with any topic, material bearing upon weathervanes comes unexpectedly in books on diverse subjects. The background knowledge that enhances enjoyment will come from very different kinds of books, according to the group being considered. In particular, however, readers will find that books on the history of art and architecture, ecclesiastical history, topography and heraldry offer some stimulating insights.

General Index

Main entries marked in bold are taken from the chapter titles.

Index of Weathervanes
by County and Town

Page numbers in bold indicate illustrations.
Page numbers in [ ] indicate unnamed reference to the weathervane indexed.